Life and Ministry of Jesus

Revised Edition

Life and Ministry of Jesus

Revised Edition

by F. Henry Edwards

Herald Publishing House
Independence, Missouri

Library of Congress Cataloging in Publication Data

Edwards, F. Henry (Francis Henry), 1897-
Life and ministry of Jesus.

"Studies in the life and ministry of Jesus appeared in church school quarterly form in 1928 and as a book in 1940. In 1950, in a revised edition"—Introd.
1. Jesus Christ—Biography. 2. Christian biography—Palestine. I.Title.
BT30 1.E35 1982 232.9 82-15399
ISBN 0-8309-0355-0

Printed in the United States of America

86 87 7 6 5

CONTENTS

INTRODUCTION

Studies in the Life and Ministry of Jesus appeared in church school quarterly form in 1928 and as a book in 1940. In 1950, in a "revised edition," a few chapter sequences were rearranged and chapters on "The Holy Spirit" and "Jesus and His Father" replaced those on "The Apostle of Our Profession" and "The Missionary Methods of Jesus."

In the manuscript now presented no basic changes have been made, but some of the chapters have been revised so as to augment from the beginning the emphasis on the divinity of the Lord Jesus Christ. Also, "The Ascension" has been discussed in an additional chapter (44).

A chapter on the "New Age" of the Spirit has been introduced (46).

The chapter, "Jesus and the Scriptures," has been spread over various chapters (43).

The earlier chapter, "Jesus in the Experience of Christianity," has been combined with "Jesus in Latter Day Saint Experience" (50, 51).

The discussion, "How Can We Know Christ," has been spread over previous chapters to make room for the "Our Lord and Savior, Jesus Christ."

The earlier editions of this book contained a chapter entitled "Christ in the Western Hemisphere" (43). When I was preparing this edition it seemed to me, and to others I consulted, that the emphasis here was not as consistent with the theme of the book as a whole as might be desired. So I rewrote that chapter. In the revised version which appears here my concern has been to indicate the major emphases on the life and ministry of the Lord Jesus as the Book of Mormon presents them. I have tried to let the book speak for itself and so have avoided, so far as I could, secondary comment which might distract from my basic purpose.

As I wrote in my introduction to the edition of 1950, this book is offered in the earnest hope that those who read it will thereby be led to a richer appreciation of the great love of our Lord for all humankind, and for every one of us in particular. Out of this I hope there will come deep interest in the teachings of the Master, and a widespread response to the call to creative repentance.

The book is intended for study rather than for cursory reading. In spite of its many limitations, I hope it will repay such study. I am emboldened to say this, since the book makes no great pretense at originality. Where I could do so, I have acknowledged my indebtedness to various authors by noting the names of books used. Some notes taken at odd moments, in libraries scattered all over the United States and England and Canada, have been used, in spite of the fact that when they were assembled there was no thought of writing this book and references to sources were not always included. Where this has occurred there has been no intended plagiarism, nor has there been any intentional failure to acknowlege indebtedness.

Since the book is not a life of the Master, I have not always followed strict chronological order, yet I have done this as fully as I could while still presenting related events in connection with each other.

My special thanks are due to Walter E. Duty, Director of the Christian Education Office, for his patience and encouragement in a task which, though pleasant, was at times somewhat difficult; to Miss Esther Brockway who did much of the typing and retyping of the manuscript; and to my daughter-in-law, Dr. Nancy T. Edwards, for her help at a time when communications broke down and rescue was urgent. Paul Wellington, editorial director of Herald House, Mrs. Evelyn Maples, and Mrs. Imogene Goodyear formed an extremely helpful rescue squad.

F. Henry Edwards

Chapter 1

THE HISTORICAL JESUS

Like the Greeks who came to Philip, *we* would see Jesus.[1] We are not the only ones who are setting out on this quest. People of every race are pursuing the same adventure of understanding. Whether we love him or deride him, we cannot ignore him. He is the outstanding person of our generation and of every generation. More and more people judge themselves with him as their standard.

Christians and non-Christians the world over acknowledge the preeminence of Jesus as a man. Many millions of our race date the other events of human history according to whether they occurred before or after his birth. All over the world it is acknowledged that his advent inaugurated a new era so different from any which had preceded it that the rise and fall of dynasties, all humanity's major triumphs and disasters, the extension of learning, the multiplication of human powers, and every other mark of our common life should be rightfully dated from the great moment when he first graced the earth with his visible presence.

Not everyone who studies the record of the early life of Jesus does so as a disciple. There are some who turn from this study to tell us that Jesus never lived, that the gospel is founded on a myth, and that the stories of the life of the Master are nothing more than the artistic creations of human minds. Since this point of view is sometimes given more weight than it deserves, it is well that at the outset we should glance briefly at some of the evidence of the historicity of Jesus. There are many. Few reputable historians support any theory which denies Jesus his place as a historical person.

Jesus was born in the Roman Empire during the reign

of Caesar Augustus. From the point of view of Imperial Rome, his brief career was too insignificant for notice. Yet his fame grew so rapidly that no less than four Roman writers of the second century refer to Jesus or to his followers in records which have been preserved to this day. How many other references have been lost is, of course, beyond conjecture.

Tacitus, the Roman historian, is best known to the general public today because of his reference to Jesus in his *Annals.*[2] This reference is admittedly an unfavorable one, since Tacitus adopts the supercilious attitude of a Roman patrician toward the humble followers of Jesus. Yet the historian does definitely refer to Jesus and his followers whom he refers to as being "commonly called Christians," and he may therefore be listed as an important witness to the fact that Jesus did actually live in Palestine as the Gospels attest.

Suetonius, who lived at about the same time as Tacitus, is a further witness. He wrote that Claudius "expelled the Jews from Rome because they were constantly raising a tumult at the instigation of Chrestus."[3] It is interesting to note in passing that the influence of Jesus in the lives of his disciples was so real that people living at a distance thought the Master must still be leading his people in person.

Pliny the Younger, while governor of Bithynia, wrote to the emperor Trajan describing the Christians in some detail and asking advice regarding relations with them. Later in the century Lucian, the satirist, wrote of the founder of the Christian religion as a Master who had persuaded a group of followers that they were all brothers and sisters and that they would live forever.

There are also several references in the writings of Jewish authors of this period. Josephus, the historian, mentions the condemnation of "James, the brother of Jesus, the so-called Messiah (or Christ)."[4] The Talmud repeatedly refers to Jesus under slight disguises.

When we remember the scant means of communication or the few incentives to record this information in the world of two thousand years ago, and take into account our own difficulties in discovering what may have been written at that distant time, we realize with astonishment how much evidence there is to support the biblical story of the early life of the Master.

The few who would have us discredit the fact that Jesus lived as a man among people usually ask us to disregard the testimony of the New Testament. They ask this on the ground that the scriptures of the early church grew out of popular myths rather than out of any factual experience. To disregard the New Testament, however, is to neglect the accepted and most available source of information regarding the life and teachings of the Master. A better way is to let the Gospels and the epistles bear their testimony and then to scrutinize their evidence so as to determine its accuracy and worth.

Let us look first at the Gospels. It is obvious that they cannot be properly called biographies. They are not even records of firsthand observation in all particulars. They are collections of reminiscences which were committed to writing, with different but supplementary purposes in view, years after the events recorded took place. The Gospel according to Mark is the shortest, but simplest, and probably the oldest of the four. Very ancient tradition affirms that the Apostle Peter was the source of Mark's information in writing the Gospel. This may well be, since the content of the Gospel bears out the tradition.

Matthew probably used the record already prepared by Mark in compiling his story of the life of Jesus. The Gospel according to Matthew was written by a Jew and for Jews, and the writer laid emphasis on those events in the life of the Master which would strengthen the faith of the Jewish Christians and enable them to defend their faith to their fellow Jews.

Luke also probably used Mark for some source material, but he wrote for a wider circle of readers than did Matthew. This was natural, for not only was he a man of broader culture than Matthew but his travels with the Apostle Paul had given him deeper Gentile sympathies than many of his compeers. He was concerned with showing Jesus as the friend of all—not only the rich but also the poor and lowly; not only the elect but also the publicans and sinners.

The Gospel according to John was written much later than the other three. John had a distinctive purpose in writing which he himself explains: "These are written, that ye might believe that Jesus is the Christ, the Son of God; and that believing ye might have life through his name."[5] John's selection of material was made with this purpose in view, and this purpose goes far to explain both the omissions and the inclusions which are characteristic of this Gospel.

Each of these writers did his work well. The fact that their narratives were prepared after an interval of many years means that those facts and phrases they recorded, those moments of humor and of tragedy, those times of indignation and of quiet peace had riveted themselves on the minds and memories of the listeners and had become increasingly significant with growing experience.

There is a simplicity and a straightforward honesty about the Gospels which stamp them with the seal of authenticity. None of the writers make any endeavor to embellish the facts. None of them take time to make obvious comment. The thoughtful reader will recognize that, even after the lapse of years, these men sensed in Jesus a person so distinctive that in painting his picture for their friends they did not dare to mar that picture by putting themselves in it. Jesus still meant so much to them that they sought only to tell his story, with the conviction that his personality would shine through and win others to him even as they themselves had been won.

This honesty was grounded in the conviction of the chroniclers that the divinity of Jesus would become more and more apparent with the passing of time. This conviction caused them to record many things about the Master which must have made it difficult for some of his contemporaries to believe in him. The stories of his liability to emotional stress and pain, of his fatigue, of his friendship with women and outcasts were not the currently approved evidences of Messiahship. Yet all these are faithfully recorded. This is an invaluable evidence that the Gospels are authentic records of a great life.

The epistles of the New Testament, especially those of Paul, bear important testimony concerning Jesus. Paul was an intellectual giant with ready access to the available sources of information, and it is impossible to believe that he was deceived about such a fact as the early life of Jesus. On the contrary, it is clear that he had had no doubts. From his writings alone we could establish the major facts of the life and ministry of Jesus. In his letters are numerous references to people and events which are now completely lost to history, but which were evidently well known at that time. Questions are raised and discussed which have no meaning if the letters are not addressed to specific people and applied to specific situations.

Over and above the foregoing is another important fact to which those who would have us discard the records of the life of Jesus, as though these records were the product of human imagination, have failed to give due weight. It is this: Only a truly great man can draw a convincing picture of the greatness in others. No wicked man could have painted the picture of Jesus which we find in the Gospels. And no artist, however good or talented, could produce such a portrait without a model, for this portrait of Jesus has qualities which not even the best would think of putting there unless he was telling the story from life.

While the collateral evidences indicate that the Lord Jesus truly lived, these of themselves do not enable us to truly "see God." This ability, as Jesus himself said, is derived from purity of heart.

The foundation of all true religion is faith in God. Christianity has a distinctive flavor in that this faith in God is inseparably connected with faith in Jesus Christ. Our faith has its roots in reality. It is not the product of thoughts or dreams. It came out of a life, a part of history. It centers in a man who was born of a woman whose name we know, who was put to death under a Roman governor whose name we also know. His life and ministry are attested by the writers of the New Testament and by the acceptance of their testimony by thousands who followed Jesus in the early generations. The Lord Jesus was crucified, died, and was buried, but he rose again by the power of God. This resurrection was no mere resuscitation; it was a newness of life. Herein lie our faith and our hope.

The references to Jesus in Tacitus, Suetonius, Pliny, Lucian, and Josephus are references to a real person. The New Testament story is centered in the life of this same real person. But in the last analysis we are not dependent on any book, not even the Bible, for evidences that Jesus lived. The whole history of Christianity and of the modern world necessitates him. There is no explanation for Western civilization without him. We know that he lived because we see all around us the evidences of his life. Bad as we are, diseased as is society, we and the social order to which we belong are incomparably better than we would have been if Jesus had never walked the highways of Galilee.

NOTES

1. John 12:21.
2. *Annals,* chapter XV, page 44.
3. *Vita Claudii,* chapter XXV.
4. *Antiquities of the Jews,* book XX, chapter 9, paragraph 1. See also book XVIII, chapter 3, paragraph 3.
5. John 20:31.

Study Helps for

Chapter 1

LESSON PURPOSE

To emphasize the fact that Jesus did actually live among us, and that his life is an indication of the meaning and possibilities of Christianity. "We have not followed cunningly devised fables."

SCRIPTURE REFERENCES

Hebrews 1:1, 2; Acts 1:1-3; II Peter 1:16-19; Helaman 5:55-62, 65.

HIGH POINTS OF THE LESSON

- It is impossible to create a purely imaginary person of the spiritual stature of Jesus.
- The differences and similarities of the four Gospels, as well as the testimony of Paul, serve to increase our understanding of Jesus.

QUESTIONS AND DISCUSSION TOPICS

1. Why is it significant that calendars record dates according to the birth of Jesus?

2. Discuss the statement, "Whether we love him or deride him, we cannot ignore him." Illustrate your answer.

3. Several nonbiblical witnesses of Roman times testified that Jesus lived. What is the special value of their testimony?

4. Why were the Gospels written? Why are they different from each other?

5. Compare the differences of the ministry of John the Baptist as written

in Matthew 3 and Mark 1:1-9. What are the differences in the testimony about Jesus' temptation in the wilderness as recorded in Matthew 4:1-10 and Mark 1:10, 11?

6. What are the distinctive characteristics of the Gospels of Matthew and Luke? To what audiences were these men directing their writing? How does the audience of writers or speakers affect the content of their message when they bear testimony of Jesus?

7. Contrast the values of the testimony of John and Paul concerning Jesus (page 12). How is your testimony similar or different from that of John and Paul? Why is it important for each Christian to have a testimony of Jesus?

8. What is the significance of the statement found in Revelation 19:10, "for the testimony of Jesus is the spirit of prophecy"? Discuss in a small group.

9. How may we know that Jesus lived on earth? How reliable is archaeological evidence of ancient civilizations as testimony of the life, death, and resurrection of Jesus?

WHAT THE LESSON MEANS FOR TODAY

People who are confronted with the life of Jesus have several options about their beliefs. Consider the following: He was simply a good man and a great teacher; he was a great prophet; he was what he claimed to be—the Son of God. The best evidence of his existence does not come from archaeology, contemporary historians, or even his letter-writing friends. Searchers for truth will find their testimony through the Holy Spirit and through the effect of the impact of Christ on those who follow him in total commitment.

Chapter 2

BEFORE THE FOUNDATION OF THE WORLD

As we have seen, Jesus actually lived and taught and was known among the people of Palestine nearly two thousand years ago. We now need to go further back than this, to the dawn of history, and to consider something which even his closest disciples did not fully understand until the events of Calvary and Easter and the forty days and Pentecost opened their eyes and quickened their understanding. It was their faith, as it is ours, that while Jesus was a man he was also much more than a man. He is the Son of God who was with the Father from before the world was created, who took upon himself the limitations of humanity for our salvation.

The Bible says that "In the beginning God created the heaven and the earth."[1] The Inspired Version adds details to this rather skeletal announcement: "I am the Beginning and the End; the Almighty God. By mine Only Begotten I created these things. Yea, in the beginning I created the heaven, and the earth upon which thou standest."[2] The King James Version agrees specifically with the Inspired Version of the Bible concerning the presence and action of the Lord Jesus Christ in creation.[3]

Evidence supporting our faith that Jesus lived with his Father before the world was is found throughout the scriptures. Let us note some of this evidence. Jesus was genuinely humble, and "made himself of no reputation,"[4] but he did not hesitate to tell the Jews of his pre-earthly life, saying: "Before Abraham was, I am."[5] To his disciples he said: "I came forth from the Father, and am come into the world; again, I leave the world, and go to the Father."[6]

When Jesus faced the agony of the judgment hall and of Calvary, he retired to Gethsemane and there prepared himself for what lay ahead by communion with his Father. Against this background, when self-deceit was unthinkable, he prayed: "Now, O Father, glorify thou me with thine own self with the glory which I had with thee before the world was."[7]

These statements form such an important part of the deepest experience of the Master that no real study of his life can fail to take them into account. If Jesus were mistaken here, it was a mistake which vitiated everything else he did and was. But he was not mistaken. Incredible as it seems, the Son of God lived with his Father before the world was.

This secret of the preexistence of our Lord was not shared with all people from the beginning. The mind of the average person was not big enough to grasp it. It was shared, however, with some of the prophets. Many centuries before Christ came in the flesh he revealed himself to the brother of Jared, saying: "Behold, I am he who was prepared from the foundation of the world to redeem my people."[8] To Moses, also, the word of inspiration came: "Thou art in the similitude of mine Only Begotten; and my Only Begotten is and shall be the Savior."[9]

When Jesus walked this earth with his friends, they knew he was much more than an ordinary man. As their intimacy with him increased, it became possible for God to illuminate their understanding, and one here and one there caught a fleeting glimpse of the Master's true nature. For the most part, however, "their eyes were holden,"[10] and it was not until the stupendous fact of the resurrection and the outpouring of the Holy Spirit had startled them into awareness that they really began to understand. Before Calvary they "followed him afar off," but in the earliest recorded apostolic preaching, Peter declared:

> This Jesus hath God raised up, whereof we all are witnesses. Therefore being by the right hand of God exalted, and having received of the Father the promise of the Holy Ghost, he hath shed forth this, which ye now see and hear. . . . Therefore let all the house of Israel know assuredly, that God hath made that same Jesus whom ye have crucified, both Lord and Christ.[11]

This declaration registered a tremendous step forward from the half-wondering recognition of the disciples that Jesus was greater than them all, to the place where they knew him to be the Son of God. They made this step forward under the guidance of the Comforter whose mission it was to testify of him,[12] and to guide them into all truth.[13] Now that their vision was enlarged, they looked beyond their own day and saw Jesus enthroned in the midst of the eternities. Having done this, they could not think that God had waited for some suitable person to be born and had then adopted this person as his Son. Guided by inspiration, they saw that the Only Begotten Son of God had lived with the Father from the beginning. Hard as it was to comprehend fully, they knew that this was the only explanation which fitted facts too clear for them to deny. Under the pressure of this knowledge, Paul, who wrote his Epistles before any of the Gospels were written, testified that Jesus

> is the image of the invisible God, the firstborn of every creature. For by him were all things created, that are in heaven, and that are in earth, visible and invisible, whether they be thrones, or dominions, or principalities, or powers; all things were created by him, and for him; and he is before all things, and by him all things consist.[14]

The Apostle Peter bore a similar testimony:

> Ye know that ye were not redeemed with corruptible things, as silver and gold, from your vain conversation received by tradition from your fathers; but with the precious blood of Christ, as of a lamb without blemish and without spot, who verily was foreordained before the foundation of the world, but was manifest in these last times for you.[15]

John the Beloved was always near to the heart of Jesus. His love blazed the trail for his insight, and every new revelation of the greatness of his friend and Master brought him new joy as well as new amazement. It is therefore not surprising that the clearest and most definite statement of the preexistent life of our Lord should come from him. In the introduction to his Gospel, John says:

> In the beginning was the Word, and the Word was with God, and the Word was God. The same was in the beginning with God. All things were made by him; and without him was not any thing made that was made. In him was life; and the life was the light of men.[16]
>
> . . . That which was from the beginning, which we have heard, which we have seen with our eyes, which we have looked upon and our hands have handled, of the Word of life; (for the life was manifested, and we have seen it and bear witness, and show unto you that eternal life, which was with the Father, and was manifested unto us); that which we have seen and heard declare we unto you, that ye also may have fellowship with us; and truly our fellowship is with the Father, and with his Son Jesus Christ.[17]

Modern revelation has also brought us the further testimony of John:

> . . . I saw his glory that he was in the beginning before the world was; therefore, in the beginning the Word was; for he was the Word, even the messenger of salvation, the light and the Redeemer of the world; the Spirit of truth, who came into the world because the world was made by him; and in him was the life of men and the light of men. The words were made by him. Men were made by him. All things were made by him, and through him, and of him.[18]

The saints of the apostolic age rejoiced in the light thrown on the meaning of their own lives by their realization that Jesus, who was their friend, was also the Lord of Creation, and that his work before history began was akin to that which they had shared with him—both motivated by love. Paul expressed this in his letter to the saints at Ephesus:

> Blessed be the God and Father of our Lord Jesus Christ, who hath blessed us with all spiritual blessings in heavenly places in Christ; according as he hath chosen us in him before the foundation of the world, that we should be holy and without blame before him in love.[19]

We did not come here by chance, nor in response to a whim, but out of divine concern for our eternal wellbeing. We are not the playthings of the Infinite; we are the sons and daughters of God for whom he planned a glorious destiny before Lucifer rebelled or the earth took form.

NOTES

1. Genesis 1:1 (KJ); Isaiah 41:20; 40:26.
2. Genesis 1:2, 3.
3. Genesis 1:2, 5; Psalm 104:30.
4. Philippians 2:7.
5. John 8:58.
6. John 16:28.
7. John 17:5.
8. Ether 1:77.
9. Doctrine and Covenants 22:4a.
10. Luke 24:15.
11. Acts 2:32, 33, 36.
12. John 15:26.
13. John 16:13.
14. Colossians 1:15-17.
15. I Peter 1:18-20.
16. John 1:1-4 (KJ). See also Psalm 105:7. The student will note that the authorized version differs from the Inspired Version at this point, but there is full agreement concerning the matter he discussed—the pre-earth life of Jesus, the Lord.
17. I John 1:1-3.
18. Doctrine and Covenants 90:1d-f; 76:3.
19. Ephesians 1:3, 4.

Study Helps for

Chapter 2

LESSON PURPOSE

To set the work of Jesus against the background of eternity, showing that our redemption is really the next step in our creation, planned by our Creator before the world was.

SCRIPTURE REFERENCES

Ephesians 1:3, 4; Colossians 1:13-17; D. and C. 90:1; Mosiah 8:53, 54.

HIGH POINTS OF THE LESSON

- Jesus was with God "in the beginning."
- Jesus was the active agent in creation. We can therefore be sure that the universe is built on love.
- The process of creation is still going forward, and our Creator, who was in it from the beginning, is still deeply immersed in the whole process.

QUESTIONS AND DISCUSSION TOPICS

1. What is the evidence that Jesus knew himself to have existed with the Father from the beginning? What difference did it make in his ministry?
2. What evidence is there that the ancient prophets were aware of the preexistence of Jesus? What difference did it make in their ministry?
3. The early Christian saints believed that Jesus was the Son of God from the beginning. What facts led them to this conviction? What did their belief require of the early Christian saints?
4. What is John's testimony about the preexistence of Jesus? Why has this testimony been repeated and confirmed to us today?
5. "I am Alpha and Omega, Christ the Lord; yea, even I am He, the beginning and the end, the Redeemer of the world" (D. and C. 18:1a). *Alpha* is the first letter in the Greek alphabet, and *omega* is the last. With this definition in mind, what does Christ mean in the opening statement of the preceding scripture?
6. What is the practical value of our belief that Jesus was an active agent in creation? Discuss this briefly.
7. What is the position of the church with regard to the apocryphal books (D. and C. 88)? What does the Apocrypha teach concerning the preexistence of Christ?
8. What does Paul mean in the statement: "He hath chosen us in him before the foundation of the world" (Ephesians 1:4)?
9. Discuss briefly the difference between two people, one of whom believes that we exist to work out the eternal purpose of our loving Creator in time and in eternity, and the other of whom believes that all our life is encompassed between birth and death.

WHAT THE LESSON MEANS FOR TODAY

Wise people fit their life plans into the greater plan of the eternal purposes of God. After he created the universe and placed people in it, he did not abandon it. The work of creation continues in the heavens and on earth. Christ continues to challenge us to grow in his likeness. Such an agelong endeavor requires our cooperation.

Chapter 3

JESUS AND THE PROPHETS

John tells us that God is love—that is, the love of God is of his very nature. When our forefathers flouted this love and insisted on walking in their own ways, God did not abandon them. Instead, he so loved the world that he gave his Only Begotten Son to teach the way of truth and life. If the Son's ministry was to be effective, however, the road had to be prepared before him. The ancient Hebrew prophets were his major trailblazers. Recognizing this, the writer of the Hebrew letter began:

> God, who at sundry times and in divers manners spake in time past unto the fathers by the prophets, hath in these last days spoken unto us by his Son, whom he hath appointed heir of all things, by whom also he made the worlds.[1]

This became part of the basic apostolic testimony.

Dr. R. B. Y. Scott wrote in 1944 that "Hebrew prophecy is the supreme element in what differentiated Israelite religion from other contemporary religions, and gave it a survival value they did not possess. Prophecy lies also at the heart of the Christian faith, for—whatever more one may say of Jesus—he was first of all a prophet."[2]

The prophets were men who had given themselves with complete abandon to the service of the God whom they knew in their own lives and through the religious experience of their people. "It was Yahweh who took me from herding the flock," said Amos simply of his call to the ministry.[3] "Here am I; send me," was Isaiah's prompt response to the call of God for someone to bear his message.[4]

The great prophets derived their spiritual power from a vivid awareness of the presence and activity in the turmoil of people's ordinary social life of the God they worshiped. They were tremendously concerned with social conditions and public issues as marking spiritual crises. They affirmed that every form of social order must be judged by spiritual consequences, and according to that judgment it will stand or fall. Isaiah said: "When you spread forth your hands, I will hide my eyes from you; even though you make many prayers, I will not listen; your hands are full of blood."[5]

Many of us think of prophets as the predictors of coming events, as, of course, the best of them were. But they were more than this. They were primarily enthusiasts for God, whose enthusiasm sometimes took strange forms—men who declared what they were convinced was the mind of God in particular circumstances or at a particular time.[6] They appealed, as did Jesus, from detail to principle, from cultus to conduct:

> Wherewith shall I come before the Lord, and bow myself before the most high God? shall I come before him with burnt offerings, with calves of a year old? Will the Lord be pleased with thousands of rams, or with ten thousands of rivers of oil? shall I give my firstborn for my transgression, the fruit of my body for the sin of my soul? He hath showed thee, O man, what is good; and what doth the Lord require of thee but to do justly, and to love mercy, and to walk humbly with thy God?[7]

Their frequent references to the future, and especially to the immediate future, resulted from their sense of the spiritual importance and moral urgency of the present. They are the contemporaries of every generation because the central truth they declare is permanently valid. What they say has the timeless quality and compelling power of authentic spiritual utterance.

The relevance of the prophets for today is not that they foresaw the course of events in the modern world. They do not *speak* of our age, but they do speak *to* it. The moral issues of their times were critical; the issues at stake today are similarly critical. If we can get past the local and temporal setting of their word as spoken to those of their ancient world, we shall find that it is spoken to us, too.[8]

The frequent references of Jesus to the prophets and

to the Psalms bear eloquent testimony to his familiarity with them. Many of the teachings of the prophets found place, often elevated, in his teachings. Among these we will do well to note the prophetic emphasis on the sovereignty of God. This was fundamental in all Hebrew religion: God was Israel's ruler and king. As far back as the earliest days of the Judges it is recorded that when Gideon was offered a crown, he replied, "I will not rule over you, neither shall my son rule over you; the Lord shall rule over you."[9]

The same awareness was evident at the beginning of the monarchy. When Saul was made king, Jehovah said to Samuel, the prophet, "They have not rejected thee, but they have rejected me, that I should not reign over them."[10]

The thought of the kingship of Jehovah over Israel is one that finds repeated expression in the Psalms, as, for example:

> The earth is the Lord's, and the fullness thereof; the world, and they that dwell therein.[11]
>
> I will extol thee, my God, O King; and I will bless thy name forever and ever. . . . All thy works shall praise thee, O Lord; and thy saints shall bless thee.[12]

The Jews of the times of Jesus regarded themselves as a specially chosen people. This tended to make the less perceptive among them insular and narrow. But in this they were not true to the greatest of their prophets and psalmists who saw and proclaimed the Father's outreach to all humankind. Isaiah wrote:

> I the Lord have called thee in righteousness, and will hold thine hand, and will keep thee, and give thee for a covenant of the people, for a light of the Gentiles; to open the blind eyes, to bring out the prisoners from the prison, and they that sit in darkness out of the prison house.[13]
>
> Behold my servant, whom I uphold; mine elect, in whom my soul delighteth; I have put my Spirit upon him; he shall bring forth judgment to the Gentiles. He shall not cry, nor lift up, nor cause his voice to be heard in the street. A bruised reed shall he not break, and the smoking flax shall he not quench; he shall bring forth judgment unto truth. He shall not fail nor be discouraged, till he have set judgment in the earth; and the isles shall wait for his law.[14]

When the time came for Jesus to begin his ministry, he did so in his hometown. His point of departure was the prophecy of Isaiah, which he read:

> The Spirit of the Lord is upon me, because he hath anointed me to preach the gospel to the poor, he hath sent me to heal the brokenhearted, to preach deliverance to the captives, and recovering of sight to the blind; to set at liberty them that are bruised; to preach the acceptable year of the Lord.[15]

Nothing could have been more significant. By this action Jesus lifted the prophetic word from its historic setting and gave it his own authority, saying, "This day is this scripture fulfilled in your ears."[16] By this declaration he announced the essential elements of his ministry to all who would follow him.

In the apostolic era the disciples found in the Old Testament many prophetic promises which they regarded as anticipating the coming of the deliverer. Of these, two in particular have been accepted by Christians down the generations as foretelling the coming of the Messiah. These include the words of Moses and those of Isaiah:

> I will raise them up a Prophet from among their brethren, like unto thee, and will put my words in his mouth; and he shall speak unto them all that I shall command him. And it shall come to pass, that whosoever will not hearken unto my words which he shall speak in my name, I will require it of him.[17]

> Behold, a virgin shall conceive and shall bear a son, and shall call his name Immanuel.[18]

> Unto us a child is born, unto us a son is given; and the government shall be upon his shoulder; and his name shall be called Wonderful, Counselor, The mighty God, The everlasting Father, The Prince of Peace. Of the increase of his government and peace there shall be no end, upon the throne of David, and upon his kingdom, to order it.[19]

Other prophecies which foretold the coming of the Messiah indicate the purpose of his coming. Isaiah wrote: "There shall come forth a shoot from the stump of Jesse, and a branch shall grow out of his roots. And the Spirit of the Lord shall rest upon him."[20]

This promise was repeated by Jeremiah: "Behold, the days come, saith the Lord, that I will raise unto David a righteous Branch, and a King shall reign and prosper, and shall execute judgment and justice in the earth."[21]

Some of the Psalms have similar emphases: "Thy throne, O God, is forever and ever; the scepter of thy kingdom is a right scepter."[22]

It is not unlikely, however, that the scriptures which Jesus read with the most sober concern were Psalm 22, the first words of which he was to quote from the cross, and Isaiah's "suffering servant" prophecy.[23]

The prophecies which have been noted were not made known within a short space of time. They were given and interpreted in the light of changing experience over a period of centuries, while the Israelites were growing from a single nomadic family to a mighty people, and while they were torn by internal dissensions, divided, scattered, regathered, separated, and reconquered. Moreover, the prophecies did not lead to a uniform understanding of what was to come. Indeed, countless varieties of interpretation were struggling for expression among the Jews in the years before "the fullness of the time was come." But they did create a spirit of expectation. When the day of Jesus came, many were looking for the Messiah, and they did have a fundamental idea of his character and calling.

NOTES

1. Hebrews 1:1-2.
2. R. B. Y. Scott, *The Relevance of the Prophets,* Macmillan Co., New York, p. 70. This is an excellent discussion to which I have referred frequently.
3. Amos 7:15, Jerusalem Bible.
4. Isaiah 6:8.
5. Isaiah 1:15, RSV.
6. See *Not as the Scribes,* H. G. G. Herklots, Student Christian Movement Press, London, p. 28.

7. Micah 6:6-8.
8. Scott, p. 14.
9. Judges 8:23.
10. I Samuel 8:7, KJ.
11. Psalm 24:1.
12. Psalm 145:1, 10.
13. Isaiah 42:6-7.
14. Isaiah 42:1-4.
15. Luke 4:18, 19.
16. Luke 4:21.
17. Deuteronomy 18:18, 19.
18. Isaiah 7:14.
19. Isaiah 9:6, 7.
20. Isaiah 11:1, RSV.
21. Jeremiah 23:5.
22. Psalm 45:6. See also Psalm 102:25-28.
23. Isaiah 53.

Study Helps for

Chapter 3

LESSON PURPOSE

To strengthen our conviction that Jesus Christ is the Son of God by showing that his coming was anticipated by godly people of earlier ages

SCRIPTURE REFERENCES

Isaiah 9:6, 7, 53; Luke 24:44-48; Mosiah 1:97-109; II Nephi 11:35, 36; I Nephi 3:52-62; Luke 1:27-38

HIGH POINTS OF THE LESSON

- Jesus Christ is the only spiritual leader of humankind whose advent and ministry have been foretold in detail.
- The purpose of the prophecies was to prepare the way of Jesus by setting up spiritual standards.
- The whole trend of Jewish national life was constructively influenced by the expectation of a great Deliverer.

QUESTIONS AND DISCUSSION TOPICS

1. What is the major purpose of prophecy? What is the value of prophecy which is not yet fulfilled?

2. In what ways can prophecy become a factor in the spiritual development of a people? Consider this in relation to the history of Israel. In the faith of the early Christians.

3. Read some of the prophecies listed in connection with the advent of Jesus. What was the value of these prophecies to those who heard them before they were fulfilled? What value do they have for us?

4. Read Luke 24:14-52, in which two disciples expressed their disappointment that Jesus, whom they believed would be their deliverer, had been slain. How did Christ relieve their anxiety as he talked to them, as related in verses 27, 44-46?

5. Under what conditions is prophecy likely to be most helpful? Who can best understand prophecy, the clever, the good, the devoutly studious? Why?

6. In view of the spiritual nature of the work prophesied of the coming Messiah, how was it that the Jews expected a political deliverer? What qualities in our own lives do we need to cultivate to understand the prophecies of Zion?

7. In what ways can the spirit of prophecy strengthen our present church life?

WHAT THE LESSON MEANS FOR TODAY

The best of the Jews expected a great Deliverer because it was like God to send them one. Today the most arresting prophecies of what lies before us are inextricably intertwined with revelations of the nature of God. It is like God to challenge us to build Zion under his guidance and to send his Son to earth again. We can trust these prophecies and shape our lives by them.

Chapter 4

THE INCARNATION

God, who created us in love, sought our responsive love from the beginning. He could not do otherwise if we were to be truly in his image. But he could not do this by command, for if he did we would not be free. So, from the beginning, he sought to make himself known to us and—of his great love—to persuade us to respond to the love which he offers us.

Being free, however, we chose to assert our freedom with scant regard for the divine purpose in our creation. Every man walked "in his own way."[1] And every time we acted in unloving rebellion our sense of the meaning of love became dim and warped. When we talked of love we meant human love, and human love is always tainted by selfishness and self-will. When we talked of good we meant good for our human purposes, not good in any ultimate sense. So language and love and understanding were corrupted and man became "sensual and devilish."[2]

In John Masefield's dramatic poem, "The Coming of Christ," four angels attempt to persuade Christ not to take the form of man in order to minister from among humans. They prophesied the suffering, the temptations, the pain, and the rejection which they see will follow such incarnation. Christ believed, nevertheless, that his coming might serve "to light the way for men from earth's unhappiness to very God." So he answered the angels:

> ...So be it then,
> But the attempt, being worthy, should be made,
> Having beheld men's misery, sin and death,
> Not to go was treason....
> I lay aside my glory and my power
> To take up Manhood. O brother Man, I come.[3]

When we as Christians talk of the "incarnation" we have in mind the coming of the Son of the living God into our world. When he did so it is our belief that our Lord bcame a true man—accepting the limitations of our humanity so as to promote our free acceptance of the will of God and make it our own. By becoming a man he did not cease to be the Son. While still loving God, yet living as a man, he made God known to us and at the same time showed us the glorious possibilities of life lived unto God.

Followers of the Lord Jesus, writing in the apostolic age, have left us their testimony:

> The Word was made flesh, and dwelt among us (and we beheld his glory, the glory as of the only begotten of the Father), full of grace and truth.[4]
>
> In this was manifested the love of God toward us, because that God sent his only begotten Son into the world, that we might live through him.[5]
>
> [Jesus]. . .took upon him the form of a servant, and was made in the likeness of men; and being found in fashion as a man, he humbled himself, and became obedient unto death, even the death of the cross.[6]

We look around us and see all sorts and conditions of people—a strange and bewildering mixture of goodness and badness, strength and weakness, purity and uncleanness, fidelity and faithlessness; of honor marred by self-interest, and dishonor lifted from the mire by unexpected elements of decency. When we try to construct for ourselves the human image that God intended, having all the virtues of these we admire most and avoiding all the defects of those whose lives fall short, we find that we and our friends cannot agree except in a very general way. Our power to see clearly is vitiated by our selfishness, class interests, hopes, fear, and pride. In our desperation we wonder whether there is anywhere a picture of the kind of person all others should strive to emulate, a standard by which we can judge what properly belongs to a person.

The Christian faith is that because of God's great love for us and his knowledge of our deep need for a perfect example, he sent his Son into the world; in his Son

Jesus, the perfect man, made in the image of God and unstained by sin, we have our true picture of what we ourselves could be.

> ...God so loved the world, that he gave his Only Begotten Son, that whosoever believeth on him should not perish; but have everlasting life. For God sent not his Son into the world to condemn the world; but that the world through him might be saved.[7]
>
> In him was the gospel, and the gospel was the life, and the life was the light of men.[8]

We frequently speak of the incarnation as though it included just the simple fact of the human birth of the Son of God. It does include this, but it also includes the whole human life of Jesus. The incarnation has to do with his birth, his growth, his steadfastness and clarity of vision under temptation, his fidelity to the truth in the presence of death, and to all that is involved in the fact that he—who is God—was also human. This was necessary because life does not belong to any one moment. Life involves growth.

Righteousness requires persistence. We may do right things individually, but we are not righteous until we are in the right way of life and our specifically right acts are woven together into a pattern.

To become a man, Jesus had to be born as a man is born and had to grow as a man must grow; he had to be tempted as a man is tempted and had to learn obedience by the things which teach a man to be obedient.[9]

Once we really get hold of this idea, we are saved from endless speculation regarding what Jesus knew at any specific period of his life. He knew what was appropriate for him to know at every stage of his growth. Such a viewpoint will also give importance to the life of Jesus in its entirety rather than in its parts. His birth, his temptation, his crucifixion, his resurrection, his ascension will not be regarded as isolated events; they will be understood in relation to his life as a whole. The manner of his birth is related to the life he was to live, and the manner of his death is the rightful climax to the life he had lived. At every stage in his life the relations of Jesus to his Father were the relations appropriate to a person of his age. The full process of identification with Divinity—the identification which comes at maturity and is a mark of real maturity—was possible only when Jesus himself was mature.

The fact that the Son of God lived among us means that we can come to know God as we never could have known him otherwise. But we must do our part. Understanding can never be imposed on us from without. This is illustrated by the fact that very few of those who visit the great art exhibitions really appreciate the pictures they go to see because they lack something in themselves. As they grow, the appeal of the pictures grows also. In much the same way many who saw Jesus saw him only as a prophet, a teacher, or miracle worker because of their own inner lack. The picture of God in Christ becomes meaningful only when understanding is illuminated by the Spirit of God. This is what Paul had in mind when he wrote, "It pleased God . . . to reveal his Son in me."[10] This revelation involves both the revelation of God in his Son and the appreciation and understanding of that revelation by those quickened by his Spirit.

Until the fairly recent past, belief in the incarnation has been associated in the minds of Christian people with belief in the virgin birth of our Lord. Although there has been revolt against this belief among some who find it unconvincing, the clear teaching of the New Testament is that Jesus cannot be explained by human forces alone. The world cannot account for him; history cannot explain him.

There are two stories of the birth of Jesus in the New Testament. The account given by Matthew is identical in both the King James and the Inspired versions.[11] The account in Luke differs slightly, but not basically.[12] Both of these narratives refer to Mary as a virgin and Luke emphasizes this by hailing Mary as such.[13] The reference is to a prophecy of Isaiah: "The Lord himself shall give you a sign; Behold, a virgin shall conceive, and shall bear a son, and shall call his name Immanuel."[14]

The Book of Mormon testimony supports that of the New Testament,[15] but the Doctrine and Covenants does not mention it even in the nearest approach to a creedal statement where it would seem that it might have been included most naturally.[16]

Belief in the virgin birth was not at first regarded as a test of faith, but the doctrine was thought of as complementary.[17] Nevertheless, the 1500 years from the time of the apostolic fathers until the Protestant Reformation, the virgin birth was one of the accepted axioms of Christian teaching. Belief in the virgin birth existed in Christian communities at the time when the gospels of Matthew and Luke were written.[18]

The story of Jesus' origin contains a vital and provocative universal message. The narratives which enshrine it can be understood by the people of all races and cultures and have formed a valuable means of teaching basic Christian doctrine. They affirm that two factors were at work in the coming of Jesus—the divine and the human. Each is vital to the total event. The participation of the Holy Spirit is significant here and for all future experiences of the disciples. The narratives are indicative of the high valuation which early Christians placed upon the personal Christ and their conviction that he was not to be explained solely in terms of human perfection.[19]

As we explore the meaning of the life of Jesus reverently and under the guidance of his Spirit, we learn more and more about life as God desires us to know and live it. Because in him Divinity was uniquely manifest, we shall not look for any future revelation which shall supersede the revelation in Jesus Christ our Lord. Because God by his Spirit dwelt miraculously in the life of Mary and so made the incarnation possible, we know that he can also dwell in our lives; when we become the willing instruments of his purpose, he can reveal his Son in us.

NOTES

1. Doctrine and Covenants 1:3e.
2. Doctrine and Covenants 17:4c.
3. This paragraph is copied from my book, *The Joy in Creation and Judgment,* pp. 119-120.
4. John 1:14, KJ.
5. I John 4:9.
6. Philippians 2:7, 8.
7. John 3:16, 17.
8. John 1:4.
9. Hebrews 5:8.
10. Galatians 1:15, 16.
11. Matthew 1:18-25, KJ; 2:1-8, IV.
12. Luke 1:26-28.
13. Luke 1:28.
14. Isaiah 7:14.
15. I Nephi 3:53-62; II Nephi 9:27; Alma 5:19.
16. Doctrine and Covenants 17:4, 5.
17. C. Thomas Boslooper, *The Virgin Birth,* Westminster Press, 1962, p. 230.
18. Ibid. pp. 216-217.
19. W. Norman Pittenger, *The Word Incarnate,* Harper & Bros., 1959.

Study Helps for

Chapter 4

LESSON PURPOSE

To show that God could be perfectly revealed only by God, and this revelation could be understood as God clothed himself in flesh and became human. To sense again the wonderful love of God which caused his Son to descend from heaven and become human for our sake.

SCRIPTURE REFERENCES

John 1:1-17, IV; Luke 1; Isaiah 9:6, 7.

HIGH POINTS OF THE LESSON

- From the beginning our heavenly Father has sought to teach us about himself. This revelation could not be fully expressed in words; it had to be a revelation in life. Jesus is the supreme revelation of God.
- Our heavenly Father has also been seeking to reveal to others by us the possibilities of our own nature. No person's life could portray this for human life has been distorted by sin. Therefore God must live in the flesh in order to help us understand him. Jesus revealed the nature of God for us.
- The incarnation is not just the birth of Jesus, but the life of Jesus: a life of communion and obedience. In Jesus the Word was made flesh.

QUESTIONS AND DISCUSSION TOPICS

1. John wrote that "God so loved the world that he gave his only begotten Son that whosoever believeth in him should not perish, but have everlasting life" (3:16). Take a few moments to meditate on this text and then ask class members to say what this means to them about God, about Jesus, about the value of people in the sight of God, about the cost to him of the love of God.
2. Jesus said to Thomas, "I am the way, the truth, and the life." What did he mean by each of these statements?
3. Why was God unable to reveal himself fully in the words and works of his prophets?
4. In what way does Jesus reveal the possibility that we may become the sons and daughters of God? How may we help each other in the way of understanding? What are the limits of our mutual helpfulness?
5. What do we mean when we speak of the incarnation?
6. Jesus taught with authority (Matthew 7:29). Note the importance of his sense of union with the Father in connection with this authority (John 12:49). Comment on the nature of ministerial authority in light of this.
7. What is the value of study of the incarnation in your own religious life? Consider the major ministries of the church as they enhance our understanding and gratitude for the incarnation: preaching, sacraments, teaching.
8. Reflect on the sacramental prayers (D. and C. 17:22-23). In what ways do the Father and the Holy Spirit sustain and give meaning to the incarnation of the Lord Jesus?

WHAT THE LESSON MEANS FOR TODAY

In the life of Jesus is the great revelation of God and of persons. It is our distinctive glory that the life of God can be revealed, to a degree, in our lives. The incarnation is made meaningful in the lives of faithful disciples.

Chapter 5

WHY JESUS WAS A JEW

Great people bring a new and distinctive force into the world, but their lives fit into the background of their people and their times. It is because they belong to the past, even while they reach forward into the future, that their lives illustrate for us the transition from the old into the new, the yesterdays into the tomorrows. If we are to understand them, it is therefore important that we know something about their backgrounds. This is especially true of Jesus, who decided for himself of what race he should be born. The question "Why was Jesus a Jew?" is no idle one. To answer it satisfactorily we must know something of Jesus and something of the people among whom he lived and worked.

It is not too much to say that Jesus could not have been born among any other people if he were to do his distinctive work in history and in human souls. Indeed, we believe that God created the Jewish people and set them apart from all others that their race might give birth to Jesus and to his early disciples, and that their religion and history might become the inheritance of a new community which Jesus would bring into being, which we know as the church.

Jesus did not begin his work in a vacuum. He was a Jew, and Jews owe their existence to the selective action and subsequent guidance of Divinity.[1] They grew from a family to a great multitude in Egypt, but because the years in Egypt had distilled slavery into their blood, God provided them a great leader, Moses, who marched them up and down almost within sight of the Promised Land but did not permit them to cross over until the generation tainted with slavery had been succeeded by a new and free generation. Through the

vicissitudes of a long history, these people were shaped by triumph and adversity, by the constant call of their destiny, and by the unfailing patience of Divinity into a truly great nation. By the time the stage was set for the earthly ministry of Jesus, the Jews had once more become a subject people under the political domination of Rome, but their distinctive genius had not been crushed out. Instead, this genius had found its richest expression in their religious life. Among them were those who could grasp the message of Jesus, and who would find in older religious literature, as well as in their own expanding experiences, compelling reasons to follow him.

In their growth toward God, the Jews were led by men of two distinct types—the prophets and the priests. The prophets were men of keen spiritual insight. Because they loved God and were in close touch with him, they brought a disturbing message concerning the obligations God had put on the children of Israel by the fact of choosing them as his peculiar people. Thus, Elijah, eight hundred years before the time of Christ, denounced the iniquity of King Ahab and of his vacillating people: "How long halt ye between two opinions? if the Lord be God, follow him; but if Baal, then follow him."[2] Said Amos, "Hate the evil, and love the good, and establish judgment in the gate."[3] Isaiah sounded the same call:

> Wash ye, make you clean; put away the evil of your doings from before mine eyes; cease to do evil; learn to do well; seek judgment, relieve the oppressed, judge the fatherless, plead for the widow. Come now, and let us reason together, saith the Lord; though your sins be as scarlet, they shall be as white as snow; though they be red like crimson, they shall be as wool. If ye be willing and obedient, ye shall eat the good of the land; but if ye refuse and rebel, ye shall be devoured with the sword; for the mouth of the Lord hath spoken it.[4]

It was not the function of the prophets to organize and systematize. Their major and important work was to illuminate, to blaze the trail of insight and of understanding. Others, the priests, must make the path into a road and the road into a highway.

> The religious teachers of Israel set to work to mark with unmistakable indications these right paths for thought and conduct. They would make the discoveries of the seers and prophets into prescriptions for the people. At every doubtful turning of the moral code, they would set up a signpost; and these signposts were "the law."[5]

It was obviously necessary that in setting up these guides for the religious life of their people, the priests should share something of the spirit of the prophets.

It was at this very point, however, that many of the priests and Jews went astray. They substituted the letter of the law for the spirit of the prophets. When the law became an end in itself that was obeyed from a sense of duty only, the law which should have liberated them became a taskmaster, driving them with the whip of fear along a dark and difficult road.

The priests did not have things all their own way, for many Jews were men of prophetic mind. By the time of John and Jesus, there was constant conflict between those who interpreted the revelations of the past in the spirit of the prophets and those who interpreted them in the spirit of the codifers, making "a man an offender for a word." Yet when we become impatient with the scribes and Pharisees whom we meet in the New Testament, we must remember that they and their predecessors did much to keep the religion of Israel free from taint and to preserve it so that the faithful among the Jews in that day were "waiting for the consolation of Israel" and living in expectancy of the coming Messiah.[6]

Unlike the people of the surrounding nations, the Jews believed in one God who made us in his own image, put something of himself into everyone, and was intensely concerned about the welfare of all. They thought of God as choosing to work with those who chose to do his will, as making covenants with carefully selected groups who were willing to become the agents of his universal and kindly purpose. They remembered that he had chosen Noah in a day of wickedness, Abraham in a day of darkness, Israel when in bondage in Egypt, and the remnant of Israel after the Captivity. Because of this distinctive faith in an energetic, divine purpose which was finding its expression in them, the Jews were ideally suited—despite their many failings—to be the people from whom the Lord should come and from among whom his earthly associates should be chosen, to provide a great literature for him and for his disciples, to dream of a kingdom of justice, and to cherish the hope of a Deliverer who would save humankind.

When Jesus began his ministry, he had available to him and accepted by the people among whom he worked the Law of Moses, the Prophets, and the Psalms.[7] The use Jesus made of this material is indicated in the fact that two of the Gospels tell us that the public teaching of Jesus began with a discourse from one of the great passages of the Old Testament,[8] and all of them show that it was here he sought much of his ammunition in his conflict with the devil.[9] Even more important than this was the use the Master made of the scriptures throughout his life as a treasury of wisdom and revelation. During his public ministry he constantly referred to them, showing an insight which must have been the product of long meditation and deep appreciation. He especially loved the Prophets and the Psalms.

Throughout the scriptures and deep in the traditions and hopes of the Jews ran their expectation of the kingdom. The kingdom was nowhere clearly defined. Sometimes one aspect was stressed and sometimes another. At its best, the kingdom ideal concerned a great people made powerful through righteousness growing out of devotion to Divinity. At other times the kingdom hope was almost purely nationalistic and even materialistic. But at least the kingdom hope was there, a hope that, when clearly understood, centered in the religious life rather than the political life of the people.

This kingdom was to be transformed at the hands of Jesus so as to be almost unrecognizable, but it was a point with which to begin. Moreover, it was treasured by the common people more than by the intelligentsia, for while the latter debated regarding the minutiae of the law, the common people sought to prepare themselves that they might be ready to welcome the Messiah who was to come as their heaven-sent leader.

Why was Jesus a Jew? Because here, among the Jews, God had prepared a place for him. Because here, in the Jews, God had prepared a people for him. It is not surprising that the nation as a nation failed to rise to the height of its most inspired leaders, for no nation has ever done that; but at least this nation developed a nucleus of men and women of genuine spiritual quality who expressed in their own lives the essential greatness of their race. To them their religion was life, their history was the record of God's great work of preparation, their literature was the expression of the word of God against the background of their history. Jesus was a Jew, in a distinctive sense, because the Jews were God's own people.

NOTES

1. Genesis 12:1, 2.
2. I Kings 18:21.
3. Amos 5:15.
4. Isaiah 1:16-20.
5. Walter Russell Bowie, *The Master, a Life of Jesus Christ,* p. 52.
6. Luke 2:25-32.
7. Luke 24:44.
8. Luke 4:17-19; Matthew 15:7-9.
9. Matthew 4:4, 7, 10.

Study Helps for

Chapter 5

LESSON PURPOSE

To show that in spite of its limitations, Jewish national life was the necessary and divinely prepared background for the ministry of Jesus.

SCRIPTURE REFERENCES

Genesis 12:1, 2; Isaiah 1:16-20; Luke 2:25-32.

HIGH POINTS OF THE LESSON

- The work of the prophets of Israel in teaching the righteous character of God
- The place of the priests in the history of Israel—their importance and limitations
- The great religious concepts of the Jews: There is but one God, who is seeking to establish his kingdom of righteousness among people who need, and shall be given, leadership from heaven and from the scriptures.

QUESTIONS AND DISCUSSION TOPICS

1. Why is it important, if we are to understand great people, that we shall know something about their backgrounds? Discuss this briefly in relation to such people as Moses, Mary, the mother of Jesus, Paul, Abraham Lincoln, Joseph Smith.
2. Name three high points in the history of Israel that show God's direction and preservation of their nation.
3. What was the function of the prophets among the Hebrew people? Name some of the great prophets. Were they accepted by the people of their time. Why?
4. What was the function of the priests in Judaism? What were the values in their work? What were some of their limitations?
5. What sound beliefs did the most devout of the Jews of the time of Christ hold about God? What were the less sound expectations of many Jews of that time? How did their belief in God prepare for the ministry of Jesus?
6. What did a Jew of the time of Jesus mean by the law? By the prophets? What part did it play in their religious life?
7. What was the attitude of Jesus toward the scriptures of his people? In what way did his life and death shed light on the scriptures? (Luke 24:25-27).
8. How is the history of Israel the story of the preparation made by God for the coming of his Son into the world? What preparation is God making for the return of his Son?

WHAT THE LESSON MEANS FOR TODAY

Our heavenly Father sought to prepare the way for the coming of his Son. He is still doing so. There is a sense in which every advance in corporate righteousness is a response to this age-long endeavor.

Chapter 6

THE BOYHOOD OF JESUS

Only two of the four Gospels mention the childhood of Jesus directly. Of these, Matthew quite evidently tells of the flight into Egypt and the return to Nazareth to strengthen his argument in the minds of the Jews that this flight fulfilled the prophecy of Hosea.[1] Luke, however, had a genuine personal interest. Perhaps he was just that kind of person; or it may be he was interested as a doctor.[2] Or, again, it may be that since he had inquired so carefully into the origins of Christianity,[3] he was anxious to give details for the sake of completeness. Whatever may have been his motivation, we owe Luke more than we at first realize for his brief but illuminating comment that "the child grew, and waxed strong in spirit, being filled with wisdom, and the grace of God was upon him."[4]

The words "filled with wisdom" might be more exactly rendered as "becoming filled with wisdom" so as to describe a continuous process of growth, for evidently Jesus grew normally in response to the life of his time.[5] Devout Christians of an earlier age found this hard to believe, and many imaginative stories of his childhood and youth were repeated and treasured by them. But there is more of divinity in the simple statement of Luke, and in the facts supporting it, than in all the fantastic stories put together.

In addition to the direct references to the childhood of Jesus given us by Luke, there are several other indications of the nature and circumstances of the boyhood of the Master. For example, the best preachers and teachers are those who can illustrate their lessons with vivid stories of human interest. Such stories have their finest appeal when they are drawn from memory rather than from imagination. Never did preacher or teacher use illustrations as freely or as effectively as did the Master. It therefore seems quite reasonable to suppose that the parables, taken generally, mirror the early life of Jesus.

There is little about the life of Jesus as it is thus reconstructed to give cause for comment unless it is the fact of its wholesome simplicity. Jesus was a boy. He was set apart by his heritage even as some boys of today are set apart by their heritage, but he was still a boy—immature, friendly, curious, growing gradually but surely toward manhood, and learning as he grew. Looking into his life through the windows formed by the parables, we can see him as he watched his mother putting the leaven to work[6] while the oven was kept hot by the "grass of the field." At first it would seem that the heaving mass was mere bubbles rising, bursting, falling, rising again in endless effervescent confusion. Then he saw that the bubbles were insignificant. The life within leavening "the whole" was what mattered. Jesus never forgot that lesson. There was also a time when Jesus found to his dismay that there was another rent in clothes which had already been patched and repatched. His mother had reached the point of diminishing returns in the clothes-patching business, and nothing could be done except to get new garments. Years later Jesus used this memory to discomfort the scribes and Pharisees,[7] but even as he did so, he probably smiled at the memory of his boyish dismay when he first learned that after a time it is futile to put new cloth on old garments.[8]

We also find help in visualizing the early life of Jesus by reconstructing the homelife of Nazareth in his day. Twenty miles from Nazareth, the blue waters of the Mediterranean sparkled in the sun, and the Mediterranean was the center of life in the civilized world.

From a hilltop nearby, Jesus could see the plain of Esdraelon, on which his vivid imagination could easily stage the battles which had taken place there in the course of his country's history. Right through the village ran the highway from Syria to Egypt, where the armies of these ancient rivals had now been succeeded by the marching legions of Rome. Here were wonderful opportunities for observation and conversation, and no boy with an imagination such as Jesus had could live in this place without gaining a liberal education in the ways of people and of nations. Even as a boy, Jesus recognized that "Go ye into all the world" was much more than an idle phrase.

Modern Nazareth is a major center of attraction for tourists. The village was probably much smaller in the days of Jesus, but it was not altogether without its importance in the life of the country. In many ways it was typical of the province. Everyone knew what happened to everyone else, and the evening gatherings of the Nazarenes around the single copious spring or the weekly gatherings in the synagogue made the village life very similar to that of a large family.

There was nothing sumptuous about the houses of peasant families in Palestine. Constant hard work probably kept bitter poverty away from the door of Joseph and Mary, but there was need for the most rigid economy at all times. The small square brick or stone dwelling place probably had a single room with a dirt floor, one door, and possibly one narrow window. The roof was flat and made of timber or boughs covered with straw and mud. This roof was reached by an outside stairway and was in much demand as an extra room, either for coolness or quiet. Under such circumstances privacy was difficult, and this may have led Jesus to form the habit of retiring to the hillside to pray. Jesus must have learned the value of communion with nature quite early.

Despite their honorable lineage, Joseph and Mary were neither rich nor powerful, but they were members of the dignified and quietly purposeful group which formed the background of the nation. They were the highest product of the long effort of Divinity to create for himself a peculiar people, zealous of good works. Avoiding all extremes, they looked forward with deep concern to the great days which the prophets had foretold. Among such people the coming of the Messiah was eagerly awaited, even if they were not quite clear as to his work and purpose. In view of this expectancy, they held childhood as something especially precious, for they believed that any of these little ones might prove to be the promised Savior.

Jesus himself is the only member of the family more frequently mentioned than Mary, his mother. There is a well established tradition that Joseph died soon after the visit to the temple;[9] if this is so, it explains rather simply the absence of further mention of him. The sayings of Jesus indicate that he had a pleasant home-life, and that Joseph was a kindly man who knew how "to give good gifts to his children."[10]

James, Joseph, Simon, and Judah and at least two girls probably composed the family group.[11] These may have been the children of Joseph by an earlier marriage or, much more likely, the children of Joseph and Mary. If the latter, then they were all younger than Jesus. He grew up in their company, sharing the discipline of the home and knowing the slight irritations and joys of such fellowship. In these simple surroundings, his capacity for leadership was first in demand, and when the children in the marketplace could find none willing to play with them, their elder brother was probably called in to maintain or to reestablish the peace.[12]

The Jews of that day had great respect for education. As soon as he could speak, the boy Jesus was taught the "Shema," the opening words of which he quoted with such telling effect in his controversy with the scribes.[13] Before long he and his fellows were singing from the psalms. Then, when he was six, he attended the elementary school attached to the village synagogue, where he was instructed in reading and writing as a further preparation for the study of the scriptures and the religion of his fathers. Much time was spent in memorizing the Law and the Prophets and the psalms, since the Jews felt that religion was the explanation of their national existence and the guide to the fulfillment of their national destiny. In addition to his religious studies, Jesus at some time must have learned Greek; he was later able to talk with Gentiles without an interpreter. At home Jesus spoke Aramaic.

The law required parents to instruct their children in the history and religion of their nation.[14] They took very seriously the injunction:

> These words, which I command thee this day, shall be in thine heart; and thou shalt teach them diligently unto thy children, and shalt talk of them when thou sittest in thine house, and when thou walkest by the way, and when thou liest down, and when thou risest up. And thou shalt bind them for a sign upon thine hand, and they shall be as frontlets between thine eyes. And thou shalt write them upon the posts of thy house, and on thy gates.[15]

Little boxes containing these words and those of Deuteronomy 11:13-21 were to be found on every Jewish doorpost, and other small boxes containing Exodus 13:2-10 and 11-16 and Deuteronomy 6:4-9 and 11:13-21 were bound on the forehead and arms of the Jews when they prayed. Moreover, such parents as Joseph and Mary went much further than the formal observances and followed the spirit of the law in teaching their children to treasure the word of God in their hearts. Much of the fluency in quoting the law and the insight in interpreting it which the Master later displayed can be traced to the rigid training and the patient and wise explanations of his early years.

Other religious observances in the home were also truly educational. Every month was ushered in at the time of the new moon with sacrifices, a feast, and a holiday.[16]

The Sabbath was welcomed with songs as a bridegroom, and each household observed it as a season of sacred rest and of joy. As the head of the house returned on the Sabbath eve from the synagogue to his home, he found it festively adorned, the Sabbath lamp brightly burning, and the table spread with the richest each household could afford. But first he blessed each child with the blessing of Israel.[17]

Then, too, there were the yearly feasts—the good cheer and merriment of Purim, commemorating the deliverance of the nation in the time of Esther; the Feast of Dedication, with its lighted candle for each member of the household; the Feast of Tabernacles, when the whole family, even to the youngest, lived in tents;[18] the Passover, when young and old relived the deliverance from Egypt, ate the unleavened bread, and united in singing the Passover psalms.[19]

Luke takes us back into the boyhood of Jesus to tell us the story of his visit to the Temple when he was twelve.[20] This may not have been the first Temple visit of Jesus, but it was important because it occurred at about the time when he became a "son of the Law" according to Jewish customs. To one who had been trained in the stricter requirements and expectations of Judaism, and who already took his religious life very seriously, such a trip could not fail to be deeply significant. Men and women from all over the country and from foreign lands went up to the holy city at the same time, and he went with the throng to the house of God, "with the voice of joy and praise," a multitude keeping holyday.[21] When he arrived with his family, Jesus went into the Temple with a new sense of responsibility, with a feeling of awe in the holy place, combined with a consciousness of his own unique relation thereto. This very site had been captured for

Jehovah by his great ancestor, David; this very Temple had been built in praise of Jehovah by Solomon and had been graced by the presence of Divinity. It is not difficult to imagine the enthusiasm and fervent zeal with which Jesus joined the other worshipers in singing the Pilgrim Psalm to the accompaniment of the music of the trumpet and of the cymbal and of the many stringed instruments and organs.[22]

For the seven days of the feast, Jesus reveled in the beauty and pageantry of the occasion. Then his parents started on the four-day journey to Nazareth. It is probable that Jesus went back for a last look at the Temple or to sit for the last time in one of the numerous discussion circles, and that his parents thought him occupied in some other part of the caravan and so did not at first bother to look for him. Whatever the cause for delay, Jesus turned naturally to the Temple when he found himself alone. Here, after three days, his distressed parents found him "sitting in the midst of the doctors, and they were hearing him and asking him questions."[23]

All of us know the reply Jesus made to the anxious questioning of his mother: "Knew ye not that I must be about my Father's business?"[24]

There has been endless speculation as to the exact meaning of this reply. We shall never know the fullness of what was in his heart at that time until Jesus himself explains it to us. But we do not have to overload the incident with a great weight of emphasis to know that here was someone who looked at life uniquely. After the experiences of the past week, it seemed to him there was only one place for his parents to look for him, and that was in the house of his Father. Moreover, in view of the homelife he had shared with them, and of this week in which all the past had been gathered up in one great experience, there was only one thing he could do in his

Father's house, and that was to be about his Father's business. Whether those around him realized it or not, life was never the same for him after that week. From that time forward, Jesus was committed to the best in the religion of his fathers and to the best in the work of his heavenly Father.

NOTES

1. Matthew 3:13-23.
2. Colossians 4:14.
3. Luke 1:2.
4. Luke 2:40.
5. Doctrine and Covenants 90:2.
6. Matthew 13:32.
7. Mark 2:19.
8. Matthew 9:22.
9. Luke 2:41-52.
10. Matthew 7:20.
11. Mark 6:4.
12. Luke 7:32.
13. Mark 12:34, 35.
14. Deuteronomy 4:9.
15. Deuteronomy 6:6-9.
16. Psalm 81:3.
17. Edersheim, *Sketches of Jewish Social Life,* p. 97.
18. Isaac Bronson Burgess, *The Life of Christ,* pp. 55, 56.
19. Psalms 113-118.
20. Luke 2:41-50.
21. Psalm 42:4.
22. Psalm 150.
23. Luke 2:46.
24. Luke 2:49.

Study Helps for

Chapter 6

LESSON PURPOSE

To indicate the influence of the boyhood of Jesus in shaping his later ministry

SCRIPTURE REFERENCES

Luke 2:21-40; 41-50

HIGH POINTS OF THE LESSON

- A major characteristic of the childhood of Jesus was its wholesome simplicity.
- Jesus grew in a home which knew the discipline of parents, of work, and of the social group.
- The education of Jesus centered in religion and in history, which were directly related.
- In the light of such training, and of his own personality, the visit to the Temple marked a natural spiritual crisis in the life of Jesus.

QUESTIONS AND DISCUSSION TOPICS

1. How important was the childhood and youth of Jesus in relation to his adult life? Reflect on the parables as indication of his early interests.
2. Analyze what Luke meant when he reported that "Jesus increased in wisdom and stature, and in favor with God and man."
3. What do we know of the home of Jesus? What were its major values? What were its limitations?
4. Who were the immediate and more remote relatives of Jesus? What were the major interests of Mary? Joseph? The other family members?
5. Why do you think the disciples left such meager records of the boyhood of Jesus?
6. Name some other factors in the life of Jesus as a youth: his reading, his acquaintance with priests, tradesmen, soldiers, the surrounding countryside.
7. What is the significance of the visit of Jesus to the Temple when he was twelve?

WHAT THE LESSON MEANS FOR TODAY

The group in which Jesus grew in "wisdom and stature and in favor with God and man" was apparently a simple and unpretentious one. The spiritual forces needed to shape the lives of great persons are available to similar families and groups.

Chapter 7

THE CARPENTER

Many of us find it difficult to imagine our Lord concerned with the tasks of village carpentry which occupied him during his young manhood, but there was nothing unusual in such work even among the families of wealthy Jews. Every Jewish boy of that day learned a trade on which he could fall back in times of necessity, and we catch many glimpses of the great leaders of the time turning from their public activities to their private business concerns. Saul, "a Pharisee, the son of a Pharisee," was a tentmaker and supported himself by his trade during his ministry.[1] Luke traveled with this tentmaker and probably worked as a doctor.[2] "The Pharisees were men of substance, cheesemongers, oilmen, corn handlers, with one or two landowners."[3] If Jesus had not worked among his fellows in much the same fashion as they did, he would have been censured as an idler who would not learn to provide for those dependent on him.

Jesus began his life as a carpenter by helping Joseph in the little shop close by their home, or possibly attached to it.[4] His first tasks were such things as handing a needed tool to Joseph or holding steady a piece of work requiring special care. Soon he was graduated from these things to the larger duties of the shop, and when Joseph died, Jesus was ready to take over the responsibilities of the business. The hours thus spent had their influence in shaping his life and providing insight into the lives of the common people, and throughout his ministry we find Jesus going back to phrases and illustrations and habits of thought which must have had their origin in the days when he was a carpenter.

Jesus tells us of the necessity of securing a good foundation before beginning to build,[5] of the builder whose uncompleted task was a constant reminder of the importance of careful planning and "counting the cost,"[6] of the man who was so concerned about building bigger barns that he forgot to live.[7] All these, and a dozen other indirect glimpses into his early life, show us a young man who planned his work carefully and very probably directed the work of a few others who shared the duties of the carpenter's shop with him. A recent translation of Mark's reference to the period (Mark 6:3) seems to confirm this point of view. It says: "Is not this the Master-Carpenter?"

Another set of facts also seems to indicate that Jesus learned to exercise authority early in life. These facts center around his ready direction of men who had themselves been accustomed to command—Peter and John who owned their own fishing boats and Zacchaeus "who was chief among the publicans." Then, too, his unquestioned leadership among the disciples was not just the natural response to his spiritual stature. He had learned how to be kind without sacrificing his dignity so that those near to him were at ease and yet never unduly familiar. He was their leader, and he acted as a leader, but he was also their friend. All this was in part the outcropping of his natural dignity, but even so it was not learned in a day. Where could he have learned it except in his home and in the carpenter's shop?

Although Jesus was probably responsible for determining the trend of the business, he also took his place in turning out the work which was to be done. We cannot imagine a man of his genius remaining in a subordinate place in the business for very long. There was not enough planning, however, for this to occupy all his time, so he probably worked right with his brothers and other companions. The story of the man who had a splinter in his eye surely goes back to a time when several men were working together in the shop, and one who could not see clearly himself tried to help out another who had just been injured.[8]

As the village carpenter, Jesus was familiar with every home in Nazareth. In the shed or sitting by the roadside under the palms, he and his brothers fashioned plows or yokes for the oxen or mended the packsaddles or chests of the journeymen passing through. At other times they were called in to repair or rebuild the barns and sheds of the neighborhood, or to build the outside stairs which made an extra room of the flat roof. As Jesus worked he talked with those who stood by, sharing their friendly comment and at the same time probing to see what they were like and what motives moved them. During these years he must have made many friends, such as those who invited him to their wedding feast,[9] and these friends came to know him for what he was then—an outstanding man. He was a stimulating person to know, with his direct but picturesque speech, his keen imagination, his quick humor, his earnestness and ready sympathy, his careful workmanship, and the many other elements of that friendly charm which later drew so many to him.

It is possible that Jesus moved his home and shop to Capernaum sometime prior to the beginning of his public ministry. An artisan in those days was likely to follow the course of business in this way almost as readily as a soldier or a trader. Such a move explains the willingness with which Peter and Andrew and James and John followed him when he invited them to do so,[10] for they probably knew him at Capernaum. This change placed Jesus in a large industrial center, for Capernaum was to Galilee what Jerusalem was to Judea, and here he found a greater variety of work than had been available heretofore. In particular, he was now in constant touch with the fishermen whose boats put into Capernaum every day from their work on the lake and whose repairs made a desirable addition to his trade.

Carpentry under such circumstances offered wonderful opportunities for friendship. Much of Jesus' work had to be done while a client was waiting for a plow to be repaired, or while another was resting on the road from one city to another, or when the fishermen came in after a night on the water. At such times people are talkative and friendly, and since they had no reason to be on their guard against him, these friendly customers probably opened their lives freely and without reserve to the scrutiny of his genius.

Jesus found other happiness in his work. He was more than a mere workman. He was a craftsman. Such a man as he was must have known real satisfaction in making the simple implements of the day as well as they could be made. Pride of workmanship is an important part of one's life. Nothing ministers so completely to the self-respect of those who love their work as the joy of definite and beautiful accomplishment—the yoke smoothly shaped to the shoulder, the chest squarely and strongly built, the door well hung in its frame, the foundation securely set for the house of a friend. All these belonged to Jesus in a sense in which they could never belong to anyone other than their maker. It is not difficult to imagine him running his hand with lingering affection along the well-rounded plow handle before passing it on to the waiting farmer.

There was no idle time in the carpenter's shop. People had little spare equipment, and when anything broke it had to be mended well and quickly. So the years brought their steady discipline, their mounting skill, the habit of careful planning, and that well-rounded wholeness of life which comes from meeting the tasks of each day intelligently and without undue haste and worry. For the Master Carpenter peace was not just stagnation; it was the pleasant hum of activity which comes when people work together in skillful goodwill and toward a common end.

The picture we have reconstructed from the scanty information of the Gospels may be faulty in some details, but is not untrue to the main facts of the life of the Master between his visit to the Temple and his appearance at the Jordan for baptism. It is not the picture we might have drawn had we not known Jesus. Except for him we might have despised the disciplines of industry. But it is the picture required by our groping understanding of the humanity as well as the divinity of the Master. He grew as we may grow. He matured in wisdom and understanding through thirty years of normal life and work. Daily he measured his strength against the disintegration and collapse which come from the wear and tear of life. In doing so he learned important lessons which he later transferred to the field of his larger activities. He always sought sure foundations in the lives of people and built thereon so firmly that wind and storm could not destroy. He led the way, making the plans and determining the course of action for those less able than he, but he also shared his work with his friends according to their strength and skill so that they might grow through sharing. Knowing life, he knew also that the finest product of any task well done is a life well built.

NOTES

1. Acts 18:2, 3; I Thessalonians 2:9.
2. Colossians 4:14.
3. *By an Unknown Disciple,* p. 115.

4. Mark 6:1-6.
5. Matthew 7:34, 35.
6. Luke 14:29-31.
7. Luke 12:18-22.
8. Luke 6:41, 42.
9. John 2:1, 2.
10. Matthew 4:12, 17-21.

Study Helps for

Chapter 7

LESSON PURPOSE

To emphasize the importance of the daily task in relation to the growth of character

SCRIPTURE REFERENCES

Exodus 31:1-6; I Thessalonians 3:11, 12; II Thessalonians 3:10-12; D. and C. 68:4; 75:5.

HIGH POINTS OF THE LESSON

- The work of Jesus helped to shape his later habits of thought and expression.
- This work provided excellent training in self-discipline; the management of others, time, and effort; and in contacts with the people of the vicinity.
- Jesus was more than a workman. He was a craftsman.

QUESTIONS AND DISCUSSION TOPICS

1. Cite some of the evidences that the Master's life as a carpenter directly affected his ministry.

2. Describe the relations of the village carpenter to the people of the village. How did Jesus use his business opportunities as a means of expressing his religious conviction?

3. What do we mean by craftsmanship? What reason do we have for believing that Jesus was a craftsman? (Matthew 11:30.)

4. One writer describes the success of the later work of Jesus in these words: "His world-transforming work was the culmination of long experience, observation, meditation, and thorough study." Note the importance of these aspects of the preparation and life of Jesus.

5. Name aspects of the leadership of Jesus among his disciples and others matured during his experience as a carpenter.

6. Consider the employment of the men nearest the Master. Did their discipleship affect their employment? What principle should guide our counsel to young people as they prepare for a lifework?

7. The prayer life of Jesus, so notable during the years of his public

ministry, probably became well established prior to the opening of that ministry. Consider its effect in the life of Jesus the carpenter.

8. What does the vocational life of Jesus teach us about the nature of stewardship?

WHAT THE LESSON MEANS FOR TODAY

One of our greatest needs in building the kingdom of God is consecrated craftsmanship. There is no development of character without it. Those whose good intentions never lead to good work are not Zion-builders; they are not good Christians; they are unfulfilled promise. No matter where we live, we have abundant opportunities for real growth through real work if we have the will to find them.

Chapter 8

JESUS AND JOHN THE BAPTIST

During the years when Jesus was growing to maturity, his kinsman John, six months his senior, was also growing up. John was a child of the desert—austere, solitary, and passionately concerned about the spiritual destiny of his people. It is quite likely that Jesus and John were well acquainted with each other. Indeed, it is almost impossible to believe that two young men, related both by blood and by their deep interest in things spiritual, should have been entirely unacquainted. Yet we cannot do more than conjecture as to the closeness of their intimacy. We know only that it was limited by the fact that Jesus lived and worked near the centers of social and industrial life and that John was constantly in the desert. We also have the direct statement of the scriptures that John "knew him not."[1] The context shows that this latter statement does not mean that John was not acquainted with Jesus but that he did not know Jesus as "the Lamb of God."

The times were ripe, and the spiritually alert among the Jews were looking for the coming of the Messiah. Malachi had prophesied that the work of the Messiah would be preceded by that of a second Elijah, a forerunner, who was to prepare the way before him.[2] As the people crowded to listen to the message of John, many of them remembered this prophecy of Malachi, and they questioned among themselves, "Can this be the promised Elijah?"[3] Then when John called himself "the voice of one crying in the wilderness,"[4] the people recognized this as a reference to Isaiah[5] wherein the prophet had stressed the judgment and testing and purifying which were to attend the coming of this Elijah, this "messenger of the covenant."

John the Baptist was an honest man. His concern for the coming of the kingdom was deep and sincere. Indeed, for John nothing else mattered; his devotion left him completely untroubled by unworthy ambition. He therefore met the questions of priests and Levites with a perfectly frank statement that he was not Elias, nor was he "that prophet." He was a "man sent from God" who "came for a witness, to bear witness of the light."[6] His work would be totally ineffective unless he was followed by the One mightier than he who would baptize "with fire, and with Holy Ghost."[7] He therefore gladly prepared the way for his greater successor, anticipating the fulfillment of the prophecy of Zacharias, his father:

> And thou, child, shalt be called the prophet of the Highest, for thou shalt go before the face of the Lord to prepare his ways, to give knowledge of salvation unto his people, by baptism for the remission of their sins, through the tender mercy of our God; whereby the dayspring from on high hath visited us, to give light to them who sit in darkness and the shadow of death; to guide our feet into the way of peace.[8]

The Gospels indicate that the work of John was well done and people of all classes flocked to hear him. His message was not an easy one but was nevertheless admirably adapted to the needs of a time when the oppression of the Romans, the wickedness of those in high places, and their own deep need of deliverance had combined to prepare the Jews for such a ministry. Yet many of the people felt that because they were "the children of Abraham," they were entitled to the special protection of Divinity as long as they observed the outward ordinances of the law. From this moral myopia John rescued them by the clear and simple sanity of his message. He declared that no matter what their heritage, to find acceptance with God they must bring forth fruits worthy of repentance, sharing their goods with the needy, doing violence to no one, making no false accusations, living honorably in the sight of all.[9]

The dominant note in John's preaching was the coming of the kingdom of God. He saw and preached that the fundamental condition of salvation in the kingdom is a change of heart and mind and life. The stark realism of John's message was reinforced by his personality. He had no time for the exaggerated ritualism of popular Judaism, nor for the legalistic hair-splitting which tithes mint, anise, and cummin and omits judgment, mercy, and faith.[10] Nor, on the other hand, did the Baptist have time for those Zealots who were constantly conspiring to bring in the kingdom of God by revolution against Rome. With an insight that truly ranks him with the greatest of the prophets, he looked right to the heart of the problem of his time and, seeing, he asked for two things—repentance based on faith in God and the coming of his kingdom and enlistment to make that kingdom possible.

John reacted against the current ceremonialism because it was so empty and misleading. Yet he had been specifically sent to baptize with water[11] and he did this extensively, making sure first, however, that the people baptized were truly repentant.[12] By this simple and direct means, the common people were convicted of sin and brought into a new fellowship of repentant believers. Many of those who were thus baptized were taught the elements of kingdom righteousness by John and later were graduated under his greater successor into full and responsible membership in the church Jesus established.

John's appeal to people was timely. His uncouth but dramatic appearance doubtless attracted many. Then, too, the boldness and the intense earnestness of the man proclaimed his absolute sincerity. Whatever his secret, it is clear that John did an important work in preparing the way for Jesus by calling people of all classes to repentance and by holding high above all mere formalism the ultimate spiritual requirements of ethical religion. It is hardly to be wondered at that Jesus recognized in John a kindred spirit and that he was glad to honor John by asking for baptism at his hands. Nor is it surprising that five of John's followers became disciples of Jesus and later were members of the Twelve.[13]

NOTES

1. John 1:33, KJ. In the Inspired Version (John 1:32) this scripture becomes, "And I knew him."
2. Malachi 4:5.
3. John 1:21, KJ.
4. John 1:24.
5. Isaiah 40:3.
6. John 1:6, 7.
7. John 1:28; Luke 3:23.
8. Luke 1:75-78.
9. Luke 3:8, 12-21.
10. Matthew 23:20.
11. John 1:32.
12. Matthew 3:7, 8, KJ; 4:34, 35, IV.
13. John 1:35-50.

Study Helps for

Chapter 8

LESSON PURPOSE

To present John the Baptist as the forerunner of Jesus and to show the timeliness and limitations of his ministry

SCRIPTURE REFERENCES

Matthew 3:1-12, KJ; 27-38, IV; John 1:6, 7, 20-28; Luke 7:18-28

HIGH POINTS OF THE LESSON

- The clear moral authority of John in preaching repentance as the indispensable prelude to kingdom-building
- The greatness of John reflected in his humility
- The important work of preparation carried on by John and its contribution to the ministry of the Master

QUESTIONS AND DISCUSSION TOPICS

1. Tell what you can of the birth and early life of John the Baptist. In what way was he related to Jesus?

2. What was the relation of the ministry of John the Baptist to that of Jesus?

3. What was the heart of John's preaching? What standard did John apply to those who came to him to be baptized?

4. What attitude did John take toward those who regarded themselves as specifically favored of God?

5. When John was thrown into prison by Herod's soldiers, why did not Jesus use his power to release him? How do you think John might have felt about this event? What lesson can you learn from this experience when you face severe difficulties and you get no immediate release?

6. Why did the people compare John with Elijah?

7. Name some who first followed John but later became prominent disciples of Jesus. What factors were important in their transfer?

8. Consider the statement of Jesus concerning the greatness of John the Baptist, but the further greatness of members of the kingdom (Matthew 11:11). What did Jesus mean?

WHAT THE LESSON MEANS FOR TODAY

Any successful attempt to build the kingdom of God in our day must include in its early stages and continuously a forthright renunciation of sub-kingdom standards and practices. The person who can persuade others to drop the search for alibis and face the facts of their own sins and consequent lack of power expresses something of the spirit of Elijah.

Chapter 9

THE BAPTISM OF JESUS

John the Baptist was divinely chosen to be the forerunner of Jesus and to baptize with water "unto repentance."[1] Prior to the time of John, and during his day, such a baptism was used to admit proselytes to the privileges of Israel. But John was seeking to create a new and greater Israel than his generation had ever known, a "chosen people" who also chose the way of God. Even the Jews must be treated as proselytes to this new Israel, for the blood of Abraham could give them no rights of citizenship without repentance.[2]

Knowing all this, Jesus sought out John and asked for baptism at his hands. John had refused to receive the Pharisees and Sadducees who came to him for baptism until they should "bring forth fruits meet for repentance."[3] For a very different reason than this, he also at first refused to baptize Jesus. In this case he knew that the candidate for baptism was more righteous than he himself was, and he said, "I have need to be baptized of thee, and why comest thou to me?"[4] John did not say it was unwise or unnecessary for Jesus to be baptized, but only that he himself was unworthy to baptize one so evidently his superior in spiritual things. In replying Jesus did not attempt to discuss any of the secondary considerations connected with his baptism. Thrusting these aside he said quietly, "Suffer me to be baptized of thee, for thus it becometh us to fulfill all righteousness."[5] Then John baptized him.

John was right at one point in hesitating to baptize Jesus, for Jesus had no need for repentance. He was not a sinner. Nothing in the story of his life hints at any powerful crises and tumults of repentance. There is no evidence of a break with his past. He carried no scars of a struggle against any lower self. But Jesus had identified himself with the people, and he now identified himself with their sin and their need. He was so truly human and so deeply loved humankind that he could not stand apart now even as he could not stand apart later when human sin sent him to Calvary.

It would be as idle to tell a woman she need not be ashamed though her husband be sentenced for fraud as to tell Jesus that he need not be baptized although all others were sinners. Jesus therefore came to John's baptism because this was the right thing for him to do and because he did his Father's will gladly. He came, moreover, because this was an opportunity to identify himself with sinners at the point where they turn to God, and it was his mission to do just this.

We shall understand the point of view of Jesus better if we keep in mind the fact that he was a Jew and was ministering among Jews. The Jews thought of salvation as a group achievement. They rarely considered the possibility of salvation for individuals except as these were incorporated into the family of God.[6] This social background of personal salvation was to be strongly emphasized in the gospel of the kingdom. The baptism of John, therefore, did more than symbolize repentance leading to forgiveness; it was the rite of admission to the fellowship of the believers. Despite his sinlessness, Jesus must identify himself with this group. The people came as recipients, while Jesus came as sovereign Lord, but both acted out of complete dedication. Quite rightfully, therefore, Jesus replied to the objection of John, "thus it becometh *us* to fulfill all righteousness." Even the Son of God must identify himself with the people of God on earth as part of his calling.

Dr. Bowie has commented on the baptism of Jesus as folllows:

Was it of himself alone that Jesus thought as he went up to John in baptism? Was there not a sense instead, in which he thought of himself and the nation as identified—made one through the vicarious association of his own soul with the burdens and needs of all his brethren? Not long ago there died in America a man whom many feared and hated because they regarded his political views as dangerous; but whom many loved with a passionate devotion because they found him to be unselfish, and because they saw in him the friend of all the weak and poor. This man, whose name was Eugene Debs, said this: "Years ago I recognized my kinship with all living things, and I made up my mind that I was not one bit better than the meanest of the earth. I said then, and I say now, that where there is a lower class, I am in it; while there is criminal element, I am of it; while there is a soul in prison, I am not free." With such words it is possible to recognize a reflection of that quality of self-forgetfulness which was supreme in Jesus—a self-forgetfulness by which the great soul identifies in spiritual fortune, and its very life, with the life of others.[7]

The baptism of Jesus marked a crisis in his life. All we know about him leads us to believe that he came to this crisis clear-eyed, having carefully counted the cost.[8] We cannot enter fully into his consciousness so as to understand by what stages he became aware of his own great heritage and calling, but it is not too much to say that he had already caught a glimpse of his unique status before God when he gently chided his mother, "Knew ye not that I must be about my Father's business?"[9] A person of his clear perception could not fail to recognize the distinction between himself and his followers, a distinction which had its roots in his free and happy relationship with his Father. Full awareness did not come in a moment, as a flash of lightning, for he "grew in grace" and "increased in wisdom and stature, and in favor with God and man."[10] It certainly matured long before John appeared in the wilderness, however, and ripened into sure conviction as John fulfilled so completely the role of Jesus' forerunner. The baptism of Jesus was therefore the natural culmination of a long personal history, the deepest elements of which were to be found in the close and enlightening communion between Jesus and his Father through prayer, obedience, and faith. In this communion Jesus saw and felt the immeasurable difference between himself and those of his generation, and in it he knew himself to be the Messiah.

The baptism of Jesus was by immersion at the hands of one whose authority to baptize was recognized by all. Immediately thereafter, as he "went up straightway out of the water," Jesus received a further baptism greater than any John could bestow.

> The heavens were opened unto him, and he saw the Spirit of God descending like a dove and lighting upon Jesus. And lo, he heard a voice from heaven, saying, This is my beloved Son, in whom I am well pleased.[11]

Whatever doubt may have remained in the mind of Jesus prior to this time was surely dispelled at this evidence of his complete acceptance with God. It was to be a long time yet before even his nearest disciples fully understood the unique relationship between Jesus and his Father. Nor would understanding ever come to them from mere words or demonstrations of power. But Jesus understood. From this time forward he was set apart, different in spite of having identified himself so completely with humanity. He was the "Son of Man"; he was the "Son of God."

NOTES

1. Matthew 3:11, KJ.
2. Luke 3:13; Isaiah 1:16.
3. Matthew 3:35.
4. Matthew 3:42.
5. Matthew 3:43.
6. Colossians 1:12-14.
7. Walter Russell Bowie, *The Master,* pp. 76, 77. Used by permission of the publishers, Charles Scribner's Sons.
8. Luke 14:25-33.
9. Luke 2:49.
10. Luke 2:52.
11. Matthew 3:45, 46.

Study Helps for

Chapter 9

LESSON PURPOSE

To show the importance of baptism in both its personal and social aspects

SCRIPTURE REFERENCES

Matthew 3:13-17, KJ; 27-46, IV; Mark 1:9-11, KJ; 7-9, IV; Luke 3:21, 22, KJ; 28, 29, IV; I Nephi 3:7-12, 71-73; II Nephi 13:6-15.

HIGH POINTS OF THE LESSON

- The close relation between repentance and baptism
- The identification of Jesus, in being baptized, with those seeking to do the will of God
- The spiritual endowment following the dedication of baptism

QUESTIONS AND DISCUSSION TOPICS

1. What were the conditions of baptism laid down by John? What did baptism mean to those immersed by John?

2. Describe the baptism of Jesus—where it took place, the events preceding it, and the actual rite.

3. Since Jesus was without sin, and the baptism of John was primarily for sinners, why did Jesus seek baptism at the hands of John?

4. What do you think of the Jewish idea that salvation is a group achievement, and that individuals are saved as they are incorporated into the family of God?

5. In what sense was the baptism of Jesus a crisis in his life? In what sense was it the natural outgrowth of his prior life? What lesson is there here for us?

6. By what authority did John baptize? Why is the question of authority important?

7. Discuss briefly the endowment received by Jesus following his baptism. What was its significance to him and to those surrounding him? Compare this experience with the instructions the Lord gave Joseph Smith in the grove. Why is this statement still valid in our time?

WHAT THE LESSON MEANS FOR TODAY

At his baptism Jesus definitely and publicly committed himself to the work of God. Every person needs to make the same public commitment.

Chapter 10

THE TEMPTATIONS IN THE WILDERNESS

Immediately after his baptism, Jesus spent forty days in the wilderness and was there tempted of the devil. This is true to life. The eve of victory has no special danger for us. We are still in the fight, straining every nerve toward our goal. Real danger comes on the morrow of victory, when we have achieved and are tempted to rest instead of pushing on to the next objective. In the moral field, as well as on the field of battle, many a person who won the first skirmish was routed in a counteroffensive. Matthew makes a point of this when he says "then"—right after his acknowledgment from heaven—"Jesus was led up of the Spirit into the wilderness." Mark also emphasizes this; he tells us that "immediately" he went to the place of temptation.[1]

Each of the first three Gospels indicates that Jesus went into the wilderness at the direction of the Spirit. The corresponding passages in the Inspired Version make even clearer what actually happened—that Jesus went into the wilderness "to be with God,"[2] but that Satan seized this opportunity to tempt him. The point for us to keep in mind is that there is no escape from temptation after a great spiritual decision or achievement. We can yield immediately to the temptation to rest on our oars; or, in planning the next step forward, we can be tempted to take the way which looks good to others in place of the way which is right in the sight of God. This was what Jesus had to face, and it is what each of us must also face. It is far better to confront the higher temptations, regardless of the guise in which they come, than to capitulate without a fight, content with past victories when the enemy is still in the field.

From the record it is clear that Jesus went into the wilderness to face frankly, in their most attractive form, the temptations that would beset him in his ministry and to vanquish them.[3] The temptations were real. The letter to the Hebrews states, "he himself hath suffered being tempted."[4]

> We have not an high priest which cannot be touched with the feeling of our infirmities; but was on all points tempted like as we are, yet without sin.[5]

Like all other real temptations, these did not come in stark nakedness; they were dressed for the occasion. Jesus faced them and won. But the glory of his victory lies in the fact that it was no easy triumph. It was a genuine struggle.

The baptism of Jesus was the initial act of his ministry. The next question which confronted him was the question every one of us must face: How can I do my part in building the kingdom? The first temptation shows one possible way. His communion with God, pursued through fasting and prayer, had left Jesus hungry, as many were hungry and many others were yet to be hungry. Conscious of his great powers, he was tempted to use these powers to turn the stones into bread. In essence the temptation was to use his powers in this way in order to prove that he was the Son of God.[6]

Well, why not? Bread is important; but if bread is important for the physical life, dependence on God is even more important for the spiritual life. Jesus kept this in mind as he met his first temptation. The word of God to him was that he must identify himself with humanity. If he was to do this, he must not use his powers to free himself from any of the limitations which circumscribe. This meant that since he had chosen to fast and was hungry, he must now wait until he could find means that were open to the average person before satisfying his hunger. If this waiting meant that he must not use powers which would show him to be the Son of God, then he would not use them. God had already spoken.[7] Let that be sufficient for the time. Any further and necessary miraculous demonstrations of his calling could come in the natural course of events. He would not only live by "every word that proceedeth out of the mouth of God"[8] but he would live by these words when God should choose to speak them.

There is also a social side to this temptation. There is no doubt that Jesus felt deep compassion for the needy. He was one of them and had lived their life with them. The temptation to use his great powers to satisfy their physical needs must therefore have been a very real temptation indeed. What would have happened if he had yielded and had spent his time and strength in feeding the multitude? There would have been neither time nor strength left for his unique work. There were plenty of stones in Judea and Galilee. If people had seen Jesus change these into bread for himself, he would have been in a worse situation than when he fed the five thousand:

> Then those men, when they had seen the miracle that Jesus did, said, This is of a truth that prophet that should come into the world. When Jesus therefore perceived that they would come and take him by force, to make him a king, he departed again into a mountain himself alone.[9]

There is nothing evil in satisfying the physical needs of people. Indeed, the church is not Christian until it recognizes the responsibility to do so. But this first temptation was not a temptation to feed people; it was a temptation to let a ministry of temporary value distract him from the ministry which was uniquely his. To this the Master dare not yield. Despite the importance of such work, Jesus knew in his heart that there is no assurance at all that better fed people will be better people. All too frequently those who have sought after God in the days of their need have forgotten him in the days of their comfort. So Jesus rejected the temptation to build his kingdom on bread. People can be trusted to be concerned about their need for bread, but they need to be reminded: "Seek ye first to build up the kingdom of God, and to establish his righteousnes, and all these things shall be added unto you."[10]

The first temptation of Jesus in the wilderness was to use his God-given powers selfishly to supply secondary needs. His next temptation[11] was to use his power presumptuously, demonstrating that he was the Son of God by a great public exhibition unrelated to any human need. Here the appeal was to the spectacular, to the sensational; the appeal of the miracle worker, the appeal which would demonstrate power rather than character.

Once again, this was what many of the Jews were seeking.[12] The great prophets had made much of signs.[13] Paul said that the difference between the Jews and the Greeks was that "the Jews require a sign, and the Greeks seek after wisdom."[14] Moreover, there was an appearance of justification for this use of signs. Later in his ministry Jesus did work miracles, and he did promise his disciples: "These signs shall follow them that believe."[15]

Jesus never used any sign as an end in itself. People must follow because the way is right, not just because it is spectacular. The tempter said: "Cast thyself down from the pinnacle of the temple." This pinnacle was a public place, where those in the courtyard could see him. The tempter was saying, "Start out well. Startle the people. Astonish them. They will always flock to see and hear a wonder-worker." The difficulty lay in the fact that the kingdom of God cannot be built that way. Spiritual ends can be achieved only by spiritual means, and the kingdom of God would only be cheapened, in the long run, by any such display of power for its own sake. What an indictment there is in this second temptation against the spectacular methods of many modern ministers, and also of their kin of our own number who seek to win converts by signs and wonders!

There remained yet one further temptation—the temptation to compromise. This, too, was in the spirit of the times. Rome had asserted her dominion over all the world. The leaders of the Jewish religion held their places by consent of Rome, and so were very careful not to incur the displeasure of Caesar. They were not very easy in their minds and hearts about this,[16] but it seemed the only practical way to get along. Jesus was yet to advise people to "render unto Caesar the things which are Caesar's," but he was also to command them to render "unto God the things which are God's."[17] For him there can be no compromise with evil. Matthew narrates this temptation as follows:

> Again, the devil taketh him up into an exceeding high mountain, and showeth him all the kingdoms of the world, and the glory of them; and saith unto him, All these things will I give thee, if thou wilt fall down and worship me. Then saith Jesus unto him, Get thee hence, Satan: for it is written, Thou shalt worship the Lord thy God, and him only shalt thou serve.[18]

This temptation is always modern, the temptation to gain "the kingdoms of the world and the glory of them" by serving the devil, in the hope that we can then use our powers to serve God.[19] Jesus knew that the way for him to become the Lord of all was to find his throne in the hearts of people and his power in a kingdom built by their willing cooperation. There was no possible shortcut for him, just as there is no possible shortcut for us. A great modern preacher has said:

> To believe that the Devil is not the lord of the world, that he cannot give the kingdom of it to whom he will, is hard at all times, intensely hard in those times when evil and brute force has established its ascendancy, and the world is crying after him. Then it seems but the condition of an obvious fact to admit this dominion of the enemy of man. Nay, it will be asserted by some as a pious duty to hold this faith. . . . I deem it impossible, while we think this, that we should not do some homage—yes, continued homage—to that power which we suppose is uppermost.[20]

It is because we must avoid giving such homage to evil

that Jesus set before us the commandment: "Thou shalt worship the Lord thy God, and him only shalt thou serve."

Such temptations as these come to good people—the temptation to "climb up another way," the temptation to build the kingdom of God by ungodly means, the temptation to let the moment obscure the vision of eternity, and the immediate gain to cloud and to deny the ultimate good. These temptations were not cheap ones, such as the temptations of pride and avarice and lust; they were deep and searching. Moreover, though "angels came and ministered unto him" after his triumph, temptation was renewed. Luke says that "when the devil had ended all the temptation, he departed from him *for a season*";[21] later, Luke tells us that the Master referred to his disciples as "they who have continued with me in my temptations."[22] So, for us, the upward way is not the way out of temptation even though it is the way to God, for every plane of life has temptations suited to it. "The saint's temptation to self-righteousness is just as real as the drunkard's temptation to self-indulgence."[23] At all times, and on every level of life, we are prone to relax when we should strive or to cherish the easy way when we should take the hard way. For us as well as for Jesus, the worst enemy of the best is the second best, the distraction of that which is good but which would prevent us from doing something better. The way to the kingdom, even after we have disciplined our lower desires, is still the way of self-denial.

The story of the temptations can have come from no other source than Jesus himself, and it may well be that this story was repeated again and again, with different emphases and in slightly different settings, as Jesus walked the dusty roads of Galilee with the small company of his disciples. This may explain why

Matthew sets the temptations in one order and Luke in another. In any event, the story of the temptations shows Jesus teaching his disciples out of his own rich experience. Not the least of the lessons he taught was the value of ready familiarity with the scriptures, which furnished an "it is written" against every critical need. This lesson is important for our day, even as it was for theirs.

NOTES

1. Matthew 4:1; Mark 1:10; Luke 4:1.
2. Matthew 4:1, IV.
3. Matthew 4:1, KJ.
4. Hebrews 2:18.
5. Hebrews 4:15.
6. Matthew 4:2-4; Luke 4:3, 4.
7. Luke 3:22, KJ; 3:29, IV.
8. Matthew 4:4.
9. John 6:14, 15.
10. Matthew 6:38.
11. This is according to Matthew.
12. John 2:18.
13. Exodus 7:9; 10:2.
14. I Corinthians 1:22.
15. Mark 16:16.
16. Matthew 22:17.
17. Matthew 22:21.
18. Matthew 4:8-10, KJ. (Note the wording in the Inspired Version.)
19. "Zion can not be built up unless it is by the principles of the law of the celestial kingdom."—Doctrine and Covenants 102:2c.
20. Frederick D. Maurice, *Lectures on the Apocalypse,* p. 216. Used by permission of the publishers, E. P. Dutton & Co., Inc. (out of print).
21. Luke 4:12.
22. Luke 22:28.
23. A. L. Garvie, *Studies in the Inner Life of Jesus,* p. 137.

Study Helps for
Chapter 10

LESSON PURPOSE

To show that temptation is inevitable and to grasp the principles by which Jesus met his temptations

SCRIPTURE REFERENCES

Matthew 4:1-10, IV; Mark 1:10, 11, IV; Luke 4:1-13, IV

HIGH POINTS OF THE LESSON

- Temptations are found on every level of life. The bad person yields to temptation on a low level and the good person conquers temptations while climbing.
- The first temptation of Jesus was to put bread before the kingdom.
- His second temptation was to replace the spiritual by the spectacular.
- His third temptation was to compromise with evil.
- Though Jesus overcame these temptations for the time, he had to meet them again in different dress.

QUESTIONS AND DISCUSSION TOPICS

1. Why did Jesus go into the wilderness of Judea? What kinds of temptations would he naturally face as he began his ministry? How is this different and similar as we move forward after making a commitment to the cause of Zion?

2. Temptation implies conflict and resistance, not capitulation without a struggle. Explain the difference.

3. What was the first temptation? Why would it have been wrong for Jesus to have yielded to this temptation? In what guise does this temptation come to us today?

4. Under what circumstances was it desirable for Jesus to feed the hungry miraculously? What problems would have evolved if he had given his whole life to this ministry?

5. Why would it have been wrong for Jesus to have cast himself down from the pinnacle of the Temple as was suggested? Jesus condemned people who sought "signs," as recorded in Matthew 12:33, 34. He commended the believers for their faith and listed "signs" that would follow (Mark 16:16-21). What is the value and limitation of miracles?

6. What is the heart of the third temptation? Describe how this temptation confronts good people today. What is the danger and/or wisdom of compromising on principles? On methods? In this connection study Doctrine and Covenants 147:6, 7.

7. From what source did Jesus draw ammunition to fight these temptations? Comment on the value of prior scripture study as preparation to meet temptations.

8. What kinds of people are most likely to be tempted by the worst? By the second best? What lesson does this hold for us?

WHAT THE LESSON MEANS FOR TODAY

The day of temptation found Jesus strong because earlier days had found him studious and devout. People are considered uneducated today when they are unacquainted with the gems of their country's literature. In a spiritual sense, persons are much more disastrously uneducated when they lack knowledge of the word of God.

Chapter 11

YOU MUST BE BORN AGAIN

When Jesus returned from the period of meditation and temptation in the wilderness, he again met John. The Baptist was accompanied by two of his disciples, Andrew and John, who were partners in a fishing enterprise.[1] These heard the Baptist greet Jesus as "the Lamb of God,"[2] and they followed after Jesus and stayed overnight with him.

The experiences of that evening so deeply impressed Andrew that immediately thereafter he sought out his brother, Simon Peter, and said to him, "We have found the Messias, which is, being interpreted, the Christ. And he brought him to Jesus."[3] It may be that Jesus had already met Peter; we can never know for certain. In any event Jesus was apparently glad to welcome this new follower and said to him, "Thou art Simon, the son of Jona; thou shalt be called Cephas, which is, by interpretation, . . . a stone."[4]

On the day after this had happened Jesus set out for Galilee. When he came to Bethsaida he saw Philip and called him also to the growing circle of his disciples.[5] Philip immediately undertook responsibility for adding another member to the group and sought out Nathanael, inviting him cleverly with the announcement: "We have found him, of whom Moses in the law, and the prophets, did write, Jesus of Nazareth, the son of Joseph."[6]

The mind of Nathanael was saturated with the teachings of the Old Testament, and he was not easily carried away by his friend's enthusiasm. Morever, he came form Cana, which is only five miles from Nazareth, and with typical local prejudice he asked: "Can there any good thing come out of Nazareth?" For a moment Philip was dismayed. Then he remembered the words and gestures of the Master and knew that the best argument for following Jesus was Jesus himself. He answered: "Come and see." Nathanael went, saw, believed, and followed Jesus first to a wedding in Cana and then to a ministry growing in significance, in the conviction that Jesus was indeed the hope of Israel and of all the world.

Soon after these events Jesus went to Capernaum with his disciples and his family and stayed there for a short time before going up to Jerusalem for the Passover. On his arrival in the Holy City he found that the great festival had been turned into a gigantic graft by the greed of the money changers, who were sustained in their places by the connivance of the chief priests. Under the system, the priests refused to accept the temple tribute in anything other than Galilean coinage. Since the poor rarely handled any but the Roman coinage, this rule called for visits to the money changers, whose profit was between 10 and 12 percent. The priests also had an arrangement by which they condemned offerings brought to the temple if these offerings had not been bought from certified dealers within the temple itself. Because of these practices resentment, din, and confusion engulfed a place which should have been reserved for quietude and prayer. Undoubtedly, many devout Jews had remarked on this time and time again, but no one seemed able to do anything about it. When Jesus took into his own hands the authority to bring this blasphemy to an end, he was assured of support from many who had hitherto been quiescent. Making a scourge of the rushes that lay on the marble pavement (or perhaps of small cords), he quickly drove out sheep and oxen. Turning to the money changers, he overthrew their tables and cried out to the sellers of doves, "Take these things hence;

make not my Father's house a house of merchandise."[7]

The action of Jesus was so obviously right that there was little public condemnation of what he had done. Certain of the Jews, nevertheless, wondered what his assumptions of leadership meant. With their minds full of the expectation of a great Deliverer—an expectation which had been quickened in the whole countryside by John the Baptist—they therefore sought out the Master to ask by what authority he did these things.[8] They failed to perceive that such an act as this carries its own authority both in the wickedness of the traffic itself and in the righteous zeal of the one who puts an end to it.

Jesus continued at Jerusalem throughout the Passover, teaching and healing the sick, and many of the curious and devout were attracted to him; but since he could not build a permanent organization with those who were merely attracted through miracles, he did not commit himself to them.[9] Their attitude was entirely different from that of the disciples who had followed him before his marvelous powers confirmed them in their faith. To these disciples Jesus was a great spiritual leader who had been entrusted by God with enormous power because of his righteousness. To those attracted by miracles, Jesus was primarily a wonder-worker. They rarely looked beyond the outward manifestations of his greatness to the character in which that greatness had its birth.

Among those drawn to Jesus was a member of the Jewish Sanhedrin bearing the Greek name of Nicodemus. This highly placed Pharisee was sufficiently concerned about the questions raised in the ministry of the Master to seek Jesus out by night that he might inquire further. We do not know why Nicodemus came at night. It may have been fear of jeopardizing his position as one of the chief men of the Jewish religious world. It may have been, on the other hand, that only at night could he find the Master free from the multitude. Or, again, it may have been that he was not yet certain enough of Jesus and his message to give public support to what was being done. Whatever the reason for his coming when he did, it is quite probable that Nicodemus did not speak for himself alone. His opening sentence makes this clear: "Rabbi, *we* know that thou art a teacher come from God; for no man can do these miracles that thou doest, except God be with him."[10] It is possible that Nicodemus came to see if there was any basis for cooperation between Jesus and those Nicodemus represented.

Jesus treated the question of Nicodemus forthrightly, saying without extended debate that there was one condition, and one condition only, on which he and those whom Nicodemus represented could get together: the Pharisees could be born again. Then, in reply to the amazed questions of Nicodemus, he elaborated. Nicodemus must be born of water and of the Spirit or he could not even see the kingdom, much less enter into it.[11] Nicodemus understood the first reference readily. It was the condition of discipleship set forth by John.[12] Disciples must be "born of water" in token of a complete readjustment of moral purpose. But, said Jesus, this was not enough. The repentant ones must also be endowed with power from on high: they must be born of the Spirit. Then, so as to leave absolutely no room for doubt, the Master reiterated his earlier statement that no line of physical descent can possibly confer spiritual status;[13] "That which is born of the flesh is flesh; and that which is born of the Spirit is spirit."[14]

For Nicodemus to believe what Jesus now told him would indeed require him to be born again. It was contrary to the whole range of his thinking. It meant that he must discard all his expectations of preferential treatment. He was just another man needing salvation. It is difficult for us to realize what a shock this must have been. His astonishment was akin to the astonishment of a French aristocrat before the revolution on being told that there was no place in France for such as he unless he should learn to think and act in terms of the common good. Or, to use a more modern illustration, his astonishment was akin to that of some modern aristocrat on being told that there is no place for him in real democracy unless he is willing to put aside all the special opportunities that privilege brings.

Shortly after the Passover, Jesus returned to Judea. By this time John the Baptist was in Samaria, but when Jesus ministered in Judea[15] it was easy to compare their work. Those who were interested in obstructing what Jesus and John were doing therefore promoted questioning between the disciples of the two leaders; but instead of producing disunion, this situation gave the Baptist a fine opportunity for further testimony to the preeminence of the Christ. Likening himself to the "friend of the bridegroom, who standeth and heareth him [and] rejoiceth greatly because of the bridegroom's voice," John declared, "He must increase, but I must decrease."[16] Surely among those born of women there was but one greater than John.[17]

Despite the generous attitude adopted by John, the Master was anxious that there should not be any further comparisons between his work and that of the Baptist. He therefore left Judea and set out for Galilee by a route which took him through Samaria. About noon he neared the city of Sychar where there was a well which Jacob had dug centuries before. At this well, with its shady roof and its seats of stone, Jesus tarried to rest while the disciples went on to the city to buy food. He had not waited long when a Samaritan woman came to draw water, and Jesus asked her for a drink. Quick to recognize him as a Jew, the woman replied: "How is it that thou, being a Jew, askest drink of me, who am a woman of Samaria? The Jews have no dealings with the Samaritans."[18] Her question was justified. A Jew might be friendly with a heathen but never with a Samaritan. The very name of the Samaritans had become a reproach to the Jews. No Samaritan was ever allowed to become a proselyte. With this simple opening Jesus nevertheless developed a conversation which soon went far beyond meat and drink to matters of eternal significance. Although Nicodemus was a ruler among the Jews and this woman was an outcast even among the Samaritans, there was a fundamental similarity between the message which Jesus brought to each of them. Nicodemus had been concerned regarding his life as a member of the governing class among the chosen people. This woman, as became a Samaritan, was concerned regarding the traditions of her fathers. But to this woman, even as to Nicodemus, Jesus brought a startling revolutionary message: "God is a Spirit; and they that worship him must worship him in spirit and in truth."[19] It is not where people worship but how they worship that matters; not tradition but truth. And the woman who had come to the well on such a commonplace task heard and understood.

The conversation with the Samaritan woman was interrupted by the return of the disciples, who marveled that Jesus should have talked with such a person. While they inquired regarding what had transpired, the woman went to the city and spread the word of what the Master had done for her. She testified to such good effect that the villagers

besought him that he would tarry with them; and he abode there two days. And many more believed because of his own word; and said unto the woman, Now we believe, not because of thy saying; we have heard for ourselves, and know that this is indeed the Christ, the Savior of the world.[20]

NOTES

1. Luke 5:7, 10.
2. John 1:36.
3. John 1:41, 42.
4. John 1:42.
5. John 1:43.
6. John 1:45.
7. John 2:13-16. It appears that this is a record of a cleansing of the temple at the beginning of the ministry of Jesus and that a second cleansing occurred during Passion Week. See Mark 11:17-19, Matthew 21:10-11, and Luke 19:44-45. If there was but one such cleansing, as some suppose, it is difficult to know just when it occurred.
8. John 2:18.
9. John 2:23-25.
10. John 3:2.
11. John 3:3-7.
12. Matthew 3:27-33.
13. John 3:7.
14. John 3:6.
15. John 3:31, 32.
16. John 3:29-31.
17. Edersheim, p. 392.
18. John 4:11.
19. John 4:24, KJ. Note the rendering in John 4:26 in the Inspired Version which emphasizes the point made in the preceding statements.
20. John 4:42-44.

Study Helps for

Chapter 11

LESSON PURPOSE

To impress the importance of rebirth as a prelude to kingdom citizenship

SCRIPTURE REFERENCES

John 2:23, 24; 3:21; 4:4-26; III Nephi 5:21-42; II Nephi 6:49; Mosiah 9:41.

HIGH POINTS OF THE LESSON

- The personal contacts which won disciples to Jesus

- The first cleansing of the Temple
- What being born again meant to Nicodemus
- What being born again meant to the Samaritan woman at Sychar

QUESTIONS AND DISCUSSION TOPICS

1. What convinced Andrew and John to become disciples of Jesus? How was Peter won? What approach was made to Philip? In spite of Nathanael's cynical attitude toward Nazareth, why did he decide to listen to Jesus?

2. Why did Jesus take it upon himself to correct the graft in the Temple? Why did this graft really concern him? How does it concern us in today's kingdom-building process?

3. John said that Jesus did not commit himself to those who were attracted to him by his miracles. What was the reason for this omission?

4. Who was Nicodemus? In what sense was he typical of honest seekers after truth?

5. To Nicodemus what was the meaning of the command to be born again? Why was so drastic a change necessary? Why both water and spirit?

6. What was John's attitude when his work was compared with that of Jesus? Name others who prepared the way for greater successes by the seventy.

7. What was the relation between Jews and Samaritans at the time of Jesus? What was the attitude of Jesus toward the woman of Sychar? What was the heart of his message to her? In view of Jesus' conversations with Nicodemus and with the woman of Samaria, consider Jesus as the breaker of barriers dividing peoples.

WHAT THE LESSON MEANS FOR TODAY

Nicodemus respected Jesus as a teacher come from God. But he did not fully realize the magnitude of the change demanded if he was to become a disciple. He must renounce his own way of life and be endowed with power for the new way of life. The terms are the same today. They will always be the same.

Chapter 12

THE GOSPEL OF THE KINGDOM

Jesus could not stay in Samaria, for his work lay in Israel. Despite the friendly reception given him, he soon took the road northward into Galilee. As he went he preached "the gospel of the kingdom of God" saying, "The time is fulfilled, and the kingdom of God is at hand; repent ye, and believe the gospel."[1]

The kingdom of God had already been proclaimed by the great prophets of Israel, including Isaiah, Hosea, and Amos. John the Baptist shared the prophetic vision of these men; he too proclaimed the coming of his kingdom and made it the basic reason for his universal call to repentance. but not even John had caught the full sweep of the meaning of the kingdom of God. It was not until Jesus took this phrase from the lips of the Baptist and endowed it with new and richer meaning that the world first caught a glimpse of the kingdom as it is guaranteed in the very nature of God.

In the days immediately preceding the coming of Jesus, practically all classes of the Jews were waiting with eager expectation for the dawning of the new era. This was the confident hope of people such as Joseph of Arimathaea, who was looking "for the kingdom of God";[2] Simeon, a devout Jew, who was looking "for the consolation of Israel";[3] and Anna, who was looking "for redemption in Jerusalem."[4] All these phrases had similar meaning, and all were indicative of the mental attitude of the pious Jew of the day.

Those who looked forward thus eagerly were none of them very clear about what they meant by the "kingdom of God" or the "consolation of Israel" or "redemption in Jerusalem," although there was general agreement that these expressions stood for a new social order founded in righteousness and responsive to divine rule. Some of the Zealots, for instance, interpreted the messianic hope and the coming of the kingdom to be the founding of an earthly kingdom, established, if necessary, by force and with its capital at Jerusalem. It was people of this type who later wanted to make Jesus their king.

Many of the Pharisees realized that there was little hope of reestablishing the throne of David by military might. Their thought of the coming kingdom, nevertheless, included at its heart the restoration of the temporal power of Israel. They looked for a miraculous demonstration of divine power, as a result of which the enemies of Israel would be overthrown and Israel and her friends given places of power and authority. In a way which was not quite clear even to them, they conceived this coming change as a great vindication of the supreme sovereignty of God; in their minds this was directly related to punctilious observance of the requirements of the law. It was this point of view, and not mere selfishness or quarrelsomeness, which later set so many of them in direct opposition to Jesus.

There were others who cherished more spiritual expectations. These were deeply conscious of the wide divergence between the righteousness proclaimed by the prophets and the realities of life around them. Despite their own eager anticipation, the selfishness of the many mocked their hopes. With touching wistfulness they waited for the coming of the great Deliverer, but nevertheless sensed in some small degree that Israel could not enter into her destiny until her people had become righteous. The preaching of John had quickened this type of expectation and had done wonders to arouse the Jews to a deeper consciousness of their own part in the deliverance to come.

When Jesus first came preaching the "gospel of the

kingdom of God," he knew that his use of this phrase was attended with some marked advantages and with other marked disadvantages. On the one hand the people felt an immediate interest in his message; on the other hand the phrase evidently meant one thing to him and something else to them. Dr. Stalker[5] has stated that the difference between them may perhaps be best expressed by saying that they placed their emphasis on "the kingdom," but he placed his on "of God." They thought of emancipation from the Romans and of becoming dominant among the nations, while the Master thought of God's being more fully revealed among the people and of the will of his Father being done on earth as it is done in heaven. It was this lack of common understanding that was behind much of the trouble between Jesus and his contemporaries. Yet some trouble was unavoidable, for the difficulty was not primarily concerned with mere phrasing. It went back much further and was a matter of spiritual vision and understanding. Jesus was very different from the Messiah whom the Jews had been expecting. The reason, of course, was that their vision of the Messiah was inadequate.

When we think of some of the reasons against the use of this term by Jesus, we know that there must have been more compelling reasons which caused him to use it. What were they? Referring to Dr. Stalker again, we quote:

> It connected his teaching with the tradition of the Old Testament and the past history of the people of God. Original and unique as Jesus is, he is never disconnected from the nation to which he belonged. His mind is saturated with the ideas of the Old Testament; his language is learned from its phraseology; the figures of the patriarchs and the pious kings occupy his imagination; and he knows himself to be the successor and the heir of the prophets. If the kingdom of God was the underlying idea of the whole Old Testament history, this was the best reason for its being the most prominent watchword of his preaching.[6]

There was still another reason why Jesus used the term "the kingdom of God" to embody the heart of his message for his own generation and for all time. This term expressed the essential relation between him and his followers. John had been the herald, proclaiming the coming of the King. Jesus was the King, coming to take charge by right. The kingdom of God is a democracy in the sense that it exists for its citizens and that their basic rights are guaranteed in the nature of the kingdom. But the kingdom of God is not a republic. It is the realm in which the will of God is supreme.

From the beginning of his ministry to its end, the appeal of Jesus was to the Jews. He preached throughout the synagogues of Galilee.[7] Then, on each visit to Jerusalem, he went to the temple and dealt directly with the responsible heads of the Jewish community.[8] Those closest to him quickly came to realize that his acceptance or rejection by the leaders of Judaism determined whether or not "his own"[9] received him.

When Jesus sent his disciples to preach in his name, they too were commanded to address their ministry to "the lost sheep. . .of Israel."[10] The disciples knew that they were participating in a struggle between a chosen people unwilling to live up to the high standards of their calling and the Son of God who must reject them if they rejected the counsel of God against themselves. If Israel had accepted its Messiah its borders would have been enlarged, its laws becoming the laws of the kingdom and its people including all the spiritual descendants of Abraham, the "father of the faithful." Since Israel did not accept its Messiah, God has brought into being a new Israel and raised up children to Abraham from the despised Gentiles, while those invited to his banquet table but lacking the garments of righteousness are cast out into the night.

When Jesus preached the gospel of the kingdom, he did not merely declare that the kingdom was about to be established; he set forth the nature and conditions of kingdom life. Yet Jesus never gave a specific definition of the kingdom. Instead, he illustrated its characteristics by many parables and word pictures, the meaning of which become clear only as they are studied carefully and in relation to each other. This reluctance to give a precise definition of what he meant by the kingdom arose out of the Master's own experience with the phrase. He knew how much it meant to him and how little it meant to those who heard him use it. He knew also that any precise definition would soon be outgrown by a people who were as yet spiritually immature but who were reaching toward God and toward the understanding he gives to those who love and serve him. So he did not try to convey his message in formal definitions about which people would have been splitting hairs from that day to this. Instead he indicated several lines of thought along which those who were eager to know would discover likenesses to the kingdom of God. He told them that the kingdom is like leaven hidden in a measure of meal;[11] like hidden treasure;[12] like a merchant seeking a goodly pearl, to obtain which he would sell all his other possessions;[13] like growing seed;[14] or like ten virgins, five of whom were wise and five foolish.[15] None of these parables indicate fully what Jesus meant by "the kingdom," but all of them contain some germ of truth which devout and thoughtful persons need to understand.

Two things were clear about the kingdom as Jesus proclaimed it: First, it is primarily the gift of God and can be built only under his direction and by his power; second, this gift of the kingdom is not available to persons of sub-kingdom quality. To a people who had excused themselves for their lack of love for each other on the ground of their common descent from Abraham, this was a shocking message. Such persons must be born again; they must learn to worship God in spirit and in truth; and if they brought gifts to the altar and there remembered that there were those who had aught against them, they were to seek forgiveness and so regain the spirit of love before they could make an acceptable offering.

The keynote of such a proclamation of the kingdom necessarily became loyalty to the God of righteousness and to Jesus as his Son and representative. This is still the keynote of the kingdom message. Whenever and wherever the kingdom is built, it will be built by God with the loyal cooperation of those who love him and who serve him without qualification and without regret.

NOTES

1. Mark 1:13.
2. Mark 15:47.
3. Luke 2:25.
4. Luke 2:38.
5. *Ethics of Jesus,* p. 46. Used by permission of the publisher, Harper & Brothers.
6. Ibid., p. 47.
7. Matthew 13:55.
8. Hastings, *Encyclopedia of Religion and Ethics.*
9. John 1:11; 6:26, 64, 65; 8:43; 10:41; Matthew 21:21-47; 23:16-40.
10. Matthew 10:5.
11. Matthew 13:32.
12. Matthew 13:46.
13. Matthew 13:47.
14. Mark 4:21-23.
15. Matthew 25:1-12.

Study Helps for

Chapter 12

LESSON PURPOSE

To clarify our concept of the kingdom presented by Jesus

SCRIPTURE REFERENCES

Matthew 4:12, 17, KJ; 11, 12, 16, IV; Mark 1:12, 13; Luke 4:14, 15, KJ; 13-15, IV; John 4:43-45, KJ

HIGH POINTS OF THE LESSON

- The kingdom of God is primarily concerned with spiritual quality.
- Jesus never defined the kingdom; instead he indicated its general character. Our understanding matures as we grow like him.
- The kingdom is both a gift and an achievement. It is made available by the power of God to those who are willing to do his will.

QUESTIONS AND DISCUSSION TOPICS

1. Why did the Jews have so many divergent ideas regarding the kingdom? What truth is common to all the viewpoints mentioned in the text?

2. What was the attitude of the Pharisees toward the coming of the kingdom? Discuss the importance of the strict observance of the law which they emphasized.

3. What advantages were derived by Jesus from the use of the phrase, "the kingdom of God"?

4. What disadvantages were inherent in the use of this phrase?

5. Why did Jesus use a phrase about which there was so much misunderstanding? Discuss the relation of common understanding of high spiritual truths and unified and inspired leadership.

6. What were the outstanding characteristics of the kingdom as preached by Jesus? Why did Jesus never define the kingdom?

7. Why did not Jesus compromise a little with the Jews in order to win them?

8. In what sense is the kingdom of God the gift of God? In what sense is it to be achieved by people? Why is new birth so important in connection with the kingdom?

WHAT THE LESSON MEANS FOR TODAY

We must achieve spiritual maturity through right living and right thinking under inspired guidance. But the primary condition of understanding is now, as always, that we shall seek the truth—not just a comfortable approximation of the truth.

Chapter 13

EARLY MINISTRY IN GALILEE

John the Baptist was arrested soon after Jesus began his public ministry. This left the preaching of the kingdom squarely on the shoulders of Jesus, and he chose to inaugurate this ministry in his hometown of Nazareth. Here he went to the synagogue "as his custom was."[1] The Jewish synagogue had no regular minister, but in the seats on the platform sat the chief of the synagogue and eight or ten of the leading elders. Any male of suitable age and character might be called out from the congregation by the person in charge to read from the Law and the Prophets and to make such comments as he might desire. Quite probably the news of the miracles of Jesus at nearby Cana and of his cleansing of the Temple at Jerusalem had preceded him. If so, this explains why Jesus was called on for the reading and comments. He read from the Book of Isaiah.[2] Then, the reading finished, he sat down to teach.

The lesson Jesus selected had to do with the coming Messiah. In essence, therefore, this sermon was the Master's declaration of his purpose and program; and since the minds of all present were filled with reports of what he had already accomplished, this made the occasion one of significant announcement. At first "all bare him witness, and wondered at the gracious words which proceeded out of his mouth."[3] Then, as Jesus read on, some faint glimmer of the true significance of the message began to dawn upon them. And then he declared:

> He hath anointed me to preach the gospel to the poor, he hath sent me to heal the brokenhearted, to preach deliverance to the captives, and the recovering of sight to the blind; to set at liberty them that are buised; to preach the acceptable year of the Lord.[4]

Some looked around and asked each other: "Who is this man to bring such a message? Is not this Joseph's son?"[5] Stirred by their growing resentment, they can almost be heard saying: "This unlearned carpenter talks as though the blessings of heaven were for everyone, for Jew and Gentile alike, for the accepted and the outcast, for those who are ceremonially clean and for those who do not even know the law."

Watching the faces of his fellow villagers, Jesus was fully aware of the opposition forming in their minds. Nevertheless he did not modify his announcement, but went on to quote from their own scriptures some of the outstanding illustrations of the goodness of God to those who were not of Israel. This was too much. Frowns were succeeded by mutterings and these by outspoken criticism which soon mounted to a roar of angry passions which drowned all remembrance of the kindliness they had at first felt because of his gracious bearing. If they could have had their way, some would have flung him down from the hilltop and stoned him;[6] but Jesus passed through their midst and went his way to Capernaum where the succeeding Sabbath found him in the synagogue, nothing daunted, preaching his message with power.[7]

As long as Jesus was content to be one of the common people, he was widely and popularly known. His fellow townspeople even rejoiced in his apparent success at Jerusalem and in Samaria and at Cana. But when the very qualities which first commended Jesus to the approval of the Nazarenes led him beyond the limitations of their understanding and their vision, they had to recognize his greatness or seek shelter behind indignant denunciation of this presumption. With a humanness which we can readily understand, they chose the latter. To accept Jesus involved renunciations they were entirely unwilling to make. Loving their own sense of special privilege more than they loved truth and righteousness, they cast the Master out of their midst.

Capernaum was quite a cosmopolitan city, and the people were free from many of the narrow prejudices which blinded the Nazarenes. It was also a major political and commercial center, and for these and other reasons Jesus henceforth made it the hub of his work in Galilee.

In Capernaum and the region round about, those who saw and heard Jesus were amazed at his quiet but clear authority: "They were astonished at his doctrine; for he taught them as one that had authority, and not as the scribes."[8] He greatly preferred to state the facts about God and about the kingdom and the conditions of citizenship in the kingdom than to enter into theological disputations. Nor did he depend on the writings of the spiritual leaders of the past to reinforce his authority as the scribes and Pharisees did. He never subordinated his authority to any of those who had gone before. On his lips old phrases, therefore, came to have new meaning; ancient truth was made to glow with living power; and the message of the prophets was sent forth once again with new wisdom and new light.

With Capernaum as his base of operations, Jesus extended his ministry throughout the neighboring countryside, preaching and healing. On these trips into the country, and also during the intervals in Capernaum, the Master steadily enriched the lives of his disciples. Many of these—like Andrew, Peter, James, and John—had been disciples of John the Baptist before they followed the Master. Others, like Matthew, may first have heard the good news of the kingdom from the lips of Jesus himself. This period was therefore important for its influence in the community and in the personal and social lives of those who were nearest to Jesus.

At the beginning of his ministry the scribes and

Pharisees regarded Jesus with the superciliousness which they tended to manifest toward those not of their particular circle. Then, as Jesus emerged as a person of much greater consequence than they had at first realized, the hostility of these leaders crystallized and became more and more apparent.

The terms *Pharisee* and *Sadducee* have an unpleasant sound for us because of their frequent derogatory use in the New Testament. Yet we must understand the contribution these men made to the development of Judaism if we are to appreciate the cause and significance of their frequent clashes with the Master. The Pharisees were strict observers of the law and firm believers in immortality and in the life of the spirit, both of which the Sadducees denied. Then, too, the Pharisees were strong advocates of the "traditions of the elders," holding that these official interpretations of the law were equally binding with the fundamental statements of the law itself. The Sadducees did not set great weight by these old traditions but were tolerant of Greek and Roman culture. The fierce exclusiveness of many Jews had been toned down in them by their good sense and—among the less honorable of them—by their opportunism. They were a nominally religious group, but their real influence was largely political.

The scribes were lawyers or teachers, skilled in the religious history and expectations of the Jews. While the scribes formed a group of their own, this group was not necessarily exclusive. One might belong to the Pharisees and be a scribe also, or one could be both a Sadducee and a scribe.

Jesus was not without appreciation for these men. He had known some of the Pharisees, for example, from the days when he sat at their feet in the synagogue school. He knew that many of them were conscientious. Their difficulty was not that they were irreligious but that their religion lacked any spiritual glow. They distrusted freedom. They felt that the only hope for national perpetuity lay in ceremonial uniformity. They contended that if the Jews were to act like other people, they would cease to be distinctive and so would forfeit their heritage of divine acceptance. There was some truth in this, but not enough to outweigh their concern for a "form of godliness" which was devoid of power.[9]

The heart of the difficulty lay in the determination of the leaders of Judaism to perpetuate Hebrew institutions rather than to achieve a better way of life. They were the conservers of the status quo. They were not all selfish or ambitious for power, although some of their number certainly had both of these limitations, but they conceived religion as something static. By restricting themselves to observance of the "law of carnal commandments," they failed to rise to the spiritual heights. So sure were they of the essential rightness of their procedure that they regarded anyone who differed from them as a menace to their temporal and eternal well-being, and they actually used their concern for spiritual things as an argument to justify the cruelty they used to suppress freedom of thought and action.

The wide cleavage between Jesus and the scribes and Pharisees is illustrated by the objections raised by the latter when Jesus ate with "publicans and sinners."[10] The rulers simply could not understand this. They felt that it indicated a loose indulgence toward sin; if it was encouraged, such indiscriminate friendliness would break down the moral fiber of the nation. Jesus told them, "They that are whole have no need of the physician, but they that are sick. I came not to call the righteous, but sinners to repentance."[11] The scribes and Pharisees, however, continued in their blind prejudice. They made obedience to the law and tradition ends in themselves, while Jesus insisted that these must minister to an inner, spiritual growth.

Relations with these leaders approached a minor crisis when the disciples plucked and ate corn as they went through the fields on the Sabbath day. The Talmudic law recognized five different species of sin in this act: to remove the husks was sifting the corn, to rub the heads of corn was threshing, to clean away the side adherences was sifting out the fruit, to bruise the corn was grinding, to hold it up in the hands was winnowing. All these acts were forbidden. The Pharisees thought that this was an excellent opportunity to put Jesus into public conflict with the law, and they challenged him.

In his reply Jesus attacked the ungodly restrictions on Sabbath observance which had grown up during the years, and which now made this holy day a curse instead of a blessing. He showed how David, of whom all the nation was proud, had eaten the consecrated bread in the house of God without authority and yet had gone unpunished since he did it in order to appease his hunger. He showed, furthermore, how at that very time the priests worked in the Temple every Sabbath, slaying the animals brought for sacrifice, drawing water, cleaving wood, building fires,[12] and yet these, too, were unpunished, since these infractions of the Sabbath were permitted under rightful authority. "Now," said Jesus, "in this place is one greater than the temple. . . . For the Son of Man is Lord even of the Sabbath."[13] Then, having stated his authority, he forever freed people from empty ceremonialism, saying "The Sabbath was made for man, and not man for the Sabbath."[14]

There was nothing trivial about the Master's handling of this problem. There was enough explosive power in his words to wreck the whole structure of Phariseeism, and but few of those who heard failed to understand. The lines were clearly drawn. There could be no compromise. Jesus must give way or be removed or the system represented by the Pharisees would be destroyed.

When Jesus set himself against entrenched interests and special privilege in religion and in society, the people who loved darkness rather than light let their resentments take control of their actions. From that time forward, if it was in their power to hurt him, Jesus was doomed.

NOTES

1. Luke 4:16.
2. Isaiah 61:1, 2.
3. Luke 4:22.
4. Luke 4:18, 19.
5. Luke 4:22.
6. Luke 4:28, 29.
7. Luke 4:32.
8. Mark 1:20.
9. II Timothy 3:5.
10. Mark 2:12, 13.
11. Mark 2:14.
12. Matthew 12:3, 4.
13. Matthew 12:5, 6.
14. Mark 2:25.

Study Helps for

Chapter 13

LESSON PURPOSE

To state the conditions under which Jesus began his kingdom ministry, the types of opposition with which he was confronted, and the methods he used to meet these difficulties. To explore his methods that we may adapt them to today's problems.

SCRIPTURE REFERENCES

Luke 4:16-30; Matthew 12:1-6.

HIGH POINTS OF THE LESSON

- The announcement of the kingdom program at Nazareth by Jesus; why he was rejected there
- The personal contacts made by Jesus in preaching the gospel in Galilee
- The attitude of the Pharisees and Sadducees
- The principles involved in Sabbath observance

QUESTIONS AND DISCUSSION TOPICS

1. How did it happen that Jesus was permitted to preach in the synagogue at Nazareth? Why did Jesus use the reading which he selected? What is the central message of this scripture?

2. How was the sermon of Jesus at first received? How was it later received? How do you account for the change? What was the immediate result of the opposition of his own people?

3. It is said that they "were astonished at his doctrine; for he taught them as one having authority, and not as the scribes." What is meant here by *doctrine* and *authority?* In what way did the authority of Jesus differ from that of the scribes?

4. Matthew relates that Jesus, walking by the sea, saw Peter and Andrew fishing. He said, "Follow me, and I will make you fishers of men. And they straightway left their nets, and followed him." Name others among the early followers of Jesus. What elements in his appeal attracted them? What reward was promised them?

5. Who were the Pharisees? What was their contribution to the development of Judaism? What was the attitude of Jesus toward them?

6. Who were the Sadducees? For what particular contribution were they noteworthy? What was the attitude of Jesus toward them?

7. Why did the Pharisees and the Sadducees grow stronger and more relentless in their opposition to the Master? What lesson does this have for us today?

8. Tell the story of the dispute over Sabbath observance. Why were the Pharisees so concerned about this? What principles did Jesus make clear in reference to the Sabbath? How do these principles apply today?

WHAT THE LESSON MEANS FOR TODAY

In the church we need people who are zealous for law observance. We cannot afford to be tossed about by every wind of doctrine. But neither can we be bound by our yesterdays. We must go forward with God, whose ultimate concern is with people and not with rituals. Spiritual safety lies in advancing, not in standing still, but we can advance safely only under the leadership of the Lord. The Pharisees were right to withstand anyone who flouted the law and offered nothing in its place. They were not right to stand against the next step forward, made under the right direction, in harmony with the law at its best.

Chapter 14

THE CALL OF THE TWELVE

During his earliest ministry Jesus did not appear to have been primarily concerned with organization. Most of his time was spent in preaching, teaching, and healing. He baptized some, although most of the actual baptizing was left to the disciples.[1] Then, too, some who had been baptized by John apparently transferred their allegiance from John to Jesus after John had borne testimony to Jesus as "the Lamb of God."[2] By the time that Jesus had concluded the first phase of his work in Galilee, however, some organization was evidently necessary. By this time the growing opposition of the leaders of the Jews had made it apparent that there was little hope of winning their support as a group, even though individuals like Nicodemus might be won. For these and many other reasons and after a night spent in prayer, Jesus now selected twelve of his disciples[3] "that they should be with him, and that he might send them forth to preach, and to have power to heal sicknesses, and to cast out devils."[4] Prior to this time several of those selected had held some authority, for they had baptized; but none of them had been apostles in the distinctive sense in which they now served.[5]

The choice of the disciples was no incidental happening. It was the response of Jesus to the need of the time and of the days that were yet to come. Fifteen centuries earlier Moses had said to the priests of Israel, "God. . .hath separated you from the congregation of Israel, to bring you near to himself. . .to stand before the congregation to minister unto them."[6] In like fashion Isaiah had surrounded himself with a group of disciples, "the children whom the Lord hath given me," that they might stand as "signs" to the house of Israel.[7]

And in the immediate past John the Baptist had had his circle of disciples. With such precedents at hand, no one appears to have been surprised at this selection of the twelve.

The timing of the choice of the twelve was critical. The early days of enthusiastic public acclaim during which the apostles-to-be had first followed Jesus were passing away. Now the opposition of the leaders and the inability of the masses to appreciate his teachings were becoming increasingly evident.

Naturally those chosen to be apostles were Jews, but they were not tradition-bound Jews. Jesus loved them and trusted them. He wrote no books; he made them his interpreters.[8] His life was their life. He dedicated himself to mining the rich possibilities buried deep in every one of them, and to opening their eyes to the value of the great treasures they carried in their earthen vessels.[9]

For their part, the twelve lived in such wholesome, wholehearted intimacy with Jesus that they caught his spirit and grew more and more loyal to him and to the truth he taught.[10] Jesus shared with them the mysteries of the kingdom which could not be shared with others,[11] so these new apostles were prepared to go forward with the work of Jesus at the close of his earthly ministry.[12] They were workers as well as pupils, learning by doing in a school of practical religion.[13]

Some of the best portraits of the twelve recorded in the Gospels consist of just a few lines, but they indicate with remarkable clarity the general characteristics of those named. Philip was so impressive personally that he is introduced to us merely as a native of the same town as his better-known associates, Andrew and Peter;[14] yet in his mouth the simple words of invitation[15] epitomize the missionary power of such unobtrusive but devoted people in any age. Then there were the two

Jameses. One of these was called "James the less."[16] The Greek original is a word meaning "the tiny one." That is not a very distinguished designation, yet this man found his place in the twelve with Peter and the other James and John the Beloved. Then, too, there were Bartholomew and Thaddeus; Simon the Zealot, a rabid anti-Roman; and Matthew (Levi), an ex-Roman taxgatherer. Judas, who bore one of the proudest names of the age, was also there; and so was Thomas the doubter, the man who wanted to be shown.

These men would have been completely unknown to history except for their association with Jesus, but they were in no sense insignificant. The fishermen among them owned their own boats and nets and employed hired servants. Peter occupied a house large enough to accommodate his family and his friends. When he was called, Matthew left a lucrative political post. If we may judge from his subsequent career, Judas was not likely to have been a poor man. The twelve are referred to as "unlearned" and "ignorant," but this simply meant that they had not received any special education in the sacred law. As a matter of fact, the Gospels and the Epistles show that Matthew, John, and Peter were all men of intelligence and of rather marked literary ability.

It is interesting to note that in choosing this first group of apostles, Jesus passed by such men as Nicodemus, Joseph of Arimathaea, and others who showed a sincere interest in his work and who had education and social standing to commend them. We cannot tell just why Jesus did choose each man of the group, especially Judas Iscariot. Nor can we tell just why he omitted men of social, political, or intellectual prominence. But we are not left entirely in the dark. It is evident that the primary qualifications of the apostles were their faith in God, their ability to break loose from the past, their courage and tenacity of purpose, and their pioneering spirit. Perhaps another qualification was that they had so little to unlearn. Paul, who had so many of the capacities which the average person would seek in a leader, was called later, after the work had been well started. Even then, the Lord had to knock Paul down to break the shackles of his past, to open his eyes to the truth, and to free his powers for apostolic ministry.

Jesus was not blind to the failings of the men whom he had selected. Even before he chose them he must have been aware of their comparative immaturity. Though they used the same words he used, repeating them after him like children, it was a long time before they came to use these words with the significance which Jesus crowded into them. Even as late as the night before his crucifixion the Lord had occasion to reproach one of the twelve, saying, "Have I been so long time with you, and yet hast thou not known me, Philip?"[17] These inadequacies, however, were more than balanced by the spiritual integrity of the eleven and their deep love for him.

Jesus was the close personal friend of his apostles, ready at all times to help them toward the light, and yet always holding something in reserve that—in reaching out for it—they might grow. Ordinarily he appears to have walked ahead of them in their journeys from place to place. There are repeated references to his summoning them and then dismissing them,[18] indicating a certain dignity in their mutual relations. Yet the Master let them manage the boat, trusting himself readily to their expertness while he slept, even during one of the sudden storms common to the Sea of Galilee.[19]

The incident where the appetites of five thousand were satisfied from the scanty resources of the twelve, borrowed from a boy, is an excellent example of the ministry of Jesus. The people needed him. They followed him when they should have been resting, coming without food in their eagerness to hear, so that he was moved with compassion and told them "many things." When Jesus had finished and the people were tired and hungry, he had them seated by companies on the green grass,[20] looking in their many-colored garments like a well-ordered flower bed. Then Jesus shared with his disciples, and the disciples shared with the people, and the circle of helpfulness reached out and out until even those who were "afar off" received not only bread and fish but also the fellowship of communion and love.

Our records are too scanty for us to trace step by step the growth of understanding among these special friends of Jesus. Nevertheless, we can imagine their standing near him as he preached to the waiting crowds or healed the sick who lined his route. Thus they gained knowledge of his message and insight into his methods. In the less frequent moments of their solitude we can hear them questioning one another, and we can see them as the impetuous Peter brought their difficulties to the attention of the Master. Untrained at first, though not unintelligent, they soon became able to speak in public and to sense the varying moods of the crowds, to handle delicately and yet with courage the growing opposition of the scribes and Pharisees and, in time, to plant the work in lands both near and far.

The Gospels reveal that Jesus' most profound and inward teaching about the fatherhood of God, his intimate care for individuals, and his available help through prayer were addressed to the disciples alone.[21] So they grew—slowly, very slowly, but quite surely—into pillars of the church; and, because there had been added to their sincerity of purpose and their personal purity and enthusiastic courage something of their Master, they were steadfast and adequate to the needs of their generation and of many generations to follow.

NOTES

1. John 4:2, KJ; 4:3, IV.
2. John 1:36, 37.
3. Luke 6:12-13.
4. Mark 3:13.
5. It is of interest to note that it was five years after the organization of the church in 1830 before the first members of the Council of Twelve were set apart, even though their place in the organization had been indicated before the church was brought into being (see Doctrine and Covenants 16).
6. Numbers 16:9.
7. Isaiah 8:16-18.
8. Acts 1:21, 22.
9. II Corinthians 4:7.
10. John 6:66-69; 11:15, 16.
11. Mark 4:10-12, 26.
12. Matthew 28:15-19; Luke 24:43-50.
13. Matthew 9:35-38, KJ; 41-44, IV; 11:1; see *The Life of Christ,* Burgess, p. 113.
14. John 1:44.
15. John 1:46.
16. Mark 15:40, KJ.
17. John 14:9.
18. Mark 8:1; 9:32; 12:49.
19. Mark 4:30.
20. Luke 9:14; John 6:10.
21. Harry E. Fosdick, *The Man from Nazareth,* 1949, p. 174.

Study Helps for

Chapter 14

LESSON PURPOSE

To study the principles involved in the choice of the twelve

SCRIPTURE REFERENCES

Luke 6:12-16; Matthew 10:1-6; Mark 3:13-19, KJ; 12-14, IV

HIGH POINTS OF THE LESSON

- Jesus waited until the time was opportune and the men were ready before he selected the twelve.
- The apostolic group is noteworthy both for those included and those omitted.
- At first these men were spiritually immature. They grew in spiritual stature through intimate personal association with Jesus, and through carrying burdens suited to their growing strength.

QUESTIONS AND DISCUSSION TOPICS

1. Who were the earliest followers of Jesus? Where had they been prior to his coming? Why was the church gradually organized? Compare this situation to the organization of the church in the Restoration movement.

2. Why were the twelve chosen? What other ministers were commissioned and sent out by Jesus?

3. What principles were followed by Jesus in the training of the twelve? Illustrate your answer if possible.

4. Who were the three most prominent apostles? Describe each one. Wherein lay his strength and where was his weakness?

5. What are the characteristics of some of the other twelve that justified their apostolic calling?

6. In what way did the feeding of the five thousand and the participation of the twelve epitomize the teaching methods of Jesus?

7. What is the primary function of the twelve? What abilities did the apostles develop with the passing of the months?

8. Name some prominent men in the early church who were not chosen for the twelve. Why was the testimony of Jesus by all of them, apostles and others, of such fundamental importance?

WHAT THE LESSON MEANS FOR TODAY

The organization of the first apostolic group had to wait until the time was ripe and the men were ripe. Organization before that time would have been disastrous; organization delayed past that time would have been wasteful of opportunity. The time limits of the occasion centered partly in external considerations but chiefly in the growth of the men involved. It still does. The building of the kingdom of God implies the selection, training, and timely appointment of the men and women needed to administer the affairs of the kingdom.

Chapter 15

THE SERMON ON THE MOUNT

Prior to the choice of the twelve, the work of Jesus had been largely public. While he may have been specially close to certain individuals, there seems to have been no inner circle to whose development he gave special attention. The choice of the twelve marked a definite change in the Master's method of ministry. He continued to preach publicly, but from this time forward his attention was primarily directed toward the training of the twelve.[1] In giving the twelve this specialized training, it was possible for the Master to follow a more orderly sequence of instruction than we find in his public sermons, which tended to be influenced by the immediate problems of members of his audience.

The best known and most fully reported sermon of Jesus is the Sermon on the Mount, which was delivered immediately after the twelve were chosen[2] and was addressed primarily to the "disciples."[3] This term *disciples* certainly includes the twelve, but it may have included some few others of those closest to the Master. "The multitude" may also have listened in on the discourse,[4] which was probably delivered on one of the slopes of the Horns of Hattin, a hill sixty feet high located about two hours' journey west of Tiberias. This is not absolutely certain, since the term translated "the mountain" denotes the high plateau country of Galilee in distinction from the lowland on the shore of the lake. In Luke's account the discourse is represented as being spoken on "a level place" in the hill country.

The importance of the Sermon on the Mount in relation to the choosing of the twelve is readily apparent. Whenever a group of people band themselves together in a common understanding, they must set up a covenant which shall express their united purpose and to which they must be loyal. Jesus did this in the Sermon on the Mount, which is the covenant and charter of kingdom citizenship. The disciples knew this. So did the later church. So do we today.

We shall study the report of the sermon given by Matthew, whose report is most complete. Luke also gives an account of the sermon, but his account is much more concise.[5] There are several possible explanations for the discrepancy betweeen these two accounts. One of these is that Matthew wrote specifically for the Jews, while Luke had the Gentiles in mind and so did not bother to report some details in which the Gentiles were not interested. Another possible explanation is that Matthew, who is fond of grouping together similar material, reported lessons given at other times as though all of these had been incorporated with what was given on the slopes of Mount Hattin.[6] In this connection it is to be noted that much of the teaching which Luke omits from his report of the Sermon on the Mount is included by Luke in other places in his gospel.[7] Then again, we must remember that it is not improbable that Jesus used similar illustrations and ways of teaching on several occasions, repeating himself deliberately for the good of his disciples. It may be that Matthew reports the Sermon on the Mount fully so as to be able to omit later repetitions of the same teaching, while Luke reports a brief account of the Sermon on the Mount bcause he is presenting much of the remaining material "in order."[8]

This sermon has been called "the moral law of the kingdom of God."[9] It bears the same general relation to the New Testament that the Ten Commandments bear to the Old Testament. This is not true in every detail, but it is a parallel which is illuminating and provocative. Since the Ten Commandments were given by God for the guidance of ancient Israel and the instruction contained in the Sermon on the Mount was given by Divinity for the guidance of the new Israel, these two are related, being motivated by the same Spirit and pointed toward the same end. All that is universally significant in the Ten Commandments is repeated in the Sermon on the Mount but on a much higher plane.

The teaching of the Sermon on the Mount is for spiritually mature men and women. It is very important that we sense this clearly. The kind of life pictured here cannot be lived by unregenerate persons but only by those who have been "born again." Others may be able to discuss the principles enunciated, but no one will really understand the Sermon on the Mount who is not already dedicated to the Christian way of life. The sermon deals with the nature of this new life which the apostles and other disciples already felt stirring within them and which is born of the Spirit of God.

The interpolations made in the Inspired Version of Matthew's narrative are particularly helpful at this point:

> Blessed are they who shall believe on me; and again, more blessed are they who shall believe on your words, when ye shall testify that ye have seen me and that I am. Yea, blessed are they who shall believe on your words, and come down into the depth of humility, and be baptized in my name; for they. . .shall receive a remission of their sins. Yea, blessed are the poor in spirit, who come unto me; for theirs is the kingdom of heaven.[10]

Although it would be difficult to justify the inclusion of these verses by studying any of the manuscripts now available, or, indeed, in any way other than by the spirit of revelation, they are in full harmony with the whole tenor of New Testament teaching. They proclaim that the new standard of living revealed in the sermon is to be built on a new relationship to Christ and this is fundamental. The teaching of Jesus applies only to those who are his disciples; others might be reformed, but they cannot be regenerated. We must beware of thinking of Jesus as the Great Teacher except as we think of him first of all as our Savior and Redeemer.

If we can overcome the partial blindness which results from our familiarity with the words of the Sermon on the Mount and can listen as the disciples listened, with the Spirit of God warming our hearts and quickening our understanding, we shall find that the dominant notes of this sermon are authority and rightness. The two are related. Jesus spoke with authority because he is who he is. He apparently had no hesitation in saying that his disciples must live for the kingdom for his sake[11] and that the eternal destiny of humanity would depend on the judgment that he would mete out on the basis of their compliance or noncompliance with his teachings.[12] The instruction contained in the Sermon on the Mount, and, indeed, all his instruction to his disciples, is therefore the authoritative instruction of one who directs by right.

The moral authority of Jesus is shown in the appeal which his moral precepts make to the inner spiritual sense of godly men and women. This, for example, is the appeal made by the Master's statement of the first and second commandments.[13] Whenever people listened to him without prejudice, the words of Jesus carried this same note of authority. The Sermon on the Mount lives and makes its appeal to those of every age and every background because it enshrines eternal truth. Its parts belong together, however, and they must be studied and applied in faith and full dedication.

NOTES

1. Mark 4:9-12.
2. Luke 6:12-49.
3. Matthew 5:1; Luke 6:17, 20.
4. The student will be interested in comparing the Sermon on the Mount as reported by Matthew and the almost identical report in III Nephi 5:44, 45-6:37; 7:1. Here the distinction is much more clear between that which

is addressed directly to the Twelve and that which has more general application; e.g., III Nephi 6:1. Note also the additional emphasis in the Inspired Version.

5. Luke 6:17-49.
6. For illustrations of Matthew's tendency to group similar incidents or teachings together, note that he gives us a group of miracles (Matthew 8, 9), a group of parables (Matthew 13), etc.
7. The passages in Luke which correspond to the Sermon on the Mount: Luke 6:20-49; 11:1-4, 9-13, 33-36; 12:22-31, 58, 59; 13:24-27; 14:34, 35.
8. Luke 1:3. In this connection note also that the Inspired Version of the Holy Scriptures interpolates two verses (Matthew 5:3, 4) in Matthew's account of the Sermon on the Mount; these verses are not added to the Lucan account in the same version.
9. Bishop Charles Gore, *The Sermon on the Mount,* p. 1.
10. Matthew 5:3-5, IV.
11. Matthew 5:11, KJ.
12. Matthew 7:22, 23, KJ; 32, 33, IV.
13. Mark 12:28-34, KJ; 33-39, IV.

Study Helps for

Chapter 15

LESSON PURPOSE

To impress the truth that the teachings of the Sermon on the Mount are directed toward believers

SCRIPTURE REFERENCES

Matthew 5:1, 2; Luke 6:17-49; III Nephi 5:44-115; 6:1-37.

HIGH POINTS OF THE LESSON

- The Sermon on the Mount was addressed primarily to the disciples. This term includes the twelve and possibly a few others.
- This sermon differs from the Ten Commandments, but carries a similar spirit and intention.
- The new standard of living envisioned in the Sermon on the Mount was illustrated in the life of Jesus but awaited more complete demonstration under the ministry of the Spirit.

QUESTIONS AND DISCUSSION TOPICS

1. To whom was the Sermon on the Mount primarily addressed? Note the relation of this sermon to the call of the twelve.

2. How does the account of the Sermon on the Mount in the Inspired Version differ from that in other versions?

3. In what respects were the teachings of the Sermon on the Mount akin to those set forth in the Ten Commandments?

4. If we feel that the principles set forth in the Sermon on the Mount should become the guide for the relations of Christian nations, what steps do you suggest might help to bring this to pass?

5. What is meant by the statement, "We must beware of thinking of Jesus as the great teacher except as we think of him first of all as our Savior and Redeemer"?

6. What difficulties impeded the understanding of the Jews when they heard Jesus saying, "It was said by them of old time. . . . but I say unto you."

7. The disciples remembered the words of the Sermon on the Mount. But note that their fuller understanding must await the coming of Easter and the Resurrection and Pentecost.

8. Compare the attitude of the apostles as they listened to the Sermon on the Mount with the attitude of the elders who came together in Ohio "to agree" concerning the word of God (Doctrine and Covenants 41:1). What conditions of understanding were present in both situations?

WHAT THE LESSON MEANS FOR TODAY

The message of Jesus far outranked the spiritual ideas of the people to whom he came. They could understand the words he spoke, but it was very difficult for them to understand the spiritual truths which he sought to convey. Many lacked the will to understand. The message made unprecedented demands on them, and so they were inclined to be critical rather than receptive. In our day the will to believe is similarly important. When our hearts are right, God can quicken new understanding within us.

Chapter 16

THE BEATITUDES

The Sermon on the Mount begins with a description of the true citizen of the kingdom of God. This description is expressed first of all in eight Beatitudes, or statements of the blessedness attaching to various types of kingdom character. It was necessary for Jesus to make this quite clear to the twelve at the beginning of their ministry, for the life of the kingdom is different in its spiritual essence and in its rewards from the life of society organized apart from God. It was important that they not judge the life of the kingdom by the standards of the world.

The Beatitudes are all related to each other. We know that they can be combined into a complete and harmonious whole because they were so combined in the life of Jesus himself. He is the chief of the "peacemakers," for his very life purpose was to make peace between God and people and among persons. When he says, "Blessed are the merciful," we are reminded that he had compassion on the multitude because they were hungry and were scattered like sheep without a shepherd, and that even on the cross he prayed for those who persecuted him. He so hungered and thirsted after righteousness that when his disciples sought recuperation in food and sleep, he said to them, "I have meat to eat that ye know not of," and between strenuous days he spent whole nights in prayer.

Behind all the Beatitudes is the presumption of meekness and lowliness of heart on the part of the disciples, a receptiveness and cooperativeness which offer service without self-assertion. A true citizen of the kingdom is a servant of God. Here also Jesus set the preeminent example, saying, "I am among you as he who serveth."[1] Yet a real servant is a person of considerable consequence. Lacking wealth with which to control the acts of others, the servant has resources to make life happy for others, and finds personal satisfaction and a sense of self-value.

"Blessed are the poor in spirit; for theirs is the kingdom of heaven." This opening "blessed" must have startled the disciples. Its essential idea is detachment from the burdens of possession. In their day Roman citizens were regarded as blessed, for they were the conquerors.[2] Pharisees, too, were popularly regarded as blessed, for they embodied the popular ideal of the Jews. Jesus passed by both the cruel Roman and the self-righteous Pharisee when he sought out people for his blessing and turned to a class variously known as "the poor," "the needy," "the meek," and "the righteous" in contrast to those commonly called "the rich," "the mighty," and "the wicked." The "poor in spirit" included such people as Joseph and Mary, Zacharias and Elizabeth, Simeon and Anna, and the shepherds of Bethlehem. They were devout but unpretentious folk who did not have time to attend to all the rites and ceremonies observed by the Pharisees but who were nevertheless kind, virtuous, industrious, unpretentious, lovable, and godly. Such as these possess the kingdom when Roman and Pharisee alike remain without.

The poor in spirit were poor in a way that reveals basic character. They regarded possessions as means but not as ends, as the furniture and equipment of life but not as life itself. The scribes and Pharisees, on the other hand, were loaded down with too much equipment for life to be able to live. Their traditions, their pride of place, their love of wealth, and a score of similar impedimenta conspired to obstruct them as they pressed toward fullness of life.

In our own day we have people who are "land poor" and "property poor." These people seem to be well-to-do, but the demands of their possessions keep them actually poor. They cannot enter into life because they will not sacrifice possessions they cannot afford to maintain. To these people and to their kin—those too eager to be ranked with the intelligentsia to have time to live, those too eager for social preference to have time for life, those who are beset by "the cares of this world and the deceitfulness of riches"[3]—the word of Jesus comes today with peculiar force: "Blessed are the poor in spirit; for theirs is the kingdom of heaven."

"Blessed are they that mourn; for they shall be comforted." This second Beatitude was every bit as startling as its predecessor, for the instinctive desire of the worldly person is to escape pain and sorrow. Almost the last we should naturally designate as blessed are those who mourn. But Jesus saw that life at its best includes capacity for deep feeling, for sympathy, for mutual understanding, and therefore for sorrow. Great love means great capacity to be hurt as well as great capacity for happiness. Those who mourn for themselves or for others are at least alive. Sir Henry Taylor knew this. He wrote:

He that lacks time to mourn, lacks time to mend.
Eternity mourns that. 'Tis an ill cure
For life's worst ills, to have no time to feel them.
Where sorrow's held intrusive and turned out,
There wisdom will not enter, nor true power,
Nor aught that dignifies humanity.

Far better the pain that is part of real life than to be "finished and finite clods, untroubled by a spark."[4]

Jesus prayed to be delivered from evil and spent much of his life in relieving pain, but he well knew that some mourning is inevitable in every life well lived—notably deep regret for sin and sympathetic sorrow with friends. He himself shared the grief of Mary and Martha; he never sought to solve such mourning as this by running away from it. Instead, Jesus permitted such mourning to sound out the deeper values of life. The writer of the letter to the Hebrews sensed the meaning of Jesus at this point when he named many of the great heroes of the history of Israel and then continued:

> Wherefore, seeing we also are compassed about with so great a cloud of witnesses, let us lay aside every weight, and the sin which doth so easily beset us, and let us run with patience the race that is set before us, looking unto Jesus the author and finisher of our faith; who for the joy that was set before him endured the cross, despising the shame, and is set down at the right hand of the throne of God. For consider him that endured such contradiction of sinners against himself, lest ye be wearied and faint in your minds.[5]

"Blessed are the meek; for they shall inherit the earth." Here again the Master brings out clearly the distinction between his way of life and the worldly way of life. Certainly neither the Romans nor the Pharisees were meek—nor, for that matter, is the "successful" modern. I remember many years ago hearing my old schoolmaster explain that the Greek word here translated *meek* was used by Zenophon for domesticated animals such as horses broken to the bridle. Here the essential idea is not lack of power but the presence of controlled power—discipline. The meek people Jesus commends are those whose passions are under the control of a great life purpose. Such do actually "inherit the earth."

Our modern life has given us limited illustrations of what the Master meant. Many of those successful in business are singularly humble. They have disciplined themselves to be receptive. They make it a point to see that anyone in their organization with a good idea has a chance to make that idea known. They must judge, of course, between the helpful and the useless, but they do not presume that all the good ideas in the business must originate with them. Such people inherit their full share of the world with which they are concerned. Perhaps an even better parallel is at hand in the lives of those of science who sit down humbly before the facts revealed in their investigations and revise theories, no matter how tenderly they have been held, which will not conform to these facts. Driven by a love for the truth which is more important to them than anything else, such true scientists enter into an inheritance which would be forever closed to them but for their singleness of purpose. When we learn to apply this same principle in the concerns of the larger life, with all our lesser concerns brought under the control of a passion for the kingdom, we, too, shall enter into our inheritance.

"Blessed are they which hunger and thirst after righteousness; for they shall be filled." The people of Palestine knew what it was to be hungry. A few of them had enough and to spare, but the vast majority lived precariously. To them the idea of hunger as blessing was particularly novel. Yet hunger is a sign of health and growth. When we cease to have recurrent feelings of hunger we are sick, and we continue to be sick until we again feel our need.

Hunger is one of the great incentives to hard work and therefore to achievement. Hunger for spiritual things is particularly blessed because it provides the spur to spiritual progress without the scourge of famine.[6] One of the major spiritual tragedies of the time lay in the self-righteousness of religious leaders. They were so sure they knew all that was worth knowing that God himself could not teach them. They lacked appetite and relish for the truth.

"Blessed are the merciful; for they shall obtain mercy." This Beatitude is more readily understood now than it was at the time when Jesus first uttered it. In that day life was coarse and brutal. The sick, the wounded, and the unfortunate were regarded as

burdens which wise people rid themselves of as quickly as possible. Unwanted children were frequently left to die. There were no hospitals, and even though disaster might call forth a feeling of pity, this emotion rarely led to organized relief. On the contrary, the public life of the time encouraged hardness and cruelty.

Jesus urged his disciples to practice mercy as a foundation for lives of reciprocity. "Be merciful," he said, "and others will show mercy to you in your hour of need." Then, extending the principle, he taught that the only hope for humankind lies in the mercy of God—his compassion and his ready forgiveness of our many transgressions—and that the wise will show the same compassion and good will that they hope to receive. This is not to put mercy on a bargaining basis but on a basis of rightness. Jesus wants us to be merciful because to be merciful is to be like God. Those who have learned to be merciful can well be treated mercifully, for they will not take advantage of the strength given them to assert their dominance over others.

"Blessed are the pure in heart; for they shall see God." We perhaps best understand what Jesus meant by this Beatitude by remembering that the Pharisees believed that God had his court above the seventh heaven, and that guardian angels of the great were free to enter this inner court where they could see the face of God.[7] The promise that the pure in heart shall see God is therefore a promise that those who are pure in heart shall rank highest among God's people and be given the same rights as the "angels of the presence."

Many of those who heard Jesus were already convinced of the great importance of purity, but the purity with which they were concerned was the external purity achieved by conformity to the ordinances of Judaism.

The purity of heart which Jesus here pronounces blessed is akin to that for which the Psalmist prayed:

> Create in me a clean heart, O God; and renew a right spirit within me. Cast me not away from thy presence; and take not thy Holy Spirit from me. Restore unto me the joy of thy salvation; and uphold me with thy free Spirit. Then will I teach transgressors thy ways; and sinners shall be converted unto thee.[8]

This purity of heart could not be achieved by mere obedience to the letter of the law; purity is not a matter of doing right things but of the doer being right with God. There is an old proverb to the effect that "unless the vessel is clean, whatever you put into it turns sour." It is so with the human heart. Unless one's heart is right with God, what one does is likely to be tainted.

Purity of heart is a living purity. It is not innocence but the outcome of conflict and a manifestation of strength. The purity of a lily comes from the nature which enables it to extract from the surrounding filth such food as will nurture its own white beauty. Similarly, the purity Jesus smiled on grows and blossoms in spite of surrounding circumstances because its roots are in the life of God.

"Blessed are the peacemakers; for they shall be called the children of God." All around the little company of the slopes of Mount Hattin were the warmakers. The more obvious of these were the Roman soldiers, but the term should certainly include also those Zealots who were willing to join any and every kind of crusade against Rome. Even among those who listened to the Master there were probably some who had a positive genius for setting people at odds against each other. Jesus blessed none of these. Instead, he pronounced a blessing on those who are aggressively concerned for peace, those who bring peace into being, those whose influence is as a leaven making for healthy and co-operative life.

As we contemplate the work of Jesus in its totality, we know in our hearts that this particular "blessed" was inevitable. Even if it should be admitted for a moment that warmakers clear away the rank and fetid undergrowth in order that we may build the kingdom of God more securely, we know that their effectiveness depends on the work of those who come afterward and who build toward unity and cooperation. "Jesus could have chained a world of slaves to the foot of his throne by merciless force, but he could not have made them hate the iniquities he abolished, nor delight in the righteousness he commanded, nor love their neighbors, nor delight to do his will. Physical force is inadequate in the realm of the spirit."[9]

Jesus promised that the peacemakers shall be called the sons of God. This is as it should be, for the spirit of love, of cooperation, of cleanliness, of mutual goodwill—the spirit of the peacemaker—is the Spirit of God. It is those who are moved by this spirit (not those who protest against war and yet are willing to enjoy the fruits of an ungodly social order), who love God and seek to spread the spirit of love abroad in the world, who shall be known as the children of God.

"Blessed are they which are persecuted for righteousness' sake; for theirs is the kingdom of heaven." In this final Beatitutde Jesus maintains the fresh vigor of the distinctive point of view which he had sounded in the earlier ones. "Those who follow me," he says, "will be persecuted. When that happens, rejoice and be exceeding glad. By your endurance under that persecution you will be admitted to the glorious company of those who suffer for righteousness' sake." The experience of godly people has fully confirmed this testimony of Jesus. The blessedness which is granted those who endure under persecution is not a reward added afterward; it is part of the experience itself. Nothing makes one's convictions so precious as the

privilege of suffering for them. To be resentful when the children of darkness refuse to receive the message of light, is to be overcome by evil. But to continue to pursue the way of righteousness in the Spirit of Christ, come what may, is to make the very hardness of the way set the heart to singing. To those who have shared the experience, it is no strange thing that after Paul and Silas had been beaten with many stripes and cast into prison and there made fast in the stocks, "at midnight Paul and Silas prayed, and sang praises unto God."[10]

The disciples needed this assurance that blessings attend persecution, and so do we. There is a widely prevalent idea that those who serve God faithfully can count on him for deliverance from pain and sickness. This is not always true. History is replete with evidences of the unfailing love of God toward his people. He frequently saves from pain and sorrow those who love him. But there are times when to deliver his disciples from lesser evils would be to deliver them over to greater evils, and our heavenly Father does not do this. He did not deliver his Son in Gethsemane, and even though Peter was saved from imprisonment in his early ministry he was later crucified. Anyone who serves God in spite of persecution is a greater person than the one who serves only when conditions are favorable; and those who serve in spite of sickness and disillusionment are greater than those who demand that their faith be constantly supported by their own relief from the pains and penalties which others suffer as part of the common lot of humanity. Our heavenly Father gladly releases us from such ills as have no hidden pearl of value for us, but he expects us to endure whether we can see this pearl or not. Paul might be saved from the viper[11] but he still had to go to Rome a prisoner in order that there he might preach the word of God.[12]

The disciples must have been astonished by these

pronouncements of blessedness in the kingdom of God. They would have been more astonished if they had not seen before them the living example of what Jesus meant. Without this example clearly realized, there are times when we think of the Christian virtues Jesus listed as weak. It is likely that we shall continue to do so except as we are possessed by the Spirit of Christ and understand what he meant to convey. For this reason it is imperative that we maintain our contacts with him. Unless we copy Jesus' virtues of sympathy, humility, integrity, compassion, singleness of heart, constructive peacemaking, and endurance for righteousness' sake as well as his faith, courage, foresight, justice, and self-discipline there is no possibility of building the kingdom.

Jesus could take for granted many of the stronger virtues among the people around him. What was needed was emphasis on passive virtues which have conquered where the more aggressive virtues have failed. All history testifies that Jesus was right:

> Though we walk in the flesh, we do not war after the flesh; (for the weapons of our warfare are not carnal, but mighty through God to the pulling down of strongholds;) casting down imaginations, and every high thing that exalteth itself against the knowledge of God, and bringing into captivity every thought to the obedience of Christ.[13]

NOTES

1. Luke 22:27.
2. Note the attitude of Paul in this connection, Acts 22:24-29.
3. Matthew 13:22, KJ.
4. Rabbi Ben Ezra.
5. Hebrews 12:1-3.
6. Admirably stated in *The Beatitudes* by Robert Russell, to which I have referred repeatedly in preparing this chapter.
7. Matthew 18:10.
8. Psalm 51:10-13.
9. Robert Russell, *The Beatitudes,* p. 96.

10. Acts 16:25.

11. Acts 28:3-5.

12. Acts 28:15, 30, 31.

13. II Corinthians 10:3-5.

Study Helps for

Chapter 16

LESSON PURPOSE

To enlarge our appreciation of the meaning of citizenship in the kingdom of God

SCRIPTURE REFERENCES

Matthew 5:3-12, KJ; III Nephi 5:47-59.

HIGH POINTS OF THE LESSON

- The Beatitudes are all related to each other and are illustrated in the life of Jesus.
- The inner meaning of each Beatitude should be explored.
- These less aggressive virtues are to be exercised in balanced harmony with such virtues as faith, courage, foresight, justice, and self-discipline.

QUESTIONS AND DISCUSSION TOPICS

1. What did Jesus mean by "the poor in spirit"? In the context of this interpretation, explain the difference between the publican and the Pharisee as they prayed (Luke 19:10-14); consider also the story of the rich man and Lazarus (Luke 16:19-31, KJ; 24-26, IV).

2. What did Jesus mean by his statement that "blessed are they that mourn"? Discuss the statement that "great love means great capacity to be hurt as well as great capacity for happiness."

3. Who were those whom Jesus called "the meek"? In what sense do the meek "inherit the earth"?

4. Discuss hunger and thirst as creative factors in human maturation. The Inspired Version adds "with the Holy Ghost" to this Beatitude. How does this addition help us better understand what Jesus meant?

5. Why did Jesus lay such great stress on the blessings awaiting the merciful? In Galatians 6:7 is this statement: "Be not deceived; God is not mocked; for whatosever a man soweth, that shall he also reap." If one sows mercy, does that person always reap mercy? What is reaped in one's own self? In society?

6. Who are the pure in heart? Why are they promised that they shall see God? Is there any adequate substitute for purity of heart? What is the relation of purity and innocence?

7. When are peacemakers blessed? Consider, briefly, the roles of peacemakers in the home, in the community, in the church. Modern revelation says "Let contention cease" (Doctrine and Covenants 134:7). What is wrong

about contention? In what spirit did Jude (v. 3) exhort the saints to "earnestly contend for the faith"?

8. No wise person seeks to be persecuted. But neither do devout Christians allow the threat of persecution to deter them from the practice of their faith. From the second century onward Christians have praised God for "the noble army of martyrs" (The Te Deum) and with Tertullian love recognized that "the blood of the martyrs is the seed of the church," and the testimony of the martyrs from Stephen onward is that there is joy in such faithfulness at last.

WHAT THE LESSON MEANS FOR TODAY

Understanding of the Beatitudes calls for dedication, prayer, and divine guidance. They do not commend themselves to worldly people. Yet they have been vindicated over and over again. In a culture which worships the aggressive virtues unduly one of our greatest needs is to offset this by the practice of these gentler Christian ways of life.

Chapter 17

THE LAW OF MOSES SUPERSEDED

The Jewish contemporaries of the Lord Jesus considered themselves subject to the Mosaic law which Paul was soon to describe as "our schoolmaster to bring us unto Christ."[1] This law had been added to earlier commands because of transgression.[2] It had now been nullified to a large extent by the way in which it was ignored and by the weight of tradition which was supposed to safeguard it but which contravened its spirit. Jesus attacked the abuses of the law evident on every hand, doing so in his personal life and affirmative teaching and also in his demonstration of the true nature of the "heavy burdens, and grievance to be borne" which their leaders laid "on men's shoulders."[3]

It should be remembered that "the law" did not include the whole of the Old Testament but only the books of Moses. The law was reinforced at the time of Jesus by what was technically known as the "tradition," a series of oral commentaries or explanations of the law. This tradition was popularly believed to have been begun by Moses and amplified down the years under the direction of the most learned scribes. It sought to make the application of the law both sure and precise in every conceivable situation, and since sincere scribes regarded the law as a direct revealment of God to Moses, they felt that it must be protected by strict observance of the tradition, whose requirements were perpetual and mandatory.

The law did not reveal the full purpose of God but provided only such intimations as would guide an immature and unresponsive people as far as they were willing to go.

It was the interpretation of the law which the rulers of

the Jews had enshrined in countless requirements and taboos, rather than the law itself, which Jesus denounced, saying to the Pharisees that by their traditions they had "made the commandment of God of none effect."[4]

Jesus himself fulfilled the law in the sense that he was true to the best in it. Moreover, he did not oppose the rulers of his people out of a lack of appreciation for what the law had done for the Jews. He did not encourage his disciples to mock and flout the law but to live above it. In particular, he said their righteousness was to exceed the righteousness of the scribes and Pharisees in the sense that theirs was a righteousness of the heart made possible by the spirit and example which he was setting before them.[5] On occasion, the Master justified his cause by appealing to the law itself. Moses, he said, would be among the first to accuse many of the traditionalists who claimed to be following him but were actually misrepresenting him.[6]

As the Pharisees were aware, Moses had specified certain foods as unclean. According to their view there was no room for argument; these foods must not be eaten. To the orthodox all searching for reasons behind the commands in the law was worse than a waste of time. Jesus, speaking with an authority which they were unwilling to admit, shocked them by giving a richer meaning to the law than any of its traditional exponents had ever done. He taught concerning ceremonially clean and unclean foods, for example, that the only spiritual contamination of food lies in its abuse. Some edibles should be avoided because they are not real foods, but they were not referred to in the tradition for this reason. Among many of the Pharisees only the letter of the law really counted.

The situation was illustrated when some of the disciples were criticized by the Pharisees for their failure to observe regular ceremonial fasts. In defense of his followers, the Master claimed the exemption provided in the law for bridal parties, referring to himself as the bridegroom and thereby more than hinting at the nature of his own authority. The Master did not ignore the place of fasting. Indeed, he gave it a very definite place in his teaching,[7] instructing his followers to fast in the spirit of worship and out of regard for spiritual values about which they were deeply concerned and not just to fulfill the letter of the law.

The major differences between Jesus and the Pharisees were twofold—in their teaching and in their practice. There were good and well-intentioned Pharisees. But many of the Pharisees had become aware that obedience to the letter of the law as develeoped by them and their forebears was not enough. Having lost their faith, but being eager to retain their social and religious eminence, they became blind leaders of the blind. Jesus said of them and of the scribes: "Ye are like unto whited sepulchers, which indeed appear beautiful outwardly, but are within full of the bones of the dead, and of all uncleanness."[8]

Jesus nourished his own spiritual life on the prophets and the psalmists and on his personal communion with God. While the Pharisees sought acceptance with God by obedience to the letter of the law, Jesus found life with God by partaking of his living Spirit.

The greatest of the prophets of Israel had proclaimed truths which belong to the ages. Micah said:

> Wherewith shall I come before the Lord, and bow myself before the high God? shall I come before him with burnt offerings, with calves of a year old? Will the Lord be pleased with thousands of rams, or with ten thousands of rivers of oil? shall I give my firstborn for my transgression, the fruit of my body for the sin of my soul? He hath showed thee, O man, what is good; and what doth the Lord require of thee, but to do justly, and to love mercy, and to walk humbly with thy God?[9]

The prophets brought the word of God. But now One greater than they was here.[10] The keynote of his message was that a new order was coming into being, fulfilling and surpassing what they had known and having laws which—of right—superseded the law of Moses.

The new order, the kingdom order, did not come by fiat; it was to be a spiritual order and spiritual achievement takes time. But it had been in the mind of God from the beginning. Foundations had been laid in the work of the prophets and in the divinely nurtured expectations of devout men and women. After John the Baptist was put in prison, therefore,

> Jesus came into Galilee, preaching the gospel of the kingdom of God; and saying, The time is fulfilled, and the kingdom of God is at hand; repent ye, and believe the gospel.[11]

The Mosaic Law was not destroyed so much as it was left behind. It was fulfilled in spirit even when it was set aside in the letter. Jesus, who gave the law, saw to the heart of each requirement and emphasized its greatest spiritual meaning. The task of Christianity is to interpret into daily living the freedom, beauty, and spiritual power of the principles enunciated by the Master.

NOTES

1. Galatians 3:24, KJ.
2. Galatians 3:19.
3. Matthew 23:4; Luke 11:46, KJ. See Galatians for the Christian substitute for this.
4. Matthew 15:6.
5. Matthew 5:20, KJ.
6. John 5:45, 46, KJ.
7. Matthew 6:16-18, KJ; 17, 18, IV.
8. Matthew 23:24.
9. Micah 6:6-8. See also Isaiah 10:1, 2; Amos 5:24.
10. Matthew 7:37; Mark 1:22, KJ.
11. Mark 1:13, 14.

Study Helps for

Chapter 17

LESSON PURPOSE

To make clear the superlative grandeur of "the perfect law of liberty" by contrasting it with the "lesser law," and showing the concern of the Master that the lesser should be superseded by the greater

SCRIPTURE REFERENCES

Matthew 5:17-48; Galatians 3:23-29.

HIGH POINTS OF THE LESSON

- Jesus never derided the law. He objected only to the attitude which made obedience to the law the whole purpose of religious life. The law was a good schoolmaster. Its purpose was to create a love for light and truth in the hearts of the people.
- The law had been the best compromise possible at the time of its promulgation. Jesus sought to fulfill its purpose by eliminating the elements of compromise.
- The Law of Moses was not destroyed by the law of the gospel; it was surpassed.

QUESTIONS AND DISCUSSION TOPICS

1. What did the Jews mean when they referred to "the law"? Why was the law elaborated with minute details? On whose authority did this elaboration rest?

2. What was the attitude of Jesus toward the Law and the Prophets? Why did he teach his disciples that they were not free to mock and flout the old law?

3. In what way was Jesus obedient to the law as a boy and as an adult? Mention two ways that, during his adult life, Jesus lived above the compromises of the law.

4. How did Jesus seek to justify his revision of the law? Why were the scribes and Pharisees so indignant?

5. Discuss the merits of the "eye for an eye" law from the standpoint of justice and mercy and the limitation of revenge. Are there principles involved that are useful for today?

6. Consider the pharisaical attitude of the older son in the story of the prodigal on the return and welcome of his younger brother (Luke 15:25-32). How does this illustrate the difference between Jesus and the Pharisees?

WHAT THE LESSON MEANS FOR TODAY

The growth of the kingdom today is impeded when we worship the letter of the gospel and ignore its spirit, or when we act as though good intentions are an adequate substitute for steady and faithful obedience to the Christian way of life.

Chapter 18

TEACH US TO PRAY

As Jesus "was praying in a certain place, when he ceased, one of his disciples said unto him, Lord, teach us to pray, as John also taught his disciples."[1] Matthew indicates that this request came during the Sermon on the Mount and gives the text of the Lord's Prayer as part of the sermon. The Lord's Prayer has been the model for all Christian prayer from that time forward. Its beauty and spiritual richness have never been surpassed.

While there does not seem to have been any specific preparation for this prayer, there does lie behind it a lifetime of general preparation. Jesus owed the richness of his prayer life to his spiritual kinship with the prophets, his quiet study of the spiritual needs of humanity, and the many hours spent in meditation and in communion with his Father. Peter wanted each moment to count in restless activity, and to the end of his ministry he was constantly urging people to be diligent in their service. While no less persistent in his concern for people's souls, Jesus valued the moments of quiet concentration and of meditative stillness as Peter never learned to do. After days of heavy mental and physical strain Jesus preferred prayer to sleep; when his burdens were heaviest, he found renewal in the presence of God where his vision was clarified and his heart again made resolute.

In answer to the request of his disciples, Jesus said, "After this manner shall ye pray."[2] The thought here seems to be that the Master did not intend to give his disciples a form of prayer to be repeated verbatim as though there were some magic in the words themselves. The prayer was an example or illustration rather than a blueprint. The context implies that it was given to them simply as a type. It illustrates those characteristics which distinguish all of Jesus' prayers—clarity, directness, sincerity, and absolute confidence in the heavenly Father.[3] Yet the prayer as it stands can never be said too frequently if it is said always in an attitude of spiritual concentration. Where this is done, supplicants do not merely repeat a form of words but seek rather to explore the mind and heart of Jesus through the gateways revealed in the phrases of this petition. From this point of view, the prayer is indeed "the Lord's Prayer," which the disciples are seeking to make their own by straining all their spiritual faculties to understand and accept.

In the endeavor to make our physical posture conform to the humility of our hearts, it has become customary for us to think of prayer as petition and submission entered into on our knees. There is no indication of the posture of Jesus at this time or that he gave the matter place in his thinking. The scriptures give ample testimony that there are as many different ways of praying as there are different individuals and occasions. The Master is reported to have prayed while prostrate on the ground.[4] Paul prayed while kneeling,[5] Jeremiah while standing,[6] David while sitting.[7] Some of the most effective prayers were offered under widely diverse conditions; thus Hannah prayed silently,[8] but Ezekiel prayed aloud.[9] The Philippians liked to pray by a certain riverside;[10] Paul prayed on the seashore.[11] David sang:

> My soul shall be satisfied as with marrow and fatness; and my mouth shall praise thee with joyful lips; when I remember thee upon my bed, and meditate on thee in the night watches.[12]

The Lord's Prayer opens with the simple form of address which is most natural on the lips and in the hearts of children. Others may ask for the gifts they desire, but those who can truly begin their prayers as

Jesus did have already begun to share in the greatest gifts of God. This opening phrase, rightly used, casts its influence over every petition that follows. It acknowledges that God is our Father and that his children belong together.

This thought is carried forward and saved from familiarity by the next phrase, "hallowed be thy name." Recognition of our kinship to Divinity must not debase our thoughts of God but must ennoble our own characters. The Jews responded to this immediately, for one of the great emphases in their earlier religious experience had been on the awesomeness and majesty of the name of God. Thus Ezekiel declared on the authority of Jehovah, "I will sanctify my great name."[13] The name of the Father here, as in the Old Testament, stands for his exalted character. To the Jew the Lord's Prayer, therefore, begins with an affirmation of reverence and of devotion. It sounds the note of awe and awe is the greatness of the emotions, the feeling of instinctive reverence in the presence of the superlatively great and good.

The order of unfoldment of this prayer is genuinely beautiful. In saying, "after this manner shall ye pray" and then setting us such a pattern for prayer, Jesus advises that in any circumstances which call for prayer—in joy or sorrow, in success or failure, in urgent need or in the quietness of meditation, in grateful praise or in bewildered questioning—the first thing to do on entering the place of prayer is to contemplate the greatness and goodness of our Father through whom we are related to the whole universe; whose name is holy, whose purpose is eternal, whose love is unfailing, and whose joy is our immortality and eternal life.

The petition for the coming of the kingdom follows contemplation of the glory of God and takes precedence over all other petitions. This plea is one to be pondered carefully in connection wtih the phrase which follows it: "Thy will be done in earth, as it is in heaven." It is essentially a pledge of loyalty even more than it is a prayer for help. Just as it is possible for disciples to partake of the emblems of the Lord's Supper unworthily,[14] and thereby to eat and drink damnation,[15] so also is it possible to come under condemnation by repeating this prayer unmeaningfully. Many are spiritually sick today because they have done this without any idea of self-commitment and so without any welling up of spiritual strength to meet their needs for the kingdom's sake. When Jesus sent out the men of the seventy, "he said unto them, The harvest truly is great, but the laborers few; pray ye therefore the Lord of the harvest, that he would send forth laborers into his harvest."[16] It is in this sense and under these conditions that the prayer for the kingdom comes readily and effectively to the lips of the disciples. The seventies could reasonably pray for more laborers when they themselves were doing their utmost. The twelve could reasonably pray for Pentecost when they needed Pentecostal powers to equip them for Pentecostal tasks. So, also, we can pray for the kingdom when we are eager for the will of God to be done in our own lives as a prelude to the extension of his will throughout the world.

In the setting thus provided, the Lord's Prayer continues: *"Give us this day our daily bread."* This petition cannot be properly understood in any place other than after the prayer for the kingdom. The gifts of God are shared with his children as an investment in the kingdom project. The prayer, moreover, is again a commitment, for it voices our common need of physical sustenance. The disciple does not ask for *his* or *her* daily bread but for *our* daily bread, the bread which all people need to do their part today in building the kingdom. For those possessing more than their share of bread for the day, this is surely equivalent to praying, "Help us to share intelligently and affectionately with those who have not, that all may have sufficient." In this petition such persons regard themselves as the ministers of distribution appointed by God, and the task of sharing is their stewardship. The one who lacks bread, on the other hand, is not here asking for God to provide bread without effort, for one of the earlier dictums of Divinity was, "In the sweat of thy face shalt thou eat bread."[17] For him, this prayer is therefore a plea for an opportunity to be self-sustaining. For the most of us the prayer is a grateful request that the strength hitherto given us for our task shall be continued, in order that we may serve the kingdom in our day and have the means of sustaining us for that service.

The prayer for forgiveness is the one completely new element in the Lord's Prayer, every other petition having been anticipated in some degree in the Old Testament. It gives us what is perhaps the clearest statement of the direct correlation between petition and performance. Luke sensed this so clearly that he rendered his version of the petition as "Forgive us our sins; for we also forgive everyone who is indebted to us."[18] The central thought here is not one of bargaining—that we will forgive our debtors their small debts if our heavenly Father will forgive us our infinitely great ones. It is a pledge that we will share in the spirit of forgiveness from which we hope to benefit. There is no reason why our heavenly Father should extend forgiveness to us if his graciousness does not create in us a spirit similar to his own. In essence our plea here is for God to lead us into ways of loving-kindness so that we who have hitherto wasted his investment will now use it for his purposes, and therefore be justly forgiven for our past transgressions.

The remaining petition says: "Lead us not into temptation, but deliver us from evil."[19] This is better expressed in the Inspired Version, which says: "Suffer us not to be led into temptation, but deliver us from evil"[20] which is in closer harmony with the Epistle of James: "Let no man say when he is tempted, I am tempted of God; for God cannot be tempted with evil, neither tempteth he any man."[21] It is not possible to escape temptation. Even Jesus did not do so. Every level of life has temptations which are specially attractive to those on that level—the temptation to drunkenness and gluttony on the animal level and the temptation to spiritual pride and self-righteousness on a higher one.

Many years earlier the psalmist wrote:

> Blessed is the man that walketh not in the counsel of the ungodly, nor standeth in the way of sinners, nor sitteth in the seat of the scornful. But his delight is in the law of the Lord; and in his law doth he meditate day and night.[22]

The model prayer of Jesus urges us to seek strength to avoid "the way of sinners" and the "seat of the scornful," where sit those who discourage us when we strive without immediate success. In place of these the Master would have us steadily pursuing the upward way where temptations fall constantly behind us. We are delivered from evil only as we constantly move into realms of greater good.

Perhaps no petition of the Lord's Prayer is voiced more frequently and more earnestly and yet more blindly than this plea for deliverance from evil. It is a part of our Christian heritage to remember the many times when God has delivered good people from sickness and from death. It is a great pity, however, that so many of us fail to ask for any greater deliverance than this. There came a time when Jesus himself asked for such deliverance, but this petition was immediately succeeded by a statement of complete devotion: "O my Father, if it be possible, let this cup pass from me;

nevertheless, not as I will, but as thou wilt."[23] It was surely possible for his Father to deliver Jesus from the evil designs of the wicked on this occasion, but it was not possible to save the life of Jesus and at the same time save his ministry. Some choice had to be made. The evil from which Jesus needed to be delivered right then was the evil of letting the prospect of a painful death blind him to the necessity for being faithful. Here is a pattern for all of us, and a window of understanding into this final plea of the Lord's Prayer. Surely it means: Deliver us from the evil of letting lesser things control the greater things, of serving the second best when we should serve the best, of being afraid for our lives when we ought to be concerned about our souls.

Commenting on the Lord's Prayer, Charles Foster Kent says:

> Noble as were the prayers with which the Jewish race voiced their faith and aspiration, there is a world-wide difference between them and the type of prayer which Jesus set before his dsiciples. The Jewish prayers bear the mark of their racial origin and point of view. Jesus' prayer is individual yet universal, concrete and practical yet deeply spiritual. . . . Reverence, loyalty, trust, contrition for sins, and a sense of the need of constant help in the battle of life are there all plainly voiced. Prayer is also defined, not as the asking for material things, but as that loyal, trustful attitude toward the divine Father which makes his good gifts possible. It is man's outreach toward God and his realization of the privileges of sonship. The spirit which characterizes this prayer is that which made possible God's complete revelation through Jesus.[24]

NOTES

1. Luke 11:1.
2. Matthew 6:9.
3. Charles Foster Kent, *The Life and Teachings of Jesus,* p. 148. Used by permission of the publishers, Charles Scribner's Sons.
4. Matthew 26:36.
5. Acts 20:36.
6. Jeremiah 18:20.
7. II Samuel 7:18.

8. I Samuel 1:13.
9. Ezekiel 11:33.
10. Acts 16:13.
11. Acts 21:5.
12. Psalm 63:5, 6.
13. Ezekiel 36:23.
14. I Corinthians 11:27; see 11:29.
15. I Corinthians 11:29.
16. Luke 10:2.
17. Genesis 3:19, KJ.
18. Luke 11:4; Matthew 6:12, 14, 15, KJ.
19. Matthew 6:13, KJ; Luke 11:4.
20. Matthew 6:14, IV.
21. James 1:13.
22. Psalm 1:1, 2.
23. Matthew 26:39, KJ.
24. Kent, *The Life and Teachings of Jesus,* p. 150.

Study Helps for

Chapter 18

LESSON PURPOSE

To appreciate the Lord's Prayer so that it becomes a basis of meditation as well as a pattern for prayer. To show that such prayer is unavailing except as it is incorporated into life lived for the kingdom.

SCRIPTURE REFERENCES

Matthew 7:7-11; 6:5-15, KJ

HIGH POINTS OF THE LESSON

- The prayer life of Jesus was not separated from the rest of his life; it was an integral part of it, both enriching that life and being enriched by it.
- The great purpose of the Lord's Prayer is to relate those who pray to the divine purpose. It follows naturally that they are rightly related to the other children of God.
- All personal gifts sought in the prayer are sought with the glory of God and the needs of the group as factors which influence both the petition and the response.
- While this prayer is repeated by many millions, it becomes a mockery unless they welcome its obligations.

QUESTIONS AND DISCUSSION TOPICS

1. List the qualities which you believe make prayer effectual. How are these qualities augmented when earnest people pray together?

2. The fact that his disciples still thought of him as praying after his ascension (Hebrews 7:24) indicates how large a place prayer held in the life of Jesus. Can you explain why this was so?

3. Discuss the importance of the opening phrases of the Lord's Prayer. How are they related to each other? What is the meaning of the phrase, "Hallowed be thy name"?

4. What is the part of the kingdom in the Lord's Prayer? Discuss the effect on the petitioner of the pledge of loyalty to the kingdom.

5. In what way is the petition for bread related to the total problem of kingdom citizenship?

6. Analyze the plea for forgiveness in this prayer. What must the one voicing this plea be willing to do? What is the effect of offering this plea without sharing in the spirit of forgiveness?

7. What is meant by the prayer for deliverance? How are people effectively "delivered from evil"?

8. List the major emphases of the Lord's Prayer. Note how each is related to the others.

WHAT THE LESSON MEANS FOR TODAY

The prayer pattern Jesus gave his disciples remains fresh and meaningful for modern-day Christians. Deeper study reveals a richness of insight often hidden by familiarity.

Chapter 19

MESSENGERS FROM JOHN THE BAPTIST

Soon after Jesus had sent the twelve on their first mission, John the Baptist was arrested and put into prison by Herod whose immoral conduct John had condemned.[1] A contributory cause for John's arrest was probably Herod's fear that the popularity of John might lead to an insurrection. The Baptist was sent to the fortress of Machaerus, a gloomy castle on the heights above the Dead Sea. From this prison John could see his childhood home and much of the country where his active ministry had been spent. This close confinement must have been particularly difficult for John to bear in view of the type of life he had led from his early manhood. It is not unlikely that he expected to be released after a short time, for there is no doubt that public opinion was with him. Yet the weeks lengthened into months and he was still incarcerated, not knowing from one moment to the next whether he would be released or whether some further change in fortune would lead to his execution.

Meanwhile Jesus was busy in Galilee—preaching, teaching, and healing. Word of his work spread through the countryside and in time reached John in prison. The news troubled John. He was glad to know of the power attending the ministry of Jesus, but this power was not being used as he had expected.

John's greatness lay in his clear perception of the need for repentance. His weakness lay in his backward-looking rigidity. He was a socially minded legalist, but a legalist nevertheless. He thought of the Messiah as one whose "fan is in his hand," who would "thoroughly purge his floor" and then "gather the wheat into his garner"; but "the chaff' he expected to be burned with "fire unquenchable."[2] Nothing of this seemed to be happening. Even he himself was left to eat out his heart in prison when surely the Messiah could have rescued him if he would. What amazed John most of all was that instead of proclaiming dire judgments on the wicked, the Master was mingling with all types of people, availing himself of the hospitality of the rich as well as of the poor, and even lending his presence at social festivities.[3]

It is not difficult to understand John's wonderment. He was a brave man who had spoken out fearlessly against Herod and was quite willing to take the consequences of this act. His problem was much deeper than concern about his own well-being; it had to do with something more important to him than life itself. It is also not unlikely that the reports brought to him by such of his disciples as remained were colored somewhat by their own bewilderment. These men had shared his expectations of a Deliverer who would come down in wrath upon the wicked and vent his fierce anger on the ungodly in high places.

With tense concern John sent two of his disciples to ask Jesus, "Art thou he that should come, or look we for another?"[4] There is no evidence that Jesus was in any way disturbed by this indication of the wavering faith of John. He had probably already sensed something of John's position. It is not hard to imagine that this may have been one of the occasions when Jesus was greatly tempted to use his miraculous powers to help his friend, and when he was restrained only by the necessity for continuing with his greater work. If Jesus had freed John, nothing would have kept the crowds from insisting upon his political leadership against Rome. At the very least, the popular clamor would have greatly impeded work which made even greater claims than friendship or patriotism. So, although Jesus left

John to pay the price of his loyalty, he understood the tremendous strain under which his friend and kinsman was laboring, and there were no reproaches when John's disciples came bearing their leader's questions.

Jesus knew that no simple affirmative or negative answer would satisfy John. Jesus was the promised Messiah, but he was not the kind of Messiah for whom John was looking, and this was too difficult to explain in words. Jesus, therefore, asked the messengers to stand by and watch the work that he was doing.[5] Then, having cured many who were crippled, plague-ridden, possessed, and blind, he told the men to go back to John and tell what they had seen but to tell it in the words of Isaiah.[6] It was as if Jesus had sent a message saying: "Do not be disturbed, John; I am not doing just what you expected of me, but I am fulfilling in detail the spiritual vision of the greatest of the prophets of the past." To John, who was eager for reassurance, this message must have been specially comforting. The Master was not doing what John would have done, but he was fulfilling the role John had anticipated; that was all John could reasonably ask.

Jesus concluded his message to John with the words: "Blessed are they who shalt not be offended in me."[7] We are not certain whether this was addressed to the messengers or to the listening crowd. It was appropriate to both, for in actual fact many had been offended to find that one who was so remarkably blessed was not using his powers in line with their expectations. They had seen a few sick people healed, a few miracles wrought among the common people, and the gospel preached to all who would listen, but this was only a pale shadow of what they felt they had the right to expect of the man who so completely met their expectations in other ways. The perceptive answer of Jesus was in reality an invitation to John to consider even more carefully than heretofore the deepest meaning of the Lord's ministry.

When the messengers of John had left, Jesus took advantage of the occasion to contrast his own work with that of his forerunner. In a few brief questions, he rescued them from their unsettled and hesitant thinking about John. "What went ye out into the wilderness to see?"[8] he asked. Was it "a reed shaken with the wind," a man of no settled opinions, with no deep convictions regarding his ministry? No, obviously that was not true. Again, "What went ye out to see?. . .a man clothed in soft raiment?" No, again the answer was obvious, for John had been entirely unresponsive to the temptations of luxury. Whatever else he was, he was sincere and earnest and self-sacrificing. Again came the question, "What went ye out for to see? A prophet? Yea," said Jesus, "much more than a prophet." Then, without hesitation, the Master named John as his forerunner[9] and pronounced him the greatest among the prophets. Yet John, despite his integrity and insight, was not to be compared with the children of the kingdom. John had seen the need for repentance and had proclaimed the wrath of God against all unrighteousness, but apparently he had no moving sense of the love of God as is portrayed in the parable of the prodigal son. He was like Moses who brought the children of Israel to the threshold of the promised land and looked over into the country which the chosen people should occupy, but who was too close to the limitations of their yesterdays to be permitted to enter into the new life himself.

In his account of this conversation concerning John, Matthew includes a statement of Jesus which is not reported by Luke:

> From the days of John the Baptist until now, the kingdom of heaven suffereth violence, and the violent take it by force. . . . For all the prophets and the law prophesied that it should be thus until John.[10]

Luke presents the same idea more clearly in another

setting.[11] The thought seems to be that the Law and the Prophets had been the guide of God's chosen people until the time of John. Now a greater light had appeared and good people were pressing into the kingdom, while those of lesser vision were seeking to wrest the kingdom ideals to suit their own interpretation, making it a kingdom of violence rather than of love.

After this mention of John the Baptist, we lose sight of him except for two brief glimpses. The first is the occasion of Herod's birthday, when Herodias—remembering John's outspoken comment on her relationship with Herod—connived with her daughter and brought about John's execution. The narrative is touchingly simple: "And his disciples [John's] came and took up the body, and buried it; and went and told Jesus."[12] There was nothing else they could do, and now there was no need for Jesus to do anything either. John had finished his work of preparation for the earthly ministry of his Master, even in this detail, for his own death was but a prophecy of what would happen to Jesus if the Lord continued his uncompromising proclamation of righteousness.

The other occasion came when the three who had shared the vision of the Mount of Transfiguration with Jesus were coming down into the valley with this experience fresh in their minds. They asked Jesus about the fulfillment of Malachi's prophecy about Elias.[13] The answer Jesus gave is not clear from the King James Version, although it does indicate that John the Baptist was the Elias whose coming had been prophesied. The Inspired Version makes this more clear, saying:

> And his disciples asked him, saying, Why then say the scribes that Elias must first come? And Jesus answered and said unto them, Elias truly shall first come, and restore all things, as the prophets have written. And again I say unto you that Elias has come already, concerning whom it is written, Behold, I will send my messenger, and he shall prepare the way before me; and they knew him not, and have done unto him whatsoever they listed. . . . But I say unto you, Who is Elias? Behold, this is Elias, whom I send

to prepare the way before me. Then the disciples understood that he spake unto them of John the Baptist, and also of another who should come and restore all things, as it is written by the prophets.[14]

In harmony with this prophecy, Latter Day Saints believe that John the Baptist continued his work of preparation when he came in the spirit of Elias, the Forerunner, to ordain Joseph Smith and Oliver Cowdery to the Aaronic priesthood that the work of preparation for the second coming of the Lord Jesus might go forward in our day.

NOTES

1. Matthew 14:2, 3.
2. Luke 3:17, KJ; 3:24, IV.
3. John 2:1, 2.
4. Luke 7:19.
5. Luke 7:21.
6. Luke 7:22; Isaiah 42:7.
7. Luke 7:23.
8. Luke 7:24.
9. Luke 7:27, 28; Malachi 3:1.
10. Matthew 11:12, 13.
11. Luke 16:16. Note the clearer statement of the Inspired Version at these two points (Luke 16:17, 18, IV).
12. Matthew 14:11.
13. Matthew 17:10-13, KJ.
14. Matthew 17:9-14, IV.

Study Helps for

Chapter 19

LESSON PURPOSE

To indicate the greatness and the limitations of John the Baptist as a means of better understanding the difficulty which Jesus had in awakening people to his own true greatness and the superlative grandeur of the message which he brought

SCRIPTURE REFERENCES

Luke 7:18-35; Matthew 11:2-19.

HIGH POINTS OF THE LESSON

- John was troubled because he had clear evidence that Jesus was the Messiah, and yet Jesus was not doing the things which John expected the Messiah to do.
- The probable reason was that John himself had been so deeply impressed with the need of the Jews for repentance that he had not yet come to understand the love of God which seeks people out and loves them into repentance.
- The Master did not decry the work of John in order to show how much greater his own work was. Instead, he emphasized the greatness of his forerunner, and then showed that his own work was even more important.

QUESTIONS AND DISCUSSION TOPICS

1. Why was John the Baptist arrested? Where was he imprisoned? What were the conditions of his imprisonment?
2. What was Jesus doing while John was in prison? Why did not Jesus effect the release of John?
3. Why did John send his disciples to Jesus? What was the purport of their questions? Why could not Jesus answer with a simple affirmative or negative?
4. How did Jesus answer John? Why was John satisfied with such an answer?
5. What is the meaning of the statement of Jesus: "Blessed are they who shall not be offended in me"?
6. What is the meaning of the phrase, "a reed shaken with the wind"? What was the Master's estimate of John? In what sense was John not to be compared with the children of the kingdom?
7. Under what conditions was John executed? What further ministry did he exercise after this?
8. What is your own estimate of John the Baptist? What was his relation to the early Christian movement? What is the special significance of the choice of such a man to help inaugurate the work of God in this dispensation?

WHAT THE LESSON MEANS FOR TODAY

Our heavenly Father cannot do much for us as long as we are self-satisfied. The first ministry of his Spirit convinces us that we are sinners, needing him and lost without him. But this, important as it is, does not go far enough. The heart of the gospel of Christ is the love of God—love strong enough to overcome all our sinning, love strong enough to persuade us toward righteousness so that punishment is unnecessary, love strong enough to make us put away all pretense and to live for the truth as God leads us to know the truth.

Chapter 20

PARABLES CONCERNING THE KINGDOM

It was not long until the early obscurity of Jesus gave way to widespread popularity, and people crowded to hear him, see him, or even to touch the hem of his garment.[1] When he could, the Master spoke in the synagogues or in the homes of his friends; but as the crowds increased he found it necessary to go to the open spaces near the seashore, or even to use a small boat as his pulpit while his hearers crowded the shore.[2]

On one such occasion, not long after the selection of the twelve, "there was gathered unto him a great multitude; so that he entered into a ship. . .and the whole multitude was by the sea on the land. And he taught them many things by parables."[3] These "earthly stories with heavenly meaning" served both to reveal and to conceal what Jesus had in mind. By comparing the truth he sought to teach with the familiar happenings of their daily life, Jesus won and held attention and then went on to win and hold understanding. His parables were like searchlights trained on the truth, revealing it clearly against the surrounding darkness.

At first it seems like a contradiction in terms to say that the purpose of the Master in using parables was to hide as well as to reveal his meaning, but this is nevertheless strictly true. These stories from life were so skillfully drawn that they yielded some truth to a casual glance, but richer truth could be mined only by those who were deeply in earnest and who would take the trouble to dig. Evidently the disciples realized something of this and were puzzled by it, for they came to Jesus after the multitude had left them and asked him why he was teaching in parables.[4] In reply Jesus made it clear that the lack of preparation on the part of his hearers set up barriers he could not immediately overcome. The people were not alert to spiritual things. If Jesus had spoken to them plainly, they would not have understood, for their hearts were not right. So he gave them stories on which they could ponder, stories which would plant a seed of truth in their hearts and minds but would not lead to argument and bitterness. These same stories were progressively meaningful to the disciples, for they were attracted by the truth and were likely to ponder it, working ever toward a richer understanding and doing so in expectant faith.

Teaching in parables was a way of separating the sheep from the goats. By this method Jesus fed the spiritual hunger of his disciples and yet refused to pass that "which is holy unto the dogs,"[5] or to cast "pearls before swine."[6] This type of teaching drew a clear line of distinction between those who heard with their ears and those who heard with their understanding. Dr. G. Stanley Hall refers to the parables as "tests of spiritual insight."[7]

Matthew records seven kingdom parables, as though they were all uttered at about the same time during this second period of the Galilean ministry. These parables are reported in other connections in the other Gospels.

Each parable was intended to answer or to illuminate a specific problem by presenting clearly some characteristic of the kingdom and of kingdom life. In studying a parable, we shall therefore do well to seek the central spiritual truth it is intended to illuminate, and then to note the bearing of the subordinate parts of the parable on this central truth. This does not mean that the secondary teachings of any of the parables are unimportant but that they should not be considered apart from the primary meaning of the story. Much damage is done to those who discover parallels where no parallels were intended, or who read into the parables meanings which are divorced from their contents. The parables listed in Matthew 13, for example, are definitely kingdom illustrations. Jesus himself said so. They should be studied with this in mind.

In his parable of the sower,[8] Jesus explained that just as the growth of a seed depends upon the nature of the soil in which the seed is planted, so also the growth of the widely scattered seeds of the kingdom depends on the receptivity of those into whose hearts these seeds fall. This parable impressed on the disciples the importance of seeking good ground in which to sow their seed, but it also taught them not to be unduly concerned that they did not always get a large crop. To sow only in good ground would require a care which they did not have the time or means to exercise; and while they were to use their best intelligence, yet they must know that the conditions of success were in other hands as well as in their own.

This parable is illustrative of the others in both its values and its limitations. Some who have sought to apply it in too great detail have seen a parallel between the "wayside" and the "stony places" and the lives of those whose hearts have been hardened in sin. Then, crowding the illustration, such persons have read into the parables that these sinners are forever doomed to reject the truth. Jesus was not concerned with this in the parable, and, as far as the parable is concerned, it may be true or it may not be true. The story does not say that none of the pathways could be broken up and fertilized and so rendered productive, nor that the stony places could not be cleared, nor that the thorns were so deeply embedded that they could not be uprooted. Jesus was concerned with just one central thought: that the harvest depends, in large measure, on the kind of soil in which the seed is sown.

In his parable of the tares,[9] Jesus was concerned with the treatment of evil. The parable was a much-needed word of warning, showing that good and evil may grow in the same soil; that it is almost impossible to uproot one without hurting the other; and that it is important to wait until the proper time before attempting to separate them. The lesson is one of patience. Then, too, there is a note of reassurance. There is a harvesttime coming. Even though it be impossible to separate wheat and tares today, there will be a time when the Lord of the harvest will separate wheat from chaff. Once again, we must not press the parable too far. According to the interpretation given by Jesus himself,[10] "the good seed are the children of the kingdom; but the tares are the children of the wicked one"; yet surely the parable is not intended to teach that the nature of the good and the bad is so fully determined that neither can change any more than wheat can change into darnel or darnel into wheat.

The parable of the mustard seed[11] is addressed to the pioneers in great causes and, most of all, to kingdom builders in every age. At its heart is one great truth: that a living seed, no matter how small, will grow according to its own nature until it is a thing of beauty and grandeur exercising a beneficial ministry both far and near and having within itself the seeds of life which reach into the far tomorrows.

From illustrating the visible and extensive growth of the kingdom in the parable of the mustard seed, Jesus turned to illustrate the invisible but far-reaching influence of the silent forces establishing the kingdom. The life of the leaven or yeast under favorable conditions reaches through the whole mass and so transforms it that every bit of the leavened mass is capable of similarly leavening other properly prepared meal. The truth here expressed can now be illustrated with thousands of examples taken from the history of God's dealings with people; but nowhere is it more clearly and tersely stated, and never was it more heartening, than when the eyes of the apostles were first opened to this great truth. The principle of the leaven is true in the individual and in society. The leaven of the kingdom will expand in one person's personality until his or her entire way of living has been changed. One good person, alert for the cause of the kingdom, will lift the moral and spiritual tone of the whole community.

The parable of the hidden treasure[12] was probably spoken to the disciples alone after earlier parables had been interpreted. There is nothing difficult about it except to those who seek to find in the story more than Jesus intended to put there. These latter will be worried about the ethical standards of the man who hid a treasure which he had found in another man's field until he was able to buy that field. But Jesus did not raise any such question. As a matter of fact, ancient Roman law allowed the recoverer of a treasure one half of its value. The point of the story is in the great value of the treasure, hidden from the eyes of the passerby, yet available for whoever would seek it and make the necessary sacrifice to obtain it.

The parable of the pearl of great price[13] again illustrates the supreme value of the kingdom, for which the merchant whose business it is to seek goodly pearls, will sell every other pearl he owns. It has been suggested that the parable of the hidden treasure and the parable of the pearl of great price together suggest that the kingdom serves practical ends and also is a thing of beauty.[14] The journey of the pearl merchant has also been pictured. He has been shown in Athens where he purchased the pearl of curiosity, and in Rome, where he secured the pearls of law and justice, and in Phoenicia, where he acquired the pearls of business and of wealth—all of which he sold in order to find money enough to buy for himself the "pearl of great price" in which all the values of the lesser pearls are combined. Again, it has been noted that the glory of the pearl is not intrinsic but is related to the insight of the beholder:

> Its sheen is invested in it by the beholding eye. The ruby and emerald possess intrinsic value, by virtue of their peculiar stain. The value of the pearl resides in its iridescence. . . . In sober truth, the glory of the pearl is not in the pearl at all. . . . In and of itself, the pearl can do nothing for the individual except to serve as a vehicle for the refraction of light.[15]

Such elaboration of the teaching of the parable is perfectly legitimate as long as it is in harmony with the central truth Jesus sought to convey, but it is not legitimate when it comes in conflict with this central truth.

The final story of this series is the parable of the drawnet. The net here specified is a large seine. The essential idea of the parable seems to be that a net so great would necessarily gather fish of every kind. In the same way, the kingdom net catches both good and bad. Just as the fish in the net must be together until the final day of separation, so will there be good and bad in the kingdom until the end. No real Christian has the right to forsake the church because there are evil people in it. How else can the church exist in such a world as ours?

In discussing this group of parables, Dr. Burgess has noted that they all bear upon the gradual growth and certain triumph of the kingdom of God, and that the various elements may be grouped as follows:

1. The results of preaching the truth of the kingdom in different circumstances are unequal (the parable of the sower).
2. The growth of evil along with the good is to be expected and endured (the parable of the tares).
3. Kingdom growth is to be gradual and in harmony with law (the mustard seed and the leaven).
4. Membership in the kingdom is of incomparable worth (treasure and the pearl of great price).

5. Though the kingdom "catches" people of all kinds, they will ultimately be separated according to their true nature and worth (the drawnet).

NOTES

1. Mark 3:10.
2. Mark 4:1.
3. Mark 4:1, 2.
4. Matthew 13:8; Mark 4:9.
5. Matthew 7:6, KJ; 7:10, IV.
6. Ibid.
7. *Jesus the Christ in the Light of Psychology,* p. 522.
8. Matthew 13:3-9, 18-23, KJ; 3-7, 17-21, IV.
9. Matthew 13:24-30, KJ; 22-29, IV.
10. Matthew 13:36-43, KJ; 35-45, IV.
11. Matthew 13:31, 32, KJ; 30, 31, IV.
12. Matthew 13:44, KJ; 46, IV.
13. Matthew 13:45, 46, KJ; 47, IV.
14. Abingdon's *Commentary,* p. 978.
15. Lloyd C. Douglas, *These Sayings of Mine,* p. 140.

Study Helps for

Chapter 20

LESSON PURPOSE

To develop appreciation for the kingdom parables leading to growing understanding of the nature of the kingdom

SCRIPTURE REFERENCES

Matthew 13:1-53; Mark 4:1-34; Luke 8:4-18.

HIGH POINTS OF THE LESSON

- Despite the ease with which we may discover the primary meanings of the parables, they do not yield their richest teachings except as we study them carefully and prayerfully.

- The key to understanding the parables is to interpret them in the light of their central messages.
- The parables point the way to understanding the nature of the kingdom, but full understanding comes from life as a whole.

QUESTIONS AND DISCUSSION TOPICS

1. What is a parable? In what sense were parables used to make the meaning of Jesus clear? In what sense were they used to convey hidden meanings?
2. What principles should we keep in mind in studying the parables?
3. What is the background of the parable of the sower? What is its central truth? What are its secondary teachings? Against what temptation must we guard in interpreting this parable?
4. What is the teaching of the parable of the tares? Why was this parable especially timely?
5. Tell the parable of the mustard seed in your own words. Tell the parable of the leaven. How are these two related? How are they dissimilar? What is the kingdom characteristic revealed by each of them?
6. To whom was the parable of the hidden treasure first spoken? What is its central message? To what other parable is this closely related? What are some secondary teachings of this parable?
7. What was the final parable of this kingdom series? What is its key teaching? Why was this helpful? What message does it contain for us today?
8. What is the central theme of these parables? What are the major lessons to be drawn from these parables as a whole?

WHAT THE LESSON MEANS FOR TODAY

The parables become meaningful as we put ourselves in the place of the early disciples and then try to understand what the Master was seeking to make clear. One of the primary conditions of understanding is that we shall share the kingdom concern of the Master and of those nearest to him. Without such concern the deeper significances of the parables will never reach us.

Chapter 21

THE FORGIVENESS OF JESUS

John the Baptist put his finger on one of the most significant aspects of the forthcoming ministry of Jesus when the Master came to him as one of those seeking baptism at his hands. John said: "Behold the Lamb of God, who taketh away the sin of the world."[1] On a later occasion, when his work on earth was complete, Jesus told his disciples that his blood was to be "shed. . .for the remission of sins"[2] and still later, when he was about to leave them to carry on his work, he opened

their understanding, that they might understand the scriptures, and said unto them, Thus it is written, and thus it behooved Christ to suffer, and to rise from the dead the third day; and that repentance and remission of sins should be preached in his name among all nations, beginning at Jerusalem.[3]

It is not too much to say that the Son of God came to earth because the problem of sin was one which only he could solve.

When Jesus proclaimed the loving-kindness of his Father, it was inevitable that he should also be concerned with sin; for sin is life lived apart from God, and sin brings both physical and spiritual death in its train. The more successful Jesus was in awakening those who heard him to the reality and awfulness of sin, the more concerned they were about forgiveness and the happier they were to find that the forgiveness he extended was as real as the sin it vanquished.

If we are to probe the mind of the Master in connection with the problem of sin and its forgiveness, it is important that we shall first give some attention to the meaning of these words in the light of the life and teaching of Jesus.

Originally *sin* meant a missing of the mark, and from this it has come to indicate the kind of life conduct which falls short of its high calling.[4] It is related to the

English word *wrong* which means *wrung* or *twisted.* But every true definition of sin must depict it against the background of the love of God, for this is how Jesus saw sin. A life of sin is a life twisted out of the proper relation to God because the sinner is unresponsive to the love of God. Sin is life lived as though the sinner wished that, for the moment and for this particular experience, God did not have to be taken into account. It is treason against the best that is in a person, as well as treason against the love of God; for when the prodigal becomes aware of this he or she always abandons sin. That is what coming to oneself requires.[5]

Sin is not just a sinful act or even one of a number of such acts. It is the attitude of unconcern or of rebellion out of which these acts spring. The Pharisee who went up to the Temple to pray could not think of any specific sins for which to ask forgiveness. He therefore proceeded to justify himself by contrasting himself with sinners in general and with the nearby publican in particular. Yet he returned to his home without forgiveness[6] because he had ignored the prophet's injunction to "walk humbly with thy God."[7] He was not an extortioner, an unjust man, or an adulterer. He observed the fasts in their season and was scrupulous in the matter of his tithing. These things were excellent as far as they went—and from the point of view of the religious leaders of the time they went far. But the Pharisee looked only on externals. His heart was not right; and until his heart was right, he was still a sinner in spite of his renunciation of specific sins. His sinfulness lay in his self-righteousness.

Jesus sought to solve the problem of human sin with the offer of divine forgiveness. This at once put both the problem and its solution on a personal plane rather than a judicial one. This is very important. Sin is primarily a personal matter, and forgiveness has to do with persons and personal relationships. The Master taught us that sin separates us from God and drives us from our Father's home and into a far country. This far country is not suited to our true natures in spite of its superficial attractiveness, and the longer we stay there the more unhealthy and unhappy we are likely to become. Lacking companionship with our Father, we are lonely and forsaken. But when we return home, we find our Father anxiously awaiting us. He runs out to meet us and greets us as his children. There are no recriminations. It is true that work which we might have done has not been done, and substance which might have been ours has been wasted; but the family hearth is still warm for us, and the love of the Father is still steadfast toward us.[8] This welcome home is what Jesus meant by forgiveness.

Such forgiveness is evidently not the same as canceling a debt. There is no bookkeeping in the transaction. Nor is it a matter of overlooking or ignoring sin. There is no willful blindness behind the reunion. It is clear-sighted, affectionate and creative. Forgiveness is available for the sinners who can be persuaded to respond to the love of God by returning home and leaving behind the husks on which they fed while in the far country. They who receive this free pardon are transformed by it, knowing that the only suitable response to such gracious and divine love is the unreserved love of their own hearts.

Our own needs set certain conditions to forgiveness. These conditions arise from the very nature of the situation and cannot be avoided. The first involves a change of heart. We who have ignored our heavenly Father, or who may have hated him and deliberately flouted his authority, must come to love and trust him. We never do this unless even here our Father takes the initiative. Every approach we make to God is actually a response to his call to us: "God so loved the world, that he gave his Only Begotten Son, that whosoever believeth on him should not perish, but have eternal life."[9] We love him because he first loved us.[10] We call our response to the love of God *faith.* It implies confident trust.

The next step is repentance. This is the natural sequence of our faith. It is a condition of forgiveness which was emphasized again and again in the ministry of John the Baptist and of Jesus, who taught that it is not possible to hold on to sin and yet experience the grace of forgiveness. we cannot serve God and mammon no matter how hard we try to do so. Repentance must be genuine, untainted by hypocrisy. Hypocrites may wear the cloak of religion and talk its language and live in its home, but they neither breathe its spirit nor abide by its laws. Because the Pharisees were so concerned about externals and so unconcerned about the true adjustment of their lives to the will of God, Jesus constantly warned his disciples to "beware of the leaven of the Pharisees, which is hypocrisy."[11]

It is also required in the nature of things that the person who seeks forgiveness shall be forgiving toward others. Forgiveness is the spirit of the family of God. It is shared between the Father and his children and also among the children themselves. "If you do not forgive," says the Master, "neither will your Father who is in heaven forgive your trespasses."[12] To make this condition even more clear, Jesus told his unforgettable story of the unjust debtor who had been forgiven a debt so large that it was impossible for him to pay it, but who soon afterwards demanded full payment from a fellow servant who owed him a trifling amount. Jesus said:

> His lord was wroth, and delivered him to the tormentors, till he should pay all that was due unto him. So likewise shall my heavenly Father do also unto you, if ye from your hearts forgive not every one his brother their trespasses.[13]

Since the essence of forgiveness is admittance to the family of God from which we have excluded ourselves by our sinning, a further step toward forgiveness is to ally ourselves with the people of God. We cannot be at one with the Father and yet separated from our fellows. When sinners would abandon their rebellion, they must enlist in the service of their Lord; there can be no neutrality in matters of eternal life. Such enlistment carries with it new allegiance to the Lord himself, new devotion to the interests of the kingdom, and new community with those committed to a similar loyalty. If forgiveness merely meant the cancellation of a debt or deliberate blindness to sin, then such enlistment might not be necessary. But since forgiveness includes free participation in family life, it can be complete only when we are in fact members of the family, pursuing the family way of life and helping attain the family goals. Even when we have become members of the family of God, we may again fall into sin; but as long as the love of the family envelops us, we will be attracted to the family standards as we would under no other circumstances.

Each of the three Synoptic Gospels states that "the Son of man hath power on earth to forgive sins."[14] As we have seen, this power was much more than the legal authority to pronounce forgiveness. It included the power to bring people to God so that they would be hungry for forgiveness. This then enabled the Father to extend forgiveness to them freely because of the changed attitude involved in their faith and without the danger of seeming to minimize the seriousness of their sinning. Jesus constantly exercised this power of forgiveness. It lay behind the reformation of Zacchaeus,[15] of the woman of Samaria,[16] and of unknown thousands of others. It was most specifically exercised at the healing of the paralytic,[17] in connection with the sinful woman at the house of the Pharisee,[18] at the healing of the sick man by the Pool of Bethesda,[19] on the occasion when the adulteress was brought to Jesus for judgment,[20] in the promise made to the dying thief,[21] in the prayer on the cross,[22] and possibly in the conversation between Jesus and Peter after Peter had denied his Lord.[23] It will be well for us to note briefly the circumstances surrounding some of these incidents.

The healing of the paralytic probably occurred toward the close of the first period of the Master's ministry in Galilee. Jesus had returned from his first preaching tour. He was at a house in Capernaum when the word of his return was noised abroad and the people flocked to see and to hear him. The house was small, and there were altogether too many people to be accommodated inside, so the Master stood where he could be heard by those outside as well. While he was thus "preaching the word" four men came, bringing a fifth who was "sick of the palsy"; but because of the crowd they could not get next to Jesus. Not to be outdone, they climbed onto the roof, broke through the thin plaster, and let the sick man down to where Jesus stood. And "when Jesus saw their faith, he said unto the sick of the palsy, Son, thy sins be forgiven thee."[24]

As far as we can judge from the direct statements of the record, the five had come with no thought other than the physical healing of the sick man. Notwithstanding this probability, it is not likely that Jesus thrust the gift of forgiveness on a man who was entirely unprepared, for this would have been quite foreign to the general tenor of his ministry. We may safely conclude, then, that the faith these men displayed was more than mere confidence in the power of Jesus to heal, even though this was foremost in their thoughts. It must have included some perception of Jesus as a man sent of God, and some recognition that the healing he brought had spiritual as well as physical significance.

We wonder why Jesus should offer forgiveness at such a time. Was it not a protest against the limitations the narrow vision of the people tended to place on him? They looked primarily for healing; but healing was only a secondary part of his ministry. The primary task of Jesus was to lead people to God. In this instance conditions were apparently ripe for Jesus to grant the paralytic an even greater blessing than he had asked. If Jesus had just healed the sick man, the crowd would have remembered him only as a miracle worker; but in healing the sick spirit as well as the failing body the Master placed himself in a new category. Since only God can forgive sins, Jesus, in the eyes of the discerning, was either a blasphemer or he was truly the Son of God.

The scribes were not slow to see the implications of what Jesus had said to the paralytic, for they were the strict guardians of Jewish orthodoxy. So they reasoned "in their hearts" as to what this could mean. Jesus saw what they were thinking, but instead of retreating he pressed home the lesson he wanted them to learn, saying:

> That ye may know that the Son of man hath power on earth to forgive sins, (he said to the sick of the palsy,) I say unto thee, Arise, and take up thy bed, and go thy way into thy house.[25]

Here was a new type of healing which reached down into the soul of the sick man, restoring his spirit that it might match his newly healthy body. Here also was a new kind of teaching, for Jesus had used the sick man's need as a means of proclaiming his own unique mission, so that all who had ears to hear might understand. Neither the scribes nor the discerning among the crowd ever forgot that day in Capernaum.

The forgiveness of the sinful woman in the house of Simon the Pharisee probably also occurred early in the Galilean ministry of Jesus. Simon had invited Jesus to eat with him and Jesus had accepted. When the meal was in progress, a woman of the streets came in. She knelt behind Jesus, anointed his travel-stained feet with oil of myrrh and with her own tears, and wiped them with her hair. The Pharisee knew what type of woman she had been, and this clouded his vision so completely that he could not see the change which her love for Jesus had wrought in her. He looked on cynically, reasoning within himself that Jesus could not be a prophet or he would repulse such a woman. For a time the Master was quiet, extending his forgiveness simply by accepting her tears and sacrifices. Then Jesus turned from the penitent sinner to one who did not realize that he also stood in need of repentance, and in one of his matchless statements put the matter plainly:

> Her sins, which are many, are forgiven; for she loved much. But to whom little is forgiven, the same loveth little. And he said unto her, Thy sins are forgiven. . . . Thy faith hath saved thee; go in peace.[26]

The healing of the infirm man at the Pool of Bethesda shows an interesting variation of the usual approach of Jesus to the ministry of healing. The paralytic whom Jesus healed had been brought to Jesus in spite of great difficulties. But Jesus sought out the man of Bethesda, apparently passing by the "great multitude" who were waiting for the troubling of the waters, and selected him from among them all.[27] As he drew near, Jesus said to this man: "Wilt thou be made whole?" When the man stated that despite his eagerness to be well he could do nothing, for there was no one to help him, the Master bade him, "Rise, take up thy bed, and walk." There the story ends for the moment. There is a hint of faith, for it was against the law for this man to take up his bed on the Sabbath. He must have had confidence in Jesus to attempt to comply, for there is no hint of repentance. The key to this situation is found later, where the narrative continues: "Afterward Jesus findeth him in the temple, and said unto him, Behold, thou art made whole; sin no more, lest a worse thing come unto thee."[28]

Evidently the Lord had allowed a little time to elapse and had then sought the man out, finding him receptive because of what had been done for him. Apparently the lesson was not wasted, for the last glimpse we have of the man of Bethesda shows him stating boldly among the Jews that Jesus had healed him.

Regardless of the great love of Jesus and the power he exercised so creatively there were some sins he could not forgive. When he was at the height of his popularity, certain scribes came down from Jerusalem. After observing his work, they charged that he was in league with the devil.[29] The scathing answer of the Master showed clearly how foolish was such an attempt to explain his power, but he was not content just to refute their statements. Instead he continued with his teaching:

> All sins shall be forgiven unto the sons of men, and blasphemies wherewith soever they shall blaspheme: but he that shall blaspheme against the Holy Ghost hath never forgiveness, but is in danger of eternal damnation.[30]

It was not that Jesus resented the insults of the scribes against himself but that their attitude was impervious to the pleadings of love. These men were well versed in the law. They were leaders of the people. They were in a position to influence many who were bewildered. Instead they preferred darkness to light; they ascribed goodness to the devil and the works of the Son of God to the power of evil. People who do this give a permanent twist to their own characters. There is no more dangerous sin. It was not hate but love which warned them that they were in danger of eternal damnation.

In his Bampton lectures delivered at Columbia University in 1950, Dr. C. H. Dodd said:

> The precepts of Christ, in judging us, expose our need for forgiveness and throw us back upon the inexhaustible mercy of God which offers such for-

giveness. Forgivenesss is clearly not merely a balm to the uneasy conscience; it is the actual creative power of God, in his kingdom, released for action when men accept his judgment and repent; and it opens up unlimited possibilities to the enterprise of the repentant and forgiven sinner.[31]

NOTES

1. John 1:29.
2. Matthew 26:28, KJ.
3. Luke 24:44-46.
4. Philippians 3:14.
5. Luke 15:17.
6. Luke 18:14.
7. Micah 6:8.
8. Luke 15:11-32.
9. John 3:16.
10. I John 4:19.
11. Luke 12:1.
12. Mark 11:28.
13. Matthew 18:33, 34.
14. Matthew 9:6; Mark 2:8; Luke 5:24.
15. Luke 19:1-10.
16. John 4:1-26.
17. Mark 2:1-9.
18. Luke 7:36-50.
19. John 5:1-18.
20. John 8:3-11.
21. Luke 23:44.
22. Luke 23:35.
23. John 21:15-19.
24. Mark 2:5.
25. Mark 2:8.
26. Luke 7:47-50.
27. John 5:3-6.
28. John 5:14.
29. Mark 3:17.

30. Mark 3:28, 29, KJ. See also Mark 3:22-24, IV.

31. *Gospel and Law,* Columbia University Press, New York, p. 62.

Study Helps for

Chapter 21

LESSON PURPOSE

To analyze the teachings of Jesus concerning forgiveness, with a view to applying them more fully in our own lives.

SCRIPTURE REFERENCES

Matthew 18:15-35; Luke 15:11-32; 18:9-14.

HIGH POINTS OF THE LESSON

- To understand the true nature of sin we must see it against the background of the love of God.
- Sin is failure to give God the right-of-way in our lives.
- Our Father is happy to forgive us, but for our sake he must impose conditions of forgiveness which are irrevocable.

QUESTIONS AND DISCUSSION TOPICS

1. What is sin? In what sense is sin an attitude rather than an act? Why was the Pharisee a greater sinner than the publican? Review this until it is quite clear.

2. In what sense was the problem of sin one which only God could solve? Why did God make it his problem?

3. How does the offer of forgiveness put the problem of sin on a personal plane? Analyze the teachings of the parable of the prodigal son.

4. Compare the forgiveness which Jesus offers and the cancellation of a debt. Why would such cancellation be valueless in any serious treatment of the problem of sin?

5. What is faith in God? What is the relation between faith and forgiveness?

6. What is repentance? What is the relation between repentance and forgiveness? What is the relation between God's forgiveness of us and our willingness to forgive others?

7. What would happen if our heavenly Father forgave us while we were yet unrepentant? Why do we need to forgive the unrepentant?

8. What is the relationshp between receiving the grace of forgiveness and accepting responsibility for allying ourselves with the purpose of God on earth? How is the grace of forgiveness related to church membership? In what sense should the church be the home of forgiveness?

9. What principles were involved in the healing of the paralytic man? In the forgiveness of the woman in the house of Simon? In the healing of the man of Bethesda?

10. Under what conditions is forgiveness impossible?

WHAT THE LESSON MEANS FOR TODAY

Our Father offers us every inducement to righteousness. Despite the heartbreak which we have caused him by our inhumanity toward each other, he holds nothing against us. We can have communion with him, however, only as we are like him. This means that if we hope to receive the benefits of his glad forgiveness, we ourselves must be both repentant and forgiving. We shall grow into persons of such quality only as our faith in God and our partnership with his people become the dominant passions of our lives.

Chapter 22

THE TWELVE AND THE SEVENTY

Jesus selected and ordained the twelve "that they should be with him, and that he might send them forth to preach, and to have power to heal sicknesses, and to cast out devils."[1] Following this selection, as we have seen, he preached the Sermon on the Mount and narrated many of the parables with the specific needs of the apostles in mind. From time to time he let the twelve share the simpler tasks of his ministry. When at last they were no longer novices, it became advisable both for their sakes and for the kingdom's sake that they should take up the responsibilities of ministry in the surrounding country without the influence of his immediate availability.

The apostles were sent out in pairs, and it is noteworthy that the Master "gave them power over unclean spirits, to cast them out, and to heal all manner of sickness and all manner of disease."[2] It is not suggested that there is any special significance to the order in which these are set forth, but it is well worth remembering that soundness of mind and body is so closely connected with kingdom preaching that Jesus associated them. In the same spirit Paul wrote to the saints many years later that "God hath not given us the spirit of fear; but of power and of love, and of a sound mind."[3]

The commission given to the twelve centered in three major points of emphasis—the people to whom they were sent, what they were to do, and the methods they should employ. At this time the twelve were sent specifically "to the lost sheep of the house of Israel";[4] they were not to go to the Gentiles or to the Samaritans.[5] This restriction was not because of lack of concern for the Gentiles or for the Samaritans but because of the imperative need for establishing a strong nucleus in the area most favorable to their teachings in order that the work would be well planted before the earthly ministry of Jesus was closed. The principle behind this instruction is an important one, not as a prohibition but as an example of missionary tactics.[6]

A further reason for the instruction that the twelve should go to the Jews lay in the fact that the apostles were as yet lacking in experience and in some of the convictions on which their later ministry would be built. Knowing this, the Master sent them to the Jews, with whom they would have much in common, rather than to the non-Jews, who would be immediately antagonized by their typically Jewish approach and point of view. Later the work of the apostles was to be broadened, but for the present they were to serve within the range of their limited abilities. The indications are that the apostles kept to the villages and small towns.[7]

The twelve were to preach and to heal. The Master said: "As ye go, preach, saying, The kingdom of heaven is at hand. Heal the sick; cleanse the lepers; raise the dead; cast out devils; freely ye have received, freely give."[8] Their kingdom preaching might not be as able nor as clear-sighted as that of the Master, but they were familiar with the note of repentance which had been sounded both by John and Jesus and which must be continued.[9] Their own kingdom expectations might still be tinged with the current Judaistic point of view, but their endeavor to explain the kingdom message faithfully and accurately was an invaluable discipline for them and put them in the way of divine guidance and illumination.[10] Limited though their powers might be, they could yet sound the note of urgent warning and thus create the sense of crisis which is never far absent from the preaching of Jesus and of those nearest to him.[11]

The instructions given the twelve for their journey were clear and straightforward. They were to make themselves one with the people to whom they ministered. They must forego all worldly possessions. By their own single-minded devotion to the affairs of the kingdom, they must indicate their conviction that their message was both important and urgent. And, finally, they were to be fearless, discounting privation and persecution in advance, and knowing that these things would work in them "a far more exceeding and eternal weight of glory."[12]

The missionaries were to take no wallet (scrip) with them for their journey. (A wallet was a small leather sack for carrying provisions.) Nor were they to put on two coats. The dress of the time was quite simple, consisting of sandals for the feet, a turban for the head, a garment not unlike a long shirt held together with a girdle, and a very simple cloak. To wear two of the shirtlike tunics was a sign of comparative wealth,[13] and it was this that Jesus forbade. The purpose of these injunctions was to seek simplicity and freedom of action. The disciples were not to burden themselves with unnecessary equipment. They traveled on foot and could obtain free lodging anywhere; their needs, therefore, were very few and simple. Most impressive to Jewish minds was the injunction to shake off the dust of their feet for a testimony against any house or city which rejected them. The symbolic act was equivalent to a solemn pronouncement that nought of the cursed thing clave to them.[14]

Although there is little reason to believe that the first missionary journeys of the apostles were attended with much persecution, it was a dangerous thing to be a lieutenant of the Master. In later years this danger became more and more acute. There was a definite reason, therefore, for Jesus to call attention to the need for special wisdom among those sent forth "as sheep in the midst of wolves."[15] All who heard must have recognized the particularly apt metaphor, for the Romans had a tradition that Romulus and Remus, the builders of Rome, had been nursed by a she-wolf, and the wolf was their national emblem.

While the twelve were absent on their first mission, Jesus continued his personal ministry. We do not know just how long they were away or how far they traveled, but it is quite possible that they were gone for several weeks and that during this time Jesus visited Jerusalem.[16] It was during this period that the disciples of John the Baptist came to Jesus with their questions as to whether Jesus was indeed the Messiah. The twelve returned at about the time of John's execution; quite likely their return was hastened by this tragedy.

Students of the Gospels have been impressed with the similarity between the commission given to the apostles and that later given to the seventy. This latter group of missionaries were advance agents sent out by Jesus soon after his departure from Galilee on his final journey to Jerusalem. Their special mission was to be his heralds in "every city and place where he himself would come."[17] The instructions to the seventy may be summarized as follows: (a) The task before them was a great one and there were few laborers; therefore they who were selected were to give of their best; (b) the movement was for men of courage; (c) they were to trust God to provide all things necessary, even though they were likely to suffer privation; (d) they were to be too enthusiastic and zealous to spend time in elaborate greetings and ceremonies; and (e) they were to be courteous, leaving their blessings with the people.

We do not know how long the seventy were absent on their mission but we are told that they returned with joy, saying, 'Lord, even the devils are subject unto us through thy name."[18] This joy centered in their inner sense of great power to do good, the new understanding of the truth gained as they explained the gospel to others, and their justifiable pride in their success. Their report was particularly heartening to Jesus who "rejoiced in spirit" that the ministry of his heralds had been attended with such an evident demonstration of spiritual power.

NOTES

1. Mark 3:13.
2. Matthew 10:1; Mark 6:9; Luke 9:1.
3. II Timothy 1:7.
4. Matthew 10:5.
5. Matthew 10:4.
6. For a parallel in the modern history of the church, see Doctrine and Covenants 118:1.
7. Luke 9:6.
8. Matthew 10:6, 7.
9. Mark 6:13.
10. Matthew 10:20, KJ; Mark 13:11, KJ.
11. Matthew 10:23, KJ; 10:20, IV.
12. II Corinthians 4:17.
13. Luke 3:11, KJ; 3:16, IV.
14. Deuteronomy 13:17.
15. Matthew 10:16, KJ; 14, IV.
16. John 5:1.
17. Luke 10:1.
18. Luke 10:17, KJ; 18, IV.

Study Helps for

Chapter 22

LESSON PURPOSE

To portray the fundamental nature of evangelical ministry

SCRIPTURE REFERENCES

Matthew 9:36-38; 11:1; Mark 6:7-13; Luke 9:1-6; 10:1-11, 17, 21.

HIGH POINTS OF THE LESSON

- The twelve and seventy were not sent just anywhere they cared to go but on specific missions, to specific people, for a specific purpose.
- The basic missionary ministries are preaching, teaching, and healing.
- The work of these ministers was characterized by deep convictions, marked urgency, and spiritual power.

QUESTIONS AND DISCUSSION TOPICS

1. Narrate the conditions attending the selection of the twelve. What were the specific duties of the apostles? How long had they been with Jesus when they were first called?

2. What were the factors that influenced the timing of Jesus in sending out the apostles on the first missionary journey? How did they travel? What authority did they possess?

3. To whom were the twelve first sent? What principles are here revealed?

4. What were the dominant notes of the apostolic ministry at this stage of their growth? Are these notes still important? Why?

5. What were the instructions given the apostles concerning their journey? What reasons lay behind these instructions?

6. How long were the twelve away on their first mission? About what time did they return? What did Jesus do in the interim?

7. Who were the seventy? Under what instructions were they sent forth? What success did they have?

8. What were the essential tasks of the missionaries at this period of the kingdom proclamation? How did these tasks change with the growth of the Christian cause? What elements remained constant?

WHAT THE LESSON MEANS FOR TODAY

The effective presentation of a great message requires the careful training of leaders, the delegation to them of authority adequate to their task, constant emphasis and reemphasis on fundamentals, sympathetic appreciation of the problems of ministry. All these were conserved in the training, assignment, and supervision of the twelve and seventy. The same principles are equally important today with reference to all ranks of the ministry of the church.

Chapter 23

THE CRISIS IN GALILEE

Many of those who came to hear Jesus had only a cursory interest in what he was trying to do. Some came to him for purely selfish reasons, seeking the healing they had heard he could give. Still others came because of the stirring within them of spiritual dissatisfaction, such as had prompted them to follow the Baptist. Others, restless under the yoke of Rome, recognized the gift of leadership possessed by Jesus and sought to use him as a means toward political freedom. Those who came for one reason frequently stayed for another. Having found physical health, some stayed for spiritual leadership. Denied political leadership, others were held by spiritual power. Coming out of curiosity, still others stayed out of conviction. No one was more aware of the heterogeneous nature of his audiences and his followers than was Jesus himself.

After the murder of John the Baptist, Jesus was the outstanding popular leader among the Jews. His headquarters were at Capernaum, which was about five miles from Tiberias and connected to it by the Roman road that ran along the western side of the Sea of Galilee. Tiberias was the new capital of Herod, who was soon informed of what Jesus was doing. Herod could maintain himself in power only by the ruthless elimination of all popular leadership. Jesus must have appeared to him as a definite threat, someone to be watched carefully and to be rendered powerless by any available means without regard to humanity or justice. That Jesus was fully aware of this and acted accordingly is apparent from the Gospels.

While events were thus moving toward a crisis, the apostles returned from their first preaching mission,[1] happy in the success which had attended them and eager to talk to Jesus without interruption from the crowd. Sensing this, Jesus invited them to retire into a desert place and rest awhile.[2] With this in mind, the little company got into a small boat and crossed to an open space near Bethsaida. The people saw them leave and passed quickly round the north end of the lake where they met the boat when it reached the shore. Touched by their eagerness, Jesus welcomed them, spoke to them of the kingdom, and healed their sick.[3] In this informal gathering of instruction and healing, the hours of the late afternoon sped rapidly away, and the disciples became concerned that the people were far from home and without food. The disciples were perfectly willing to share what they had, but their total resources were five barley loaves and two small fishes. To their amazement Jesus told them to have the people sit down on the green grass of the hillside in orderly groups of fifty or a hundred. When this was done the Master blessed the food and gave it to the disciples, and they served the multitude. All ate and were satisfied, and twelve baskets of remnants were gathered up.

The people who were thus miraculously fed were Jews who were looking eagerly for a great Deliverer. When they realized what Jesus had actually done, they remembered the promise of Moses: "The Lord thy God will raise up unto thee a Prophet from the midst of thee, of thy brethren, like unto me; unto him ye shall hearken."[4]

They remembered, also, how Moses had fed their ancestors in the wilderness with manna from heaven, and a murmur ran down the ranks, "This is of a truth that prophet that should come into the world."[5] Jesus heard what was happening and knew that the situation was serious. If the incipient movement was permitted to grow, Herod would soon have abundant justification for his suspicions and would undoubtedly throw the weight of his authority against Jesus and his associates. If Jesus wanted political power, here was an excellent opportunity. If he did not want such power, here was a major threat made even more difficult by pressure from some of his own disciples such as Simon the Zealot and Judas. Because of these things, the Master urged the disciples into the boat and sent them to the other side of the lake.[6] Then he sent the multitude away, also. Finally, he betook himself to the mountaintop for solitude and prayer.

Late that night the disciples started back across the lake in search of Jesus, but the winds were contrary. The disciples could not use their sails, and so were unable to reach the shore. As they still labored, Jesus came to them, walking on the water. When the disciples saw him, they were afraid, but he reassured them, saying, "Be of good cheer; it is I; be not afraid."[7] Peter seems to have been the first to recover his equanimity. With his usual eagerness to test any new experience, he sought permission to come to the Master. Jesus gladly consented, and Peter did well until, thinking of himself, his faith failed him, and he began to sink; whereupon Jesus stretched forth his hand and led Peter back to safety in the boat.[8] When Mark was recounting this experience many years later, he showed surprise that men who had so recently watched Jesus multiply the available food in order to satisfy their hunger should now be so amazed at his power to come to them amid the tempest.[9] But they *were* amazed. Every step forward in the self-revelation of Jesus startled them with all the force of a new searchlight turned on life.

The next day after the feeding of the multitude, the people came together again in the place where they had been so miraculously fed, but Jesus was not there. This intrigued them, for they had seen the disciples go away in the only available boat, and they could not imagine how the Master had crossed the lake. Crowding into some more ships which had come over from Tiberias, they crossed back to Capernaum and at length found Jesus in the synagogue.[10] Their interest still centered in their miraculously supplied feast of yesterday, but already the influence of the miracle was waning. After all, some argued, Jesus had merely fed them with barley loaves and fishes whereas Moses had given them "bread from heaven." Moreover, Jesus had fed them but once and Moses had sustained the people day after day. Undoubtedly Jesus was the most marvelous miracle worker they knew; they felt, however, that they must be quite sure of what they would get out of championing Jesus before they followed him, for the risks involved were great. They came this morning, therefore, seeking a further sign. Knowing their hearts, Jesus met them on their own level and astonished them by making a parable of what had transpired. They wanted bread from heaven, so Jesus said, "I am the bread of life."[11] They wanted a miracle which would be repeated day after day, so Jesus said to them, "He that cometh to me shall never hunger; and he that believeth on me shall never thirst."

Here, then, was the crucial test. The night before, when they would have made him king, Jesus had hustled his disciples away, had sent the crowd home, and had retired to the mountain to pray. Now, when their calmer judgment had reminded them of the dangers of the insurrection they had contemplated and they had come back for reassurance, Jesus chided them for making too much of the loaves and fishes; he deliberately assumed the role of spiritual leader instead of that of political deliverer. Jesus now stated more clearly than ever before that in spite of his unwillingness to be their political savior, he was still truly the Messiah and that eternal life, not just political freedom, was available for all who would put their trust in him.

Jesus had made a profound impression on his more thoughtful followers, and the decision which he now required them to make was not an easy one. If they were looking for a leader in the revolt against Rome, then clearly Jesus was not the one they sought. His rejection of the role of a worldly Messiah did not explain away his miraculous powers, however, nor did it explain away the curious warmth they felt in their hearts when they listened to his marvelous teachings or pondered on the meaning of his parables. Soon the most clear-sighted of them realized that the choice was not merely whether or not they would follow Jesus; it was a choice between the old way of life and a new. If they were to follow Jesus, it must not be because of loaves and fishes and hope for political emancipation from Rome. They must follow him, if they followed at all, for a deeper reason than this—a reason which involved turning their backs on all their earlier standards of life, their prior expectations of the great Deliverer, and their worldly anticipations of the kingdom. It is not to be wondered at that "the Jews therefore strove among themselves,"[12] and even that many "of his disciples, when they had heard this, said, This is a hard saying; who can hear it?"[13] and "from that time many of his disciples went back, and walked no more with him."[14]

The crisis brought on by the resolute refusal of Jesus to lower his standard to the expectations of his time reached even into the Twelve. Judas was greatly disturbed,[15] yet Judas was shrewd, and it is probable that he continued with Jesus because he recognized the power of the Master and hoped to persuade Jesus to change his mind. The rest of the twelve were also disquieted, but their intimate communion with the Master was beginning to bear fruit. They had at last begun to sense the primary importance of the "bread from heaven." They were like the blind man who, in the early stages of healing, could not see clearly but did see men as trees, walking.[16] So Peter, speaking for the majority of them, said, "Lord, to whom shall we go? thou hast the words of eternal life. And we believe and are sure that thou art that Christ, the Son of the living God."[17]

This crisis in Galilee was a turning point in the life of Jesus. The Master could henceforth expect that Herod would seek every opportunity to destroy him and his work. This was natural. Much more tragic was the fact that after months of patient endeavor, during which time some had joined the circle of his disciples, so very many were still unable to see beyond the loaves and fishes. They still thought of the kingdom as essentially a kingdom of this world. They wanted a leader who could give them security and riches and power. They did not want one who would require them to abandon their old standards, to practice a repentance which should go to the very root of life itself, and to trust him with their temporal and eternal destinies. Henceforth, Jesus must work in constant fear of death and in constant danger of defeat. Since he was a man, as well as the Son of God, these things must have meant much to him. His only hope lay in that small group he had chosen to be with him—and, as he said, one of them was to betray him.

NOTES

1. Mark 6:30, KJ; Luke 9:10, KJ.
2. Mark 6:31, KJ; Mark 6:32, IV, calls it "a solitary place."
3. Luke 9:11.
4. Deuteronomy 18:15.
5. John 6:14.
6. Mark 6:45, KJ; 47, IV.

7. Matthew 14:27, KJ; 23, IV.
8. Matthew 14:28-32, KJ; 24-27, IV.
9. Mark 6:51, 52, KJ; 54, 55, IV.
10. John 6:59.
11. John 6:35.
12. John 6:52.
13. John 6:60.
14. John 6:66.
15. John 6:64, 70, 71.
16. Mark 8:22-25, KJ; 23-26, IV.
17. John 6:68, 69.

Study Helps for

Chapter 23

LESSON PURPOSE

To show that the work of Jesus in calling people to repentance was more important than any other work to which he might have given himself

SCRIPTURE REFERENCES

Matthew 14:13-23; Mark 6:31-46; Luke 9:10-17; John 6:1-15.

HIGH POINTS OF THE LESSON

- Jesus had by this time become an outstanding person among the Jews, the rallying point for Jewish patriots in their resentment of Rome.
- If Jesus wanted political power, here was his opportunity. If he did not, the pressure of the people was likely to detract from what he did want to do.
- The choice which Jesus made did not arise from disregard of the importance of their need or from lack of patriotism, but from devotion to even more primary needs. If he had become the king of the Jews, he could never have become the Savior of the world.

QUESTIONS AND DISCUSSION TOPICS

1. For what reasons had his followers been attracted to Jesus prior to this time? For what reasons had they remained with him? Discuss the significance of this change.

2. What political and popular effect did the death of John the Baptist have on Jesus? What new dangers did this introduce into the life of Jesus?

3. Why did the feeding of the five thousand produce such a deep impression on the Jews? In what ways did it intensify the critical situation produced by the death of John?

4. What circumstances were connected with Jesus' walking on the Sea of

Galilee? What was the effect of this incident in the lives of the disciples? How did it affect the body of the Jews?

5. Recall some of the questions in the minds of the Jews after they had had time to think over the miraculous feeding of the five thousand. What assurances did they want? What type of leader were they seeking?

6. Discuss why Jesus rejected the opportunity to become a popular patriotic leader. What chances of success did he have? What would have happened if he had yielded to the need of his people?

7. What was the attitude of the twelve in this crisis? What made them continue to follow Jesus even though they did not yet fully understand his purpose?

8. Discuss Jesus' estimate of the importance of repentance in view of this crisis. What other options were available to him?

WHAT THE LESSON MEANS FOR TODAY

There is but one basic reason why people should join in building the kingdom of God today—the love of God. Other reasons may stem from this primary one but unless this is first, we shall at some point abandon our unique test in order to promote secondary causes. The kingdom cannot be built by worldly people except as they learn the meaning of repentance under the guidance of Jesus.

Chapter 24

SIGNS AND AUTHORITY

The popularity of Jesus was still great enough to alarm the leaders of the Jews. Since he would not compromise with them and they would not submit to him, this popularity was a threat directed against their most vital concerns. These leaders were divided into two major groups—the sincere but blind worshipers of the law and those whose major interest was not primarily religious but personal. The sincere legalists were against Jesus because they thought he was attacking the authority of the distinctive institutions of Israel and was therefore a menace to the better life of his own people. The opportunists were against Jesus because they thought the people might give him power which they themselves coveted. A few of the leaders, like Nicodemus, believed.

The situation was critical, and the enemies of the Master forgot their secondary differences in order to unite against Jesus as their common foe. Their major point of attack centered in the authority of the Master. This point of attack was well chosen, for the Jews had long been deeply impressed with the importance of authority in religion. It was the sign of the sovereignty of God. There were many illustrations in their own history of the dire consequences following those who assumed authority to which they were not entitled. Korah, Dathan, and Abiram had been swallowed up in a fissure of the earth;[1] swift death had overtaken Uzza when he dared to steady the ark;[2] King Saul lost his crown for offering a sacrifice he had not authority to prepare; and King Uzziah was sticken with leprosy because he sought to burn incense on the altar.[3] With such history in the background of their thinking and of the thinking of the Jews who were looking on, the scribes and Pharisees "tempting him, sought of him a sign from heaven."[4]

This demand for a sign was in strange contrast to the accusation which these men had formerly made that Jesus was an emissary of Beelzebub and worked wonders by the power of evil,[5] yet their request was not without precedent. Many of the prophets had worked miracles, and Aaron's rod had budded as evidence that God had accepted the tribe of Levi for the work of the priesthood.[6] The request was also in full harmony with current expectations. The Jews looked for the authority of the Messiah to be attested by many miraculous signs. Under the procurator Fadus, a certain Theudas drew thousands to the Jordan where he promised that Israel would once more walk through on dry ground. Under Felix another pretender promised to throw down the walls of Jerusalem, as Joshua had thrown down those of Jericho, and so persuasive was he that thirty thousand gathered on the Mount of Olives to see the miracle come to pass. A few years later another imposter led the Samaritans to the top of Mount Gerizim in great numbers with the promise that there he would perform mighty miracles. To one less clear-sighted than Jesus, this request for a sign might therefore have come as a temptation to silence all further dispute with a miracle of irresistible grandeur. But the Master had met this very temptation in the wilderness. With his customary directness, Jesus therefore declared that no miraculous signs would be given. The evidences of his authority lay deeper than any such signs could penetrate.

As a matter of fact, Jesus had already given many signs of his miraculous powers. He had duplicated the marvelous deeds of Moses and other heroes of Jewish history before the very eyes of his questioners, and often, as at Nain, his miracles had been performed near the very places where earlier men of God had done wonders. There would therefore be nothing distinctive about a further miracle such as the multitude had already seen. The request of the scribes and Pharisees was rather for a special demonstration which should so surely come from heaven that henceforth there could be no possible doubt of the authority of the one giving such a sign. The request meant that neither the character of Jesus nor his teachings nor anything associated with his name or his ministry had yet convinced them. Indeed, they did not know what they wanted except that it must be so spectacular as to silence all questioning. Jesus must convince them against their will, a will already set against him, or regardless of his other credentials they would oppose him.

In his account of this incident, Mark has preserved one significant fact which escaped the other Gospel writers. He tells us that Jesus "sighed deeply in his spirit,"[7] revealing the depth of his disappointment at the perversity lying behind this question. Then he explained that no sign would be given but the "sign of the prophet Jonas."[8] Now the evidence for the miraculous preservation of Jonah from the "great fish" is extremely scanty.[9] As far as we have any record, only those who believed Jonah himself had any kind of evidence that this miracle ever happened. In a similar way, Jesus promised his generation that they should have a sign, but that this sign should be available only to those who believed. It would not be a sign for the multitude but for those "witnesses chosen before of God."[10]

There was another parallel between "the sign of the prophet Jonas" and the "sign" now offered by Jesus. The message of Jesus, like that of Jonah, involved a clear call to repentance. To such a call the people of

Nineveh had responded gladly, heathen though they were. The scribes and the Pharisees, who could not see that the Master's authority was indicated in the moral quality of his message, therefore ranked themselves as lower in the spiritual scale than the heathen. Even the queen of Sheba put them to shame, said the Master, "for she came from the utmost parts of the earth, to hear the wisdom of Solomon; and, behold, a greater than Solomon is here."[11] The people of this generation, who of all generations had been most highly favored, had been too blind to see their opportunity. Other generations, under the ministry of lesser prophets, had been moved to repentance; but this generation, under a far greater ministry, had condemned itself by its waywardness.

It was hardly to be wondered at that shortly after this experience Jesus charged his disciples to "beware of the leaven of the Pharisees, and the leaven of Herod."[12] On another occasion Jesus said that the leaven of the Pharisees was hypocrisy, or acting as though appearance matters more than inner reality. In this situation, however, it is clear that Jesus had in mind the spiritual irresponsibility which the Pharisees manifested in demanding a sign when they were already confronted by evidence greater than any other generation had ever known. In the very nature of things, no mere sign could possibly bring conviction.

The Jews were mistaken in demanding extraneous signs before they could believe the truth. The ultimate evidence of genuine spiritual authority does not lie in one's commission; it is intrinsic in one's message and life. When the Pharisees sought evidence of authority in miracles, they acted as though the function of the Messiah was to astound them and to compel their belief, rather than to convince them by a moral appeal which would transform their lives and make possible the building of the kingdom of God.

Jesus illustrated the importance of signs when he gave the apostles his final commission, saying "these signs shall follow them that believe."[13] The best sign of the kingdom is the growth of the kingdom among people of God. Miracles may attract the curious but they do not build character. When miracles follow after faith, however, they confirm that faith by showing that genuine miracles are not mere magic but are among the legitimate fruits of righteousness. When Jesus gave his generation the "sign of the prophet Jonas," by rising from the dead and appearing to many, this revelation was reserved for the faithful. These could be trusted to learn the great truth that the ultimate authority of Jesus lies in his rightness and his spiritual excellence, and that his power grows out of this authority. If Jesus had appeared to the multitude, they would have recognized his power and many of them would have been frightened, but they would have been converted to power and not to righteousness. This was at the heart of the issue between Jesus and his enemies. When these enemies asked the Master for a sign from heaven, they wanted a demonstration of coercive power. Jesus gave them a sign from heaven, the demand for repentance, which surely originates with God, but they did not recognize it. Later, in his resurrection from the dead, he gave a further sign from heaven to those who believed. Those who believed understood. There was no promise to those who did not believe.

NOTES

1. Numbers 16:1-33.
2. I Chronicles 13:10.
3. II Chronicles 26:18-21.
4. Luke 11:17.

5. Matthew 12:24, KJ; 12:20, IV.
6. Numbers 17:3-10.
7. Mark 8:11.
8. Matthew 12:39, KJ; Luke 11:29, KJ.
9. Jonah 1:17; 2:10.
10. Acts 10:41.
11. Luke 11:32.
12. Mark 8:15.
13. Mark 16:16.

Study Helps for

Chapter 24

LESSON PURPOSE

To show that the authority of Jesus centered in his moral rightness and that although miracles might bring helpful confirmation to the believer, they have a secondary place and not a primary one.

SCRIPTURE REFERENCES

Matthew 15:39; 16:1-12, KJ (15:37; 16:1-7, IV); Mark 8:10-21, KJ; Alma 16:51-56.

HIGH POINTS OF THE LESSON

- The demand for an external sign, unaccompanied by efforts toward moral excellence, is evidence of spiritual immaturity.
- The call to repentance has unsurpassed moral authority.
- Miracles are an evidence of power which has its roots in righteousness.

QUESTIONS AND DISCUSSION TOPICS

1. What types of persons opposed Jesus at this period of his ministry? Why did each group oppose him?

2. Why did these men question Jesus concerning his authority? What is the importance of authority in ministry?

3. Why was Jesus asked for a "sign"? When and how had Jesus already met this temptation to prove his authority by giving miraculous signs?

4. What was meant by the "sign of the prophet Jonas"? In what way were the people of Nineveh morally superior to the scribes and Pharisees?

5. Discuss the importance of the sequence involved in the promise of Jesus. These signs shall *follow* them that believe (Mark 16:17).

6. What did Jesus mean by the "leaven of the Pharisees"? Why did Jesus call the Pharisees hypocrites?

7. What is the teaching of Paul concerning "the working of miracles" among the diverse gifts of the gospel? (Read I Corinthians 12:10 against the background of I Corinthians chapters 12 and 13.)

8. Why did Jesus refuse to give miraculous signs to the Pharisees and yet promise his apostles that certain signs should follow the believer? Discuss the principle involved as related to our day.

WHAT THE LESSON MEANS FOR TODAY

Our immediate task is obviously to respond to the highest call of God that we know. As we do this, we shall come to know God and become more and more like him. So will it be possible for him to bless us in ways which will then seem natural but which would not appear entirely miraculous.

Chapter 25

"THOU ART THE CHRIST"

The days of his first popularity in Galilee were now over, but his immediate disciples were still loyal to him. Jesus therefore used the opportunities provided by his retirement for their further instruction. The apostles in particular had some experience by now, and their growing understanding gave the Master a foundation on which to work.

As the little company journeyed northward away from Galilee, they came to Caesarea Philippi, magnificently located amid three valleys on a terrace in an angle of Hermon and almost shut in by towering cliffs and thick woods. We do not know exactly where Jesus and the Twelve were when they came to the crux of conversation, carried on as they walked, but it is not unlikely that from where they were they could see the great white temple of Caesar Augustus, the Roman emperor who was worshiped as a god and who typified the power of this world. Lower down but still very probably within sight of Jesus and his companions was a vast grotto sacred to the Greek god Pan. In such an environment the conversation flowed naturally along lines centering in the nature and purpose of God, and thence into a discussion of the current reaction to their message and to Jesus himself.

Caesarea Philippi was a new city, widely known for its marble theater and its many palaces. Near it lay the rich cities of the coast with their great buildings, their harbors filled with ships from all over the world, and their other multiplied evidences of prosperity. In few other places could the disciples have been so deeply impressed with the "kingdoms of this world and the glory of them." In view of their background, filled with expectations of the coming Messiah who should lead them in asserting the dominance of the Jewish people in all the world, it is not unlikely that the Twelve were thinking somewhat wistfully of what might be done, even here, under such leadership as Jesus could give them if he would. As if interpreting their thoughts, Jesus said to them: "Whom do men say that I, the Son of man, am?"[1] The disciples answered that some said that the spirit of the martyred John the Baptist had entered into him. Others told him that current speculation named him as the reincarnation of Elijah or of Jeremiah or of one of the other prophets. Here was no suggestion that Jesus was the Messiah; he had refused to do the things which the common people expected the Messiah to do, and many had lost faith in him.

This current gossip was important, but it was not all-important. The understanding of these friends and disciples of Jesus, on the other hand, was of major significance. They had already done some proselyting and they were to do more. It was imperative that they should not give a wrong impression of Jesus or of his message. Jesus, therefore, made his question much more direct by saying, "Whom say ye that I am?" and Simon Peter answered and said, "Thou art the Christ, the Son of the living God."[2]

Many months before this time, Andrew had brought his brother, Simon Peter, to Jesus with the words, "We have found the Messias, which is, being interpreted, the Christ."[3] Peter had apparently accepted his brother's estimate of the Master. Nathanael had also joined the small group, saying, "Rabbi, thou art the Son of God; thou art the King of Israel."[4] But as the small group stood at attention, the eyes of every man on their leader, Jesus could not have been asking for a simple reiteration of what these men had told him so long before. What he sought was their verdict now, when he was a fugitive, discredited by the religious leaders of their people and rejected by the great majority of those he had sought to save. What were their deepest convictions about him now that he had disappointed them in so many of their cherished expectations and had denied them the places they might have occupied if he had chosen to come as a conqueror?

Peter answered for the apostles. Through all their bewilderment, one conviction had grown steadily with them. They were not yet fully sure what messiahship meant, but at least they were sure that—whatever it meant—Jesus was the answer to their hopes. The trouble with the great body of the Jews was that they had come to look for a person who would do great things for them without sufficient regard for what they must do for him—one who would save them rather than one who would challenge them. When Jesus demanded great things of them, they decided he could not be the one for whom they were looking. The apostles were like everyone else except in one thing: they were close enough to Jesus to know that—no matter how many preconceived notions they must abandon—they must follow him and no other. There was a world of meaning in the earlier words of Peter, "Lord, to whom shall we go? thou hast the words of eternal life. And we believe and are sure that thou art that Christ, the Son of the living God."[5]

The answer Peter now gave, and in which the other apostles concurred, must have warmed the heart of Jesus. It was not an easy answer, and it did not mean that all the problems existing in the minds and hearts of these men had been solved. Jesus was well aware of this. But Peter's confession of faith did give a foundation on which Jesus could build, for it was not the verdict of ordinary experience. The verdict of the times had already been given by those who had ceased to follow Jesus. The verdict of the apostles rested on an inner conviction wrought in their minds and hearts by the revelation of God.[6] Indeed, that was the only way in which they could gain such a conviction as they now had. It was not a matter of words only, but of power and of the Spirit of God bringing deep assurance.[7] It meant that Peter and his fellows were at last convinced by a power greater than themselves that Jesus was the way, the truth, and the life.[8] Where Jesus might lead them they were not yet sure, but at least they were committed to him. Whatever else the answer of Peter meant, it at least indicated that the apostles were convinced that Jesus was the fulfillment of the highest anticipations of the greatest seers of their people.

Jesus was not slow to build on what had been achieved. He could not continue his work in Galilee. The people were so set against him that the only way to win them was to fulfill their hopes of a political deliverer, and the bare possibility that Jesus might attempt this made it likely that Herod would imprison him and execute him as he had John the Baptist. On the other hand, Jesus could not abandon his ideals and his followers by seeking permanent refuge outside the borders of Palestine. Even though he had avoided imprisonment up to now, it was quite clear to Jesus that the issue could not be postponed much longer. He must give what time he could to the further training of those who were to continue his work, and then he must fulfill the destiny marked out for him by Isaiah, who had seen that the Messiah must save his people through suffering.

The narrative states that

> From that time forth began Jesus to show unto his disciples, how that he must go to Jerusalem, and suffer many things of the elders, and chief priests, and scribes, and be killed, and be raised again the third day.[9]

Here was an immediate and heavy strain on the newly confessed faith of the apostles. As Jesus sought to make his destiny clear to their groping minds, the very love Peter bore for him made the impetuous disciple unwilling to face the facts. He who had so recently confessed that Jesus was the Christ now burst out: "God forbid, Lord. This must not be!" Jesus answered, almost sharply, "Get behind me, you Satan! You are a hindrance to me! Your outlook is not God's but man's."[10] Perhaps the very sharpness of the rebuke was called forth by Jesus' memory of that day in the wilderness when he had faced a temptation identical with this as the tempter had said to him, "He shall give his angels charge over thee, to keep thee; and in their hands they shall bear thee up, lest at any time thou dash thy foot against a stone."[11] Temptation was stronger now that it came out of the deep affection which Peter had for him.

The apostles did not learn the true nature of Jesus' messiahship at this time, for later they were to contend about who should have the chief seats in the kingdom,[12] but the groundwork was laid. As later events showed, this lesson would not be fully learned even at the time of the Crucifixion, but afterward Jesus could point back to the instruction he was now giving and could convince the apostles that his self-delivery into the hands of the Jews was a carefully premeditated act. They could not yet see Jesus as the "suffering servant" whose great work had been foretold by Isaiah but they were on the way to understanding. A chief element in that understanding was their firm conviction, made stronger by their open confession, that all their hopes for the future centered in Jesus.

In the prophecy of his own suffering, Jesus laid the foundation for these men to understand a fundamental principle of the Christian enterpise in every age: "If any man will come after me, let him deny himself, and take up his cross, and follow me."[13] It will not be enough for disciples today, any more than it would be enough for disciples of that day, to forego secondary things. True disciples must deny *themselves.* They must refuse to follow their own way of life in order to follow the kingdom way of life. They must refuse to follow the traditions of their people in order to rely on the "exceeding great and precious promises" of the Lord Jesus Christ.[14] They must be "determined not to know anything among you, save Jesus Christ, and him crucified" in order that their "faith should not stand in the wisdom of men, but in the power of God."[15] This does not mean that life shall be supine or unintelligent or that the burdens of life shall be cast onto the shoulders of others. It does mean that the life of the disciple cannot be self-centered; it must be Christ-centered. When the apostles confessed that Jesus was the Christ, they affirmed their obligation of loyalty to him. They had yet to learn the full meaning of that which their hearts told them. The way ahead was to be very dark, but it was a way which led to transforming glory won out of the heart of pain.

NOTES

1. Matthew 16:14.
2. Matthew 16:15, 16, KJ; 16, 17, IV.
3. John 1:41.
4. John 1:49.
5. John 6:68, 69.
6. Matthew 16:17.
7. I Thessalonians 1:5.
8. John 14:6.
9. Matthew 16:22.
10. Matthew 16:23, Moffatt's translation.
11. Luke 4:10, 11.

12. Mark 10:37.

13. Matthew 16:24, KJ; 16:25, IV.

14. II Peter 1:4.

15. I Corinthians 2:2, 5.

Study Helps for

Chapter 25

LESSON PURPOSE

To show that when the apostles confessed "thou art the Christ" they did not yet know what this would demand of them, but they did know that they must be faithful no matter what the demands might be.

SCRIPTURE REFERENCES

Matthew 16:13-20, KJ; 14-21, IV; Mark 8:27-30, KJ; 28-31, IV; Luke 9:18-21.

HIGH POINTS OF THE LESSON

- Once the apostles accepted Jesus as their long-expected Deliverer, he thereafter claimed their allegiance by right.
- They were as yet unaware of the paths into which his leadership would direct them, but they did know that he was the only leader who could now satisfy the longing of their souls.
- Jesus built on the knowledge thus gained and showed that it must lead to willing self-denial for his sake.

QUESTIONS AND DISCUSSION TOPICS

1. Where was Caesarea Philippi? How did Jesus and his disciples happen to be there? What circumstances made their discussion here inevitable?

2. What were the common reports of the day concerning Jesus? Why did none of the apostles suggest that the people regarded Jesus as the Messiah?

3. Some of the disciples had previously confessed that Jesus was the Christ. What was the essential difference between their prior confessing and the one they now made?

4. What expectations of the Jews concerning the Messiah did Jesus refuse to fulfill? How did the expectations of the apostles change as they became better acquainted with Christ?

5. Why had the apostles now reached their verdict that Jesus was the one they sought? What special aid had they received? Under what circumstances do people receive such aid?

6. What external circumstances led Jesus to give special attention to the spiritual needs of his disciples after this time? In what way did the confession of Peter help Jesus to give the apostles this special attention?

7. Why did Jesus now begin to place particular emphasis on his coming sufferings? How did the twelve receive this ministry? What principle which he was now illustrating did he commend to them?

8. Consider the importance of worship in maturing our understanding of the nature and demands of the lordship of Jesus.

WHAT THE LESSON MEANS FOR TODAY

Jesus rightfully expects us to follow his moral leadership, but that is not enough. We shall not follow him gladly until we sense his unique relation to us and ours to him. When we recognize that he leads by right, rooted in the fact that he made us and that he loves us and died for us, we shall join gladly in the great adventure of life through self-denial.

Chapter 26

"I WILL BUILD MY CHURCH"

When Peter made his great confession of faith, the Master said to him:

> Blessed art thou, Simon Bar-Jona; for flesh and blood hath not revealed it unto thee, but my Father who is in heaven. And I say also unto thee, That thou art Peter; and upon this rock I will build my church, and the gates of hell shall not prevail against it. And I will give unto thee the keys of the kingdom of heaven; and whatsoever thou shalt bind on earth, shall be bound in heaven; and whatsoever thou shalt loose on earth, shall be loosed in heaven.[1]

The interpretation of this statement has occasioned commentators considerable difficulty. It is clear, however, that the church was already in process of being built, so we cannot interpret the passage to mean that the church was yet to be founded on Peter. Nor can the foundation have been the understanding which Peter now possessed that Jesus is the Christ; this understanding was to be greatly enriched in subsequent experiences, especially at the first Easter and during the period prior to the Ascension. It seems, therefore, that the only tenable interpretation is that the church is built on the conviction born in the souls of people by the revelation of God that Jesus is the Christ. He is the way, the truth, and the life;[2] in him "we live, and move, and have our being,"[3] and he therefore has rightful and final authority in the lives of good persons by reason of their own willing surrender to his direction.

This revelation is an adequate foundation, for it is renewed in the lives of successive generations. It becomes more and more meaningful as experience is enlarged and interpreted under the influence of the Spirit of God. Such a conviction as this holds people close to the heart of God and makes possible the progressive achievement of the divine purpose among them.

There is a sense in which ancient Israel was the prototype and forerunner of the church of Jesus Christ. It is in this sense that Stephen referred to "the church in the wilderness."[4] This already existent church was not completely discountenanced by Jesus. Instead, it was caught up in the new movement and was thereby fulfilled in much the same way as the old law was caught up and fulfilled in the law of the gospel. All the authority and excellencies attaching to the old covenant were transferred to this new "nation," so Paul could later write: "He taketh away the first, that he may establish the second"[5] and "if that which is done away was glorious, much more that which remaineth is glorious."[6] On this point Dr. Smith says:

> From the illustrations adopted by St. Paul in his epistles, we have additional light thrown upon the condition of the church. Thus the Christian church is described as being a branch grafted on the already existing olive tree, showing that it was no new creation, but a development of that spiritual life which had flourished in the patriarchal and the Jewish church.[7]

It is important that we understand this combination of continuity and discontinuity between the people of Israel and the church of Jesus Christ. The church was a continuation of Israel in the sense that here the purpose of God which had been pursued in Israel was pursued still further and on a larger scale. The church was a discontinuance, on the other hand, in the sense that the authority of the old was transferred to the new; those who persisted in rejecting Jesus as the Christ were themselves rejected, their authority annulled, and their law superseded.

The Christian church from the first believed itself to be the old Israel reconstituted. Paul boldly appropriated the ancient Jewish heroes as the "fathers" of the new movement[8] in much the same way as naturalized Americans regard Washington and Lincoln as belonging to them as well as to native Americans. The same assumption lies behind the ministry of James,[9] Peter,[10] and

John, the letter to the Hebrews, and the book of Revelation. James addressed the Christians as the "twelve tribes."[11]

The reconstituted church, the one which Jesus told Peter he would build on the sure foundation of his revealed and rightful leadership, was brought into being during the earthly ministry of Jesus. There was evidently a time when the old and the new overlapped, for Jesus said that John was outside the kingdom;[12] yet he himself was baptized by John and so were many of his disciples. But a crisis between the two seems to have been reached somewhere about the time of the murder of John the Baptist. By that time Jesus had preached the good news of the kingdom throughout Galilee and had been rejected by the Jews as a whole and by their leaders. All this took place before the conversation at Caesarea Philippi, the scene of Peter's confession, and the promise of the Lord Jesus; and from that time forward it is clear that Jesus gave himself with the utmost care to the training of the twelve as his apostles—the rulers and pastors of the Israel that was to be.[13]

One of the chief reasons why the Jews were about to be rejected and their place taken by the new Israel was that their leaders had made "the word of God of none effect" by their tradition.[14] Quite naturally, therefore, Jesus followed his statement that he would now build his church by provision for the authorized leadership of that church, saying to Peter:

> I will give unto thee the keys of the kingdom of heaven; and whatsoever thou shalt bind on earth, shall be bound in heaven; and whatsoever thou shalt loose on earth, shall be loosed in heaven.[15]

The Jews well understood that Jesus meant by this authority to "bind" and to "loose" the official right to prohibit or to permit, the right to govern in harmony with the terms of their appointment. This right was confirmed on the apostles after the Resurrection.[16]

There is no reasonable doubt that Jesus did organize

his church and authorize and train his apostles to lead that church after his own earthly ministry had ceased. There is a sense in which the church is portrayed as completely identified with the kingdom.[17] Thus Jesus used the present tense quite definitely in the Beatitudes; for example, "Blessed are the poor in spirit; for theirs is the kingdom of heaven."[18] Nevertheless, other sayings of the Master indicate that the kingdom is essentially progressive and is to be achieved gradually.[19] Yet again the kingdom is referred to as future and perfect.[20] The reconciliation of these divergent uses of the term "kingdom of God" seems to lie in the fact that the church at its best merges into and becomes the kingdom, but the kingdom in its richest and finest sense lies ahead as a goal to which the church is always progressing. As the church realizes its destiny and a greater portion of its members are "born of the Spirit" as well as being "born of water,"[21] the church will become more and more truly the kingdom of God.

Unfortunately, the church is never exclusively composed of twice-born men and women. Adequate baptism involves an inner change. When there is no inner change no kingdom citizenship is conferred, for we have the authority of Jesus himself for believing that unless one is "born of water and of the Spirit, he cannot enter into the kingdom of God." We may safely believe, therefore, that the full identification of the church with the kingdom awaits the full conversion of all church members and their progressive spiritual renewal.

NOTES

1. Matthew 16:18-20.
2. John 14:6.
3. Acts 17:28.

4. Acts 7:38.
5. Hebrews 10:9.
6. II Corinthians 3:11.
7. *Smith's Bible Dictionary* 1:454. This question is admirably discussed in W. H. Kelley's *Presidency and Priesthood.*
8. II Corinthians 10:1, or his argument in Galatians 3:16, Romans 9:6, and Romans 11:5, 16, KJ.
9. Acts 15:13-18.
10. I Peter 1:1, 2.
11. James 1:1.
12. Matthew 11:11.
13. In view of the status of Dr. Gore in the Church of England, his discussion of this point in his book *The Holy Spirit and the Church* is most illuminating and helpful.
14. Mark 7:13.
15. Matthew 16:20.
16. John 20:21-23.
17. Matthew 11:11, 12; Luke 7:28; 16:16, KJ.
18. Matthew 5:3, KJ.
19. Mark 4:26-32, KJ; Luke 13:18, 19.
20. Mark 9:1, KJ; 14:25; Luke 13:27, 28.
21. John 3:3-5.

Study Helps for

Chapter 26

LESSON PURPOSE

To present the church as an essential instrument in the achievement of the world purpose of Jesus Christ

SCRIPTURE REFERENCES

Matthew 16:14-20; Mark 8:28-31; Luke 9:18-21.

HIGH POINTS OF THE LESSON

- The church is built on the revelation that Jesus is the rightful leader of all humankind.
- The church is the "new Israel," inheriting all that was best in the earlier Israel and continuing the purpose of God in her.
- The church is the prophecy of the kingdom, and the building of the kingdom is the major purpose of the church.

QUESTIONS AND DISCUSSION TOPICS

1. Name some interpretations of the statement of Jesus to Peter, "Upon this rock I will build my church." Which of these do you believe to be the correct interpretation? Why?

2. In what sense is the church a continuation of Israel? What special values were conserved for the early church by this point of view? What difference will this point of view make in our interpretation of the prophecies addressed to Israel and as yet unfulfilled?

3. Why were the Jews rejected? What was the effect of this rejection?

4. What provision did Jesus make for the leadership of the church he was building? Under what circumstances were various priesthood offices added to the church? How does this compare with the early Restoration?

5. What is the meaning of the authority to "loose" and to "bind"? By whom is this authority exercised today? How is such authority related to the building of the church?

6. What different emphases may be placed on the statement, "I will build my church"? What varieties of meaning are involved?

7. In what sense is the church identical with the kingdom? In what sense do they differ?

8. Why did Jesus build *his* church rather than reform any of those existing prior to his coming? Why did he build a church at all? Why should we be concerned about church building? How is a church vital to the extension of the kingdom of righteousness?

WHAT THE LESSON MEANS FOR TODAY

People belong together. Good people are impeded by the wickedness of others and bad people are helped by the goodness of others. When the Jews as a people failed to meet the requirements of their calling, they were rejected in spite of the fact that there were many good individuals among them. Having rejected those who rejected him, the Master built a new people (including many Jews) whose purpose it was to give corporate expression to his will (I Peter 2:9-10).

Chapter 27

THE TRANSFIGURATION

The week immediately following the conversation at Caesarea Philippi was spent in that vicinity and was probably devoted to further thought and discussion of what lay ahead of Jesus. All of us know how thought tends to be clarified in conversation, and it is not unlikely that Jesus encouraged the apostles to talk freely concerning his messiahship and the self-denial this involved. There was need for such conversation, for the idea of service through sacrifice was difficult for them to understand. They knew the meaning of the words, but incorporation of the principle into their lives involved a major adjustment in their habits of thought and ways of living. They were not unwilling to make sacrifices, but they expected these sacrifices to be rewarded by the gift of important places in the kingdom. The call for sacrifice without thought of reward seemed unreasonable.

Looking back across the centuries, we find it easy to be surprised at the spiritual dullness of those who were nearest to the Master. We cannot understand why they did not immediately grasp the import of the lessons Jesus took such pains to make clear to their minds and hearts. Our failure to understand this is itself an indication of the difficulty which confronted Jesus in teaching them. We ourselves know the great phrases of the gospel but have not yet perceived their true meaning. For twenty centuries people calling themselves disciples have sought to compromise between the way of Jesus and the way of this world. This attempt to compromise is likely to continue while our Christianity lacks the illumination of understanding into which we are guided by the Holy Spirit of God.

Matthew, Mark, and Luke tell us that at the end of the week spent near Caesarea, the Master took Peter, James, and John and went up into a mountain to pray.[1] The mountain referred to was probably Mount Hermon, which towered in snowcapped grandeur above Caesarea Philippi and offered ample opportunity for solitude. This was the second time that Peter, James, and John had been selected from among the twelve as participants in a special endowment of spiritual power, for they previously had been chosen to witness the raising of the daughter of Jairus.[2] Later, the same three were to be special witnesses of the agony of Jesus in Gethsemane.[3] Just as the selection of the Twelve from among the larger number of disciples was made because of the work they were to do and not because Jesus had any special affection for them rather than for the others, so now this repeated selection of Peter, James, and John to share the inner secrets of his ministry seems to indicate that their calling was in some sense distinct from that of their fellow apostles.

Matthew and Mark both say that Jesus took these three apostles into the mountain "and was transfigured before them."[4] Luke adds the information that it was "as he prayed" that "his countenance was changed, and his raiment became white and glittering."[5] This period of prayer evidently lasted for some time, for while the Master prayed the three apostles gave way to their fatigue and slept.[6]

While Jesus prayed he was visited by Moses and Elias. While his heavenly visitants were talking with him the disciples awoke and saw them and felt something of the glory which rested on them and on Jesus. It had been fifteen centuries since Moses had died at Nebo[7] and nine centuries since Elijah had been taken to heaven without seeing death,[8] but the reality of their appearance does not seem to have been questioned by

Jesus or the apostles. Matthew, Mark, and Luke also show by their narratives that they believed the supernatural experience to be perfectly understandable in the attendant circumstances. In these sophisticated days, when the reality of the unseen is a matter of speculation with most of us, it will be well for us to remember that to Jesus and those nearest to him, this bridging of the centuries was a matter of experience and not of conjecture. Out of the strength of this experience Peter wrote many years afterward:

> We have not followed cunningly devised fables, when we made known unto you the power and coming of our Lord Jesus Christ, but were eye-witnesses of his majesty. For he received from God the Father honor and glory, when there came such a voice to him from the excellent glory, This is my beloved Son, in whom I am well pleased. And this voice which came from heaven we heard, when we were with him in the holy mount.[9]

John also wrote, as if in reference to this same occurrence:

> The same word was made flesh, and dwelt among us, and we beheld his glory, the glory as of the Only begotten of the Father, full of grace and truth.[10]

It is significant that the heavenly visitants were Moses the lawgiver and Elias, one of the most notable among the prophets. As the wondering disciples looked on, they saw that the Master was in full harmony with both of them, even as they were with each other. To those who were accustomed to observing signs and parallels, as were the Jews, this could not fail to mean that Moses and Elias recognized that Jesus was exactly what he claimed to be—the fulfiller and not the enemy of the Law and the Prophets.

The messengers from the living past talked with Jesus "of his death" which "he should *accomplish* at Jerusalem"[11] as though this dreaded ordeal was not something to be avoided but something to be achieved, a hard victory which only he could win. The assurances Jesus received must have done much to strengthen him in his conviction that he was choosing the right course.

Yet the Master still moved forward in faith, and with only such certitude as was available to him as a man of God. Rich though this experience was, it did not take away from Jesus the effort of faith nor the strain of doubt. In the Garden of Gethsemane he was yet to pray that, if possible, the cup of his humiliation should pass from him. But the Transfiguration did give Jesus all possible renewed assurance of the reality of the unseen world and of the great plan of salvation which was being worked out through the centuries with its center and culmination in him.

Meanwhile, the bewildered apostles looked on in rapt amazement. Peter made a clumsy attempt to prolong the experience, suggesting that he and his fellow apostles might build huts in which to house the heavenly visitors as worshipers were housed at the Feast of Tabernacles. Then, when the great revelation seemed to have reached its culmination and Moses and Elias were about to depart, "there came a voice out of the cloud, saying, This is my beloved Son; hear him."[12] Hitherto, these Jews had listened to the words of the Law and the Prophets. They had just seen that both were ministers serving Jesus. Now the voice of God spoke, and all that hitherto had been symbolized and hinted at was now made clear and mandatory: "Hear him." Old things were passed away; all things had become new. It is small wonder that after the experience was concluded, "they saw no man, save Jesus only."[13]

The more we understand of the heart and mind of Divinity, the more sure we are that our heavenly Father adjusts his self-revelation to the growing need and understanding of those who love and serve him. This being true, there was a definite reason why the transfiguration experience should occur when it did. Jesus had spent a difficult week with those who sensed something of his greatness but who were unable to reconcile the idea of his messiahship with his apparent defeat. They had been schooled too long in the idea that suffering and defeat are evidences of divine disapproval. Now, worn by the strain of the week, yet resolute in his determination to follow the path which led by way of Jerusalem to death, Jesus sought comfort and reassurance in the presence of his Father. His complete dedication and his dire need provided ample justification for pulling aside the veil which separates time and eternity, and so Jesus shared for a moment the glory which Moses and Elias had won and which he himself was so soon to regain in his Father's presence.

On the way down from the mountain, Jesus charged the apostles, saying, "Tell the vision to no man, until the Son of man be risen again from the dead."[14] The use of the term *vision* by Jesus cannot mean that the experience was not real. It was so unusual as to be almost unique—a visual experience shared simultaneously by three men. Perhaps we can take a hint from the testimony of Joseph Smith and Sidney Rigdon concerning the vision which they shared. They wrote:

> We, Joseph Smith, Jr., and Sidney Rigdon, being in the Spirit on the sixteenth of February, in the year of our Lord one thousand eight hundred and thirty-two, by the power of the Spirit our eyes were opened, and our understandings were enlightened, so as to see and understand the things of God.[15]

The Transfiguration confirmed the disciples in their faith that life persists after death, in their assurance of a divine purpose which runs through all the ages and unites them in one, in their knowledge of the authority of Jesus, and in their growing realization that the Law and the Prophets find their fulfillment in Christ Jesus. On the other side of the picture, we need to remember that even this transcendent experience did not lead to full and immediate understanding on the part of the apostles. The Spirit of God within must interpret the meaning of the experience without. This does not happen in a moment; it involves time-consuming spiritual growth. But as they grew they understood, and in the years which followed they lived by this understanding and sought to pass it on. Those who had not shared the vision of the mountaintop nevertheless shared their testimony. We too may share it as our understanding is also illuminated by the light within.

NOTES

1. Matthew 17:1-14; Mark 9:2-13, KJ; 1-11, IV; Luke 9:28-36.
2. Mark 5:37, KJ; 29, IV; Luke 8:51.
3. Matthew 26:37, KJ; 34, IV; Mark 14:33, KJ; 38, IV.
4. Matthew 17:1, 2, KJ; 1, IV; Mark 9:2, KJ; 1, IV.
5. Luke 9:28, 29.
6. Luke 9:32.
7. Deuteronomy 34.
8. II Kings 2:11.
9. II Peter 1:16-18.
10. John 1:14.
11. Luke 9:31.
12. Luke 9:35.
13. Matthew 17:7.
14. Matthew 17:8.
15. D. and C. 76:3a; see also 76:3e.

Study Helps for

Chapter 27

LESSON PURPOSE

To impress the reality of the unseen world and the continuity of the purpose of God down the ages

SCRIPTURE REFERENCES

Matthew 17:1-14; Mark 9:2-13, KJ; 1-11, IV; Luke 9:28-36; II Peter 1:16-18.

HIGH POINTS OF THE LESSON

- The Transfiguration occurred when those nearest the Master were struggling to reconcile the idea of Jesus as the Messiah with his announcement that he must suffer death at the hands of the Jews.
- After this the bridging of the centuries was a matter of experience for those who saw Moses and Elias and not just a matter of conjecture.
- Those who were to lead the church after the ascension of Jesus now knew that they were engaged in an agelong endeavor. They glimpsed the preparation of the centuries for their own day and were therefore much more willing to trust the future success of their enterprise to the guidance of God.

QUESTIONS AND DISCUSSION TOPICS

1. When did the Transfiguration occur? Why did it take place when it did?

2. On what occasions were Peter, James, and John selected for specially intimate association with Jesus? What was the probable significance of this selection?

3. What may we safely conjecture about the prayer of Jesus on the mount of transfiguration? What other major crises in the life of Jesus were preceded by periods of earnest prayer?

4. What lasting effect did the Transfiguration have on the apostles? What is the significance for us of this visit from the remote past?

5. Who were the heavenly visitants? What was the special significance of the visit of each of them? What did they discuss with Jesus?

6. What was the culmination of this experience? Why did this come at the end of the Transfiguration rather than at the beginning?

7. What was the immediate reaction of the apostles to the Transfiguration? As they grew in spiritual stature so this experience became more meaningful to them (II Peter 1:16).

8. Tell briefly of the first vision of Joseph Smith, the ordination to the Aaronic priesthood, and the vision of April 3, 1836. What did such experiences do for the leaders of the early church?

WHAT THE LESSON MEANS FOR TODAY

Our faith in the reality of the unseen world and in the continuity of the divine purpose down the ages is a reasonable faith. Christianity is built on the firm foundation of what God has actually done for his children—the creation, the Incarnation, the Resurrection, the Restoration. The Transfiguration has its place in this list of the times when God broke through into history. Out of their sure knowledge the apostles testified concerning it.

Chapter 28

LAST DAYS IN GALILEE

As Jesus and the three who had been with him in the mount of transfiguration came down to the plain, they found the other nine apostles in the center of a small group who turned eagerly toward them as they drew near. The first to reach Jesus was a man who had brought his epileptic son to the disciples in the hope that they would heal him. The disciples had failed.

It was evident that while Jesus was away, the scribes had sought to undermine his authority by taunting the nine apostles for their inability to effect the cure. Jesus asked that the boy be brought before him. As he came, the lad was seized with a violent attack which flung him to the ground. The immediate necessity was for healing, but the more fundamental necessity was for faith. Jesus met both needs. Using the lad's condition as a means of approach, he impressed on the father the importance of faith in God in order that the blessing might be made possible. Then he healed the boy. Later, when the disciples came to Jesus and asked why they could not heal the lad, the Master impressed them also with both the importance and the power of faith, saying:

> If ye have faith as a grain of mustard seed, ye shall say unto this mountain, Remove to yonder place, and it shall remove; and nothing shall be impossible unto you.[1]

Mark adds that in situations such as this, where they were under the fire of criticism from their enemies, they needed such quiet confidence in God as could come only by fasting and prayer.[2]

Leaving the vicinity of Caesarea Philippi, Jesus and his disciples passed southward toward Galilee, evidently traveling secretly[3] in order that Jesus would have more time with his disciples—or possibly to avoid any public clamor which would hinder the work Jesus had to do.

As they walked, Jesus again sought to prepare these men, whose understanding was so dear to him, for the tragedy which awaited them at Jerusalem and from which he could see no escape. Peter, James, and John had been helped toward understanding by the Transfiguration, but their stubborn conviction that Divinity means power to overcome rather than power to suffer still made it hard for them to understand. The other nine were even more bewildered. They recognized that Jesus was repeating the idea which had seemed so novel when he first mentioned it at Caesarea Philippi. The words about taking up their crosses were no more familiar, but they were not much more intelligible than they had been at first. Sensing something of their own spiritual ineptitude, the disciples became afraid to question Jesus further and lapsed into silence or into muttered conversation among themselves.[4]

When the travelers arrived at Capernaum, one of the temple taxgatherers came to Peter and asked whether Jesus had paid the customary half shekel tax assessed against adult Jews for the support of the temple.[5] The incident was more important than appeared on the surface, and Peter came to Jesus for his advice. With quiet humor the Master pointed out that kings and princes do not pay taxes, and that therefore he should not be taxed to support his Father's house. Nevertheless, he said, pay the tax "lest we should offend them [cause to stumble]."[6] It is highly probable that this incident, simple as it was, was remembered again and again during the later ministry of the apostles, and persuaded them to "go the second mile" in matters which were not important instead of hampering their work by unyielding insistence on their rights. Paul, for example, met some of the scruples of the Jews in this way.[7]

When they arrived at Capernaum, Jesus asked the disciples what they had been discussing among themselves after they had ceased questioning him on the highway. They had hoped Jesus had not noticed, for they had been discussing who was the greatest among them; such a conversation now seemed unworthy. Ignoring their embarrassment, Jesus sat down and called a little child to him. With his arm around the child, the Master declared that there is no place for anyone in the kingdom of God who does not learn to be humble as a little child. Then, pressing the lesson home, he said:

> Whosoever shall receive this child in my name, receiveth me; and whosoever shall receive me, shall receive him who sent me; for he who is least among you all, the same shall be great.[8]

Preeminence in the kingdom evidently does not depend on any of the standards by which people are accustomed to judge the importance of other people. It depends on humility, teachableness, kindness, and instinctive friendliness such as that of little children. Authority in the kingdom, moreover, does not depend on the more obvious credentials persons may carry but on the fact that they are sent by the king.

It is not unlikely that the discussion by the way had been occasioned by the fact that—when they had been taken to the mount of transfiguration with Jesus—Peter, James, and John had for the second time been selected from among the apostles to share an intimacy denied the others. The debate concerning which of them was greatest was readily understandable under the circumstances, for the nine who had been left in the valley were chagrined because of this seeming partiality as well as their inability to help the epileptic boy. Understandable though the situation was, it was vitally important that no jealousy now come between these men, separating them from each other and from Jesus. The Master therefore addressed himself first to this problem. To solve it he reverted once more to the principle which he had presented so clearly in the Sermon on the Mount. Not only must they be humble but they must be in the work for the work's sake, just as little children go into a game for the game's sake.

Taking advantage of this instruction, Jesus broadened his teaching so as to emphasize the responsibility of his followers for each other. Everyone must care for every other one, for all are infinitely precious to their Father in heaven. Every one of these men who now listened so intently was like the sheep who had strayed from the fold and had been brought back only after great effort and danger.[9] Occasions of offense might occur among them; they must therefore take every precaution to keep these difficulties in the smallest possible circle and see to it that every offense was settled as soon as possible. If a disciple's sense of responsibility must extend even to the little children,[10] it must certainly extend to the body of the saints,[11] and be especially strong among members of the apostolic group.

Against this background Jesus reiterated a statement made to Peter at Caesarea Philippi,[12] except that he now specifically included the other members of the Twelve in the circle of those having authority to "loose" and to "bind." In view of the circumstances under which this commission was confirmed on them, it was not possible for the apostles to think that their authority was an arbitrary one. It was an authority to be exercised in a spirit of kindliness and in harmony with fundamental principles. It was to be directed toward the maintenance of the spirit of peace and of spiritual effectiveness among the citizens of the kingdom. It was an authority which centered in the manifestation of the Spirit of Christ, which is the spirit of conciliation, of forgiveness, and of mutual forbearance.[13]

As Peter listened to Jesus, a very practical question arose in his mind. Surely there must be some limit to such conciliation, he thought. He wanted to be generous but he also wanted some rule to guide his action, for his Jewish upbringing had taught him to think in terms of rules. With the utmost sincerity Peter therefore asked, "Lord, how oft shall my brother sin against me, and I forgive him? Till seven times?"[14] "No," said Jesus patiently, "until seventy times seven." Peter had once more missed the point, and in doing so had provided still another illustration of the fundamental problem confronting the Master in his relations with his disciples. They did not yet talk the same language. Peter wanted to help, but the root of the matter was not in him. Like the masterly teacher that he was, Jesus was not discouraged by Peter's limitation; he was encouraged by Peter's desire. Building on this, the Master told the beautiful and effective parable of the unprofitable servant, the chief thought of which is that we all should welcome the privilege of serving each other in the same spirit as our heavenly Father has blessed us. The need of others gives us an opportunity to copy in a small way the unmeasured graciousness of our heavenly Father toward us.[15]

This series of conversations grew out of the concern of the Master for the spirit in which his disciples must work together. When the right spirit prevails, each member of a social group can be used according to his or her capacity, and this is one of the fundamental ideals of the Christian enterprise. This very ideal requires that some whom God has blessed with distinctive talents, for reasons which are good in his sight, shall occupy places of prominence in the group. The nine apostles knew this, as did Peter, James, and John; for all the Twelve had evidently been chosen for distinctive nearness to the Master from which other good men were excluded. Now Jesus impressed them that all gradations of authority must be exercised in the right spirit, and none of them must think that his official preeminence gave him prior rights in the sight of God. Such rights are the fruits of a quality of life, not of prominence in ministry.

While the disciples were wrestling with this new point of view, John came to Jesus and said, "Master, we saw one casting out devils in thy name, and he followed not us; and we forbade him, because he followed not us."[16] The very fact that John mentioned this difficulty under these circumstances was itself a request for the Master to review what he had done in the light of the teaching which he had just given them concerning forgiveness. Jesus immediately took up the friendly challenge and applied the spirit of his teaching to this new problem. Despite his limitations, the man complained of had been seeking to do good and had been attempting this in the name of Jesus. So Jesus said, in effect, "Do not rush to condemn such a man. It is true that he is not yet with us; but if he is honestly trying to do the same things that we are trying to do, we should at least be grateful that he is not in the camp of the enemy. Whoever helps in the work in no matter how small a way, in a genuine effort to further the Cause, shall in no wise lose his reward."[17] The same problem confronts the disciples of our day, and the answer of Jesus is still applicable.

NOTES

1. Matthew 17:20.
2. Mark 9:29, KJ; 26, IV.
3. Mark 9:30, KJ; 27, IV.
4. Luke 9:45.
5. About thirty cents.
6. Matthew 17:24-27, KJ; 23-26, IV.
7. Acts 21:18-26.
8. Luke 9:48.

9. Matthew 18:10-14.
10. Matthew 18:10.
11. Matthew 18:15-17.
12. Matthew 16:19, KJ; 20, IV; 18:18.
13. Note that modern revelation states in reference to the official decisions of the presiding quorums of the church, "The decisions of these quorums, or either of them, are to be made in all righteousness, in holiness and lowliness of heart, meekness and long-suffering, and in faith and virtue and knowledge; temperance, patience, godliness, brotherly kindness, and charity, because the promise is, if these things abound in them, they shall not be unfruitful in the knowledge of the Lord" (Doctrine and Covenants 104:11i).
14. Matthew 18:21.
15. Matthew 18:22-34.
16. Mark 9:36.
17. Mark 9:39-41, KJ; 37, 38, IV.

Study Helps for

Chapter 28

LESSON PURPOSE

To come to a better understanding of the spirit of mutual consideration and forbearance which must motivate true disciples, and to see that this spirit must be extended as far as possible to those not of the faith.

SCRIPTURE REFERENCES

Matthew 17:24-27, KJ; 23-26, IV; Mark 9:14-50, KJ; 12-50, IV; Luke 9:37-50.

HIGH POINTS OF THE LESSON

- Even the twelve confused public recognition with success and had to be taught that success lies in service.
- Genuine spiritual authority depends on possession of the spirit of forbearance and mutual consideration.
- Disciples must work with those who do not yet see clearly whenever this can be done without a sacrifice of principle.

QUESTIONS AND DISCUSSION TOPICS

1. Describe the situation which confronted Jesus when he came down from the Mount of Transfiguration. Why did Jesus say that the disciples had failed to heal the afflicted boy? What did the father mean when he said, "Lord, I believe; help thou mine unbelief"? Under what circumstances can we share his feeling about the growth of faith?

2. As they walked together Jesus warned his disciples that he should be delivered into the hands of men. They did not understand what he meant "and they feared to ask him." Why do you think they were afraid?

3. What reason did Jesus give for not being required to pay the Temple tax? Why did he pay it? Is this principle important today?

4. Who are the greatest in the kingdom of heaven? Is such preeminence important among persons of exalted spiritual stature?

5. Why was it so important for the twelve to eliminate jealousy? What effect would the rise of jealousy have had on the jealous apostle? On the group? On inquirers? On the work? Consider John 17:11, 21.

6. What is the law of the church concerning offenses? Whose responsibility is it to remove causes of offense? If there is ill-feeling between me and my brother or sister, should I (a) refrain from the Communion until it is settled or (b) settle it so that I may partake?

7. Tell the story of the lost sheep. What are the lessons of this story? Tell the story of the unprofitable servant. What are the lessons of this story?

8. John told Jesus that they saw one casting out devils, and they "forbade him, because he followed not us." How did Jesus resolve this problem? In the light of his answer, how shall we regard other branches of Christianity and other community groups?

WHAT THE LESSON MEANS FOR TODAY

"Blessed are the peacemakers."

Jesus taught the disciples that all parties to a conflict are under obligation to approach its solution in the spirit of fraternity. This is not an incidental matter, but is fundamental to sound kingdom building.

Chapter 29

THE GOSPEL IN PEREA

It is apparent from the Gospels that after the crisis in his ministry in Galilee, Jesus planned to be in Jerusalem at the next Passover season. Many of the Galileans and the leaders from the other provinces would certainly be there. Then, if ever, he could speak to the heart and conscience of the nation. Even though he should fail to win the leaders or any great number of the people, he knew he could make his visit so memorable that forever afterward those who believed in him would remember the Passover for its association with him rather than because of its original significance. With this in mind, the Master spent the intervening period in intimate communion with his disciples. He tried in a thousand and one ways to open their eyes to the true riches of the kingdom and to the responsibilities and opportunities which were theirs.

When the time came, Jesus "steadfastly set his face to go to Jerusalem."[1] Leaving Capernaum with his disciples, he avoided Tiberias by going south on the other side of the lake and then took the west Jordan road toward Judea. From somewhere in the vicinity of Scythopolis, he sent messengers to discover whether the direct road through Samaria was open to Jewish pilgrims. The Samaritans would not receive him, and when James and John saw this, these "sons of thunder" wanted to call down fire from heaven on the Samaritans as a punishment for their lack of hospitality. Instead, Jesus merely led the way to another village; in that act was punishment enough. It may be that some John, Peter, Paul, or possibly a Eunice, Lois, or Dorcas lived there waiting to be called forth to such new life as Jesus brought to Lazarus and to every other man or woman who welcomed him. This is all conjecture; we do not know. All we know is that those Samaritans did not welcome Jesus when they had a chance to do so, and so he passed them by. When he did, they passed into oblivion.

Since the Samaritan road was barred, Jesus crossed the Jordan into Perea where John the Baptist had found such a responsive welcome. With the seventy going ahead and preparing the way for him, he walked from village to village teaching the crowds that gathered to hear him, healing their sick, and lending the benediction of his presence to young and old. It is a little difficult to know what part of the Gospel records refers to this period, for the narrative in Mark occupies only one chapter[2] and in Matthew two chapters.[3] In Luke the account is extended through ten chapters[4] and contains some of the most interesting events of the life of Jesus and some of his most precious teachings. Some of these teachings may have been repetitions of instruction given in Galilee, and some may be differently presented in Matthew because of that writer's tendency to group similar narratives together. Whatever the reason, we cannot be absolutely certain whether several of the incidents Luke includes here really belong to this period or to a different time. There are enough events which clearly belong here, however, to show the general character of the ministry Jesus exercised during these significant weeks.

One of the parables for which we are indebted to Luke concerns the good Samaritan. As was the case with many of the most illuminating teachings of Jesus, this story was called forth by a question. "A certain lawyer," we are told, "tempted him."[5] Evidently the man was rather keenly aware of his own ability, and in the pride of this awareness propounded a question which seemed perfectly simple but which was really one of the most searching he could have asked: "Master, what shall I do to inherit eternal life?" Jesus referred his questioner to the law, and when the lawyer quoted this correctly, said in effect, "All right, you know the law; now do it." How neatly the tables were turned. Then it was the lawyer who was being tested. Desiring to justify himself, the man asked, "Who is my neighbor?"

Against this background Jesus told his story of an incident that might have occurred any day on the Jerusalem-Jericho road. The two cities were only twenty miles apart, but Jerusalem was nearly 2,600 feet above sea level and Jericho was nearly a thousand feet below sea level. The road between the two cities was so full of twists and turns that it had become the happy hunting ground of robbers who attacked their victims and then escaped around the curves and into the limestone caves. As Jesus talked, those who heard him could picture the road with the traveler lying half dead, the priest hurrying by on the other side, too busy to be concerned in such a commonplace situation. They could see the Levite, too, as he passed quickly by lest he become a victim. They had seen this kind of thing happen and enjoyed the humor of the first allusions; but it was a little more difficult for them to accept the Samaritan, one of their despised neighbors, as the hero of the story. In the telling, Jesus left no possible doubt that the Samaritan was the hero.

For two thousand years this parable has carried its message to all kinds of people in all kinds of circumstances. It is a lesson which is so true as to be beyond dispute. Yet we may read that story many times before we realize how adroitly Jesus changed the emphasis. The lawyer has asked, "Who is my neighbor?" but when Jesus had finished this parable he said to the lawyer, "Which now of these three, thinkest thou, was neighbor unto him that fell among the thieves?" The lawyer's attitude was, "Who is a neighbor to me?" The attitude of Jesus was, "Who proved himself a neighbor to the man in need?" The difference in point of view is vital.

From Perea Jesus made a brief visit to Jerusalem to participate in the Feast of Dedication. Here, as always, Jesus was trying to open the eyes of the Jewish people to the true nature of God and his kingdom and to cause them to repent as individuals and as a people of the kind of life which obstructs the purpose of God in the name of God. Jesus sought to explain this in his story of the good shepherd. All of his hearers were familiar with the material of this story, for many of them were shepherds; the others knew good shepherds as important members of their community life. Jesus likened himself to the shepherd who walks ahead of his sheep, eastern fashion, leading them and clearing the way for them, knowing every one by name and protecting them with his own life against marauders of every kind. "A stranger they will not follow," said Jesus, "for they do not know him and cannot trust him and do not feel safe with him."[6]

The essence of the distinction between the good shepherd and the hireling was expressed by Jesus in a sentence which has become one of the watchwords of the Christian evangel: "I am come that they might have life, and that they might have it more abundantly."[7] The hireling comes for his own purposes. He cares nothing for the sheep, but steals and destroys and kills. The good shepherd, on the other hand, lives that his sheep may have more abundant life as they follow him in green pastures and beside the still waters, fearing no evil even though he leads them through the valley of the shadow of death. And so they come at last to that sheepfold, to which the shepherd is gathering other sheep, through the dark watches of the night into the glorious light of the new day.[8]

Jesus also likened himself to the door to the sheepfold, the one by whom the sheep enter the fold. All who have a right within the sheepfold must go past him, and all who enter any other way are thieves and robbers no matter how sincere and earnest they are or claim to be. Since he is the door, he opens the way for all who come in the right spirit and with the right purpose. There is no need for anyone to break in; the only reason anyone would seek to break in is that such a one is unwilling to pass scrutiny in the doorway.

While he was walking in Solomon's court during his visit to the Temple, certain of the Jews asked Jesus boldly, "How long dost thou make us to doubt? If thou be the Christ, tell us plainly."[9] It was hard for them to see that this was just the problem which confronted Jesus. If he did say, quite simply, "Yes, I am the Christ," then they would ask him to prove his claim by doing the things they expected the Messiah to do, chief of which was to reassert the political independence of the Jews. With infinite patience, the Master explained that the answer to their question lay in the kind of work he was doing. Here was the evidence of his messiahship. They did not recognize this evidence because they did not think as God thinks. They were looking at the King, but they could not really *see* him because they lacked kingly qualities within themselves. Their difficulties arose out of the lifelong habit of giving first place to secondary things, worshiping power and success instead of honor and truth and service.

In the teaching of this period is also a parable told by Jesus to illustrate the unfailing love of God for his children, and the ways in which many have separated themselves from that love. The story of the prodigal son[10] is one of the brightest gems of world literature. It tells of the younger son of a well-to-do farmer who became impatient of the restraints of homelife and asked for the share of the family estate which would normally come to him upon his father's death. Taking his inheritance, he went to a "far country and there wasted his substance in riotous living." After a time his resources were dissipated, and he "began to be in want." Soon, in utter destitution, he was reduced to the worst ignominy which could befall a Jew: his vaunted independence had led him to the hogpen. Here "he came to himself" and started back home with only one asset, his memory of his father's love. Expecting nothing and deserving nothing, he approached his old home; but there he was met and welcomed while yet a long way off by the father who loved him.

The story might have ended there. If it had, the strictly religious Jews would have felt that it was intended solely for those who had left the faith of their Father and the rich treasures of his home. But with consummate genius, Jesus went on to paint the picture of the brother who had remained at home. This man was a typical Pharisee, strict in his observance of the proprieties but cold and conceited and lacking affection for his brother. This older son was lost, as well as the younger one. He had missed the finest thing that his home had to offer—the love of his father, which should have taught him how to love his brother. Both sons needed to wake up to the opportunities which were theirs. Each of them needed something his father could give but which he must make an effort to take, and without which he could never really enter into the joy of his father's presence.

NOTES

1. Luke 9:51.
2. Mark 10.

3. Matthew 19:1 to 21:1.
4. Luke 9:51-19:27.
5. Luke 10:26.
6. John 10:1-14.
7. John 10:10.
8. Psalm 23.
9. John 10:24.
10. Luke 15:11-32.

Study Helps for

Chapter 29

LESSON PURPOSE

To present and clarify the teachings of Jesus in Perea

SCRIPTURE REFERENCES

Luke 9:51-62; 10:27-37; John 10:1-21; Luke 15:11-32

HIGH POINTS OF THE LESSON

- To have Jesus pass us by is by far the worst possible punishment for our blind failure to welcome him.
- A worldly person asks, "Who is my neighbor?" A godly person asks, "To whom can I be neighborly?"
- We do not have to persuade our Father to love us but we must do our part, whether this means returning from a far country or waking up to the privileges of a home we have never left.

QUESTIONS AND DISCUSSION TOPICS

1. Why was Jesus eager to spend the Passover in Jerusalem? How did he spend the months immediately preceding the Passover?

2. Describe the incident in the Samaritan village. What were the results of the protest by the Samaritans? What is the significant teaching of this incident?

3. What were the circumstances under which Jesus was asked "Who is my neighbor?" Is your neighbor necessarily a friend? What difference does this make?

4. What is the central teaching of the story of the Good Shepherd? With what psalm is this story associated? Analyze the meaning of this psalm.

5. Why were some of the Jews especially provoked by the story of the Good Shepherd? Consider pride as an enemy of understanding.

6. In the days of Jesus a sheepfold was merely a fenced-in enclosure with a small opening for the sheep to enter. At night the shepherd slept lying across this opening. In what sense is Jesus the "door" into the fold? Who are those who climb up another way?

7. When Jesus walked in the temple in Solomon's porch, the Jews asked him, "How long dost thou make us to doubt? If thou be the Christ, tell us plainly." Why was this impossible? See John 10:25-38.

8. What are the chief lessons of the parable of the prodigal son? What lesson do you draw from the attitude of the older brother?

WHAT THE LESSON MEANS FOR TODAY

Jesus addressed himself to the problems which arise out of our common humanity. Our fashions of speech and our modes of dress have changed since he lived in Palestine, but the most vital questions of the day still center in our relationship to the Father and to our neighbors. People are still trying to enter the kingdom in some way other than by the Door. We are still plagued with pharisaical elder brothers who keep the law without love. We still need to listen to the Master Teacher.

Chapter 30

MARRIAGE AND THE HOME

Christianity was in many ways the completion of Judaism. It is not possible therefore to regard the Christian law of marriage as a code first instituted during the earthly ministry of our Lord. Indeed, anyone who might 'ook into the New Testament, whether Gospels or Epistles, for a full and self-contained code of law on marriage would be disappointed. The actual passages in the Gospels containing Jesus' teaching are few; we do not find any directions as to a number of important matters on the subject, and the same is true, though to a slightly less extent, of the Epistles.[1]

During the earthly life of Jesus too-easy divorce was a national scandal. The problem was not that the Jews did not know the provisions of the Law of Moses relating to marriage and divorce but that these had been interpreted in such fashion as to denude them of the purpose and the restraints which originally had been built into them.

During his Perean ministry a group of Pharisees asked Jesus whether it was lawful for a man to put away his wife for every cause.[2] It may have been that some of the Pharisees were sincerely desirous of securing the guidance of the Master, for the elevation of standards of marriage was recognized to be of great importance to the whole nation. It is much more likely, however, that the majority of these men knew that the question would involve Jesus in serious difficulties, and it was this which prompted their inquiry.

As part of the background it will be well to remember that there were two schools of thought among the Jews concerning marriage and divorce—that of Hillel and that of Shammai. The Law of Moses stated:

When a man hath taken a wife, and married her, and it come to pass that she find no favor in his eyes, because he hath found some uncleanness in her; then let him write her a bill of divorcement, and give it in her hand, and send her out of the house. And when she is departed, out of his house, she may go and be another man's wife.[3]

The school of Hillel interpreted this fragment of the law to mean that a man might divorce his wife for any cause that seemed adequate to him—because he had ceased to love her, because he had seen someone he liked better, or even because she had cooked his dinner poorly. The school of Shammai, on the other hand, contended that divorce was never justifiable except on the basis of an offense against chastity. As was quite natural among people who had been trained in obedience to the letter of the law rather than to its spirit, the interpretation of Hillel and his followers was far more popular than that of Shammai. Because of this division, and the resulting laxity, marriage had lost its sanctity and its security; women were degraded into chattels, children were robbed of parental care, duty and responsibility were flouted, and the social and spiritual foundation of the people were undermined.

The situation had been illustrated for the whole nation a short time prior to the questioning of Jesus by the Pharisees. Herod had married his niece Herodias, the wife of his half brother, Herod Philip, and to clear the way for this had divorced his own wife. John the Baptist had been so deeply incensed by this marriage that he had denounced it publicly—and had paid for his daring with his life.[4]

In view of this situation, it is clear that when the Pharisees "came unto him, tempting him" concerning marriage, they required Jesus to sanction a situation which was a stench in the nostrils of good people or else to set himself in public opposition to Herod, to the school of Hillel, and to many of the most influential people of the nation.

The physical threat involved does not seem to have

troubled Jesus at all. His sole concern was to answer the Pharisees in such a way as to make clear the will of God concerning marriage, and to win good men and women to the principles he laid down.

"What did Moses command you?" he asked. The Pharisees answered that Moses had permitted a man to put away his wife by writing her a bill of divorcement.[5] They were on safe ground so far, they thought. This set forth the issue even more clearly than before: Was the interpretation of Hillel right or was that of Shammai to be followed? To the chagrin of the Pharisees, Jesus ignored both Hillel and Shammai; he even passed judgment on Moses. He said that the great lawgiver had found the custom of divorce prevalent among his people. Knowing their hardness of heart, he deemed it prudent to regulate rather than to forbid a practice so universal. Moses did this by requiring a husband to deliberate long enough to write out a bill of divorcement before casting his wife aside. This legal requirement was an attempt to reduce the number of divorces growing out of passionate resentments which might be dissipated if tempers had time to cool.

A law given under these circumstances was necessarily a compromise. If the Pharisees really wished to understand the will of God in the matter, said Jesus, they must go back to the beginning of things and see what had been ordained in the creation. According to this law, written into our nature, God wills that a husband and wife shall belong to each other so intimately as to become one, each living in the life of the other. The bond between them should be stronger than that between persons and their parents. Husband and wife ought to "cleave" to each other; this word *cleave* implies a mutual adherence which nothing can separate.[6]

Continuing with this line of thought, Jesus pointed out that when a man puts away his wife for a trivial reason, and so causes her to seek elsewhere the companionship and the sense of mutual completion which she ought to find with her husband, this man shares guilt for her sins. Charles Foster Kent says that the teaching of Jesus in this connection can best be translated: "Whosoever shall divorce his wife in order to marry another, commits adultery against her. And if she divorces her husband in order to marry another, she commits adultery." What we have here is not so much a command as an unvarnished statement of facts: To secure a divorce in order to marry another may give legal sanction to unchastity but it does not change the basic wrongness of such an act.[7]

There can be little doubt that Jesus and the early apostles deplored the practice of easy divorce prevalent in their day. The instruction given by Jesus was communicated to Paul, who later wrote to the saints in Corinth:

> Unto the married I command, yet not I, but the Lord, Let not the wife depart from her husband; but if she depart, let her remain unmarried, or be reconciled to her husband; but let not the husband put away his wife.[8]

Also in his first letter to the Christians at Thessalonica, Paul said:

> You remember the injunctions we gave you, by authority of the Lord Jesus. It is God's will that you should be consecrated, that you abstain from sexual vice, that each of you should learn to take a wife for himself chastely and honorably, not to gratify sensual passion like the Gentiles in their ignorance of God. . . . God did not call us to be impure, but to be consecrated; hence he who disregards this, disregards not man but the God who gave you his Holy Spirit.[9]

There is also little likelihood that Jesus intended to make pronouncement which should be applied in legalistic fashion in every one of the homes whose members sought to follow him. Jesus did not work that way. He was concerned, rather, to set forth the principles which are pertinent to the situation and to illustrate and invoke the spirit in which these principles should be applied.

In considering the teaching of Jesus in this connection, it will be helpful to keep in mind such factors as the following:

> Marriages at the time of Jesus were arranged on the basis of family interests. Compatibility rather than the medieval idea of romantic love was often the major personal factor involved.
>
> The women of the time of Jesus were not economically independent. If they were divorced, they were likely to face urgent problems of survival.[10]

These factors were important and were undoubtedly in the mind of Jesus:

> He built his teaching on the statement of divine intention in marriage.[11]
>
> He gave the husband/wife relation primacy—that husband and wife shall be one flesh.[12]
>
> He sought to prevent divorce by eradicating its roots in unchastity.[13]
>
> This counsel was not concerned primarily with mutual affection developed prior to marriage but rather with the obligation undertaken in marriage that the partners shall act lovingly toward one another. This outgoing concern, he taught, can become the prelude to deeper and deeper affection as it is maintained.
>
> He sought to delay hasty divorce by his reminder that a man resolved to divorce his wife should "give her a writing of divorcement."[14]
>
> His attitude was forward-looking, dwelling on the existing and forthcoming needs of the sinners involved. For instance, he refused to condemn the woman taken in adultery when her paramour went unpunished.[15]

Again, when the Samaritan woman showed her concern over acceptable worship, he ignored the complications of her married life and shared with her one of the great conversations recorded by John.[16]

NOTES

1. See *What Is Christian Marriage?* by Arthur T. Macmillan, Macmillan & Co. (1934), p. 38.
2. Matthew 19:3; Mark 10:2.
3. Deuteronomy 24:1, 2.
4. Matthew 14:5-11, KJ; 4-10, IV.
5. Deuteronomy 24:1, 2; Mark 10:4.
6. Matthew 19:4-6.
7. Doctrine and Covenants 42:20.
8. I Corinthians 7:10, 11.
9. I Thessalonians 4:2-5, 7, 8, Moffatt.
10. Matthew 5:32, KJ; 36, IV.
11. Matthew 19:4-6.
12. Mark 10:7-9.
13. Matthew 5:28, KJ; 30, IV.
14. Matthew 5:31, KJ: 35, IV; Mark 10:4.
15. John 8:7-11.
16. John 4:6-24, KJ; 7-26, IV.

Study Helps for

Chapter 30

LESSON PURPOSE

To clarify and impress the importance of Christian standards for homelife

SCRIPTURE REFERENCES

Matthew 19:3-15; Mark 10:2-16; Luke 18:15-17

HIGH POINTS OF THE LESSON

- Jesus would not tolerate a double standard of morals.
- He regarded marriage as a spiritual union which both the parties and those connected with them should do their utmost to perpetuate.
- This attitude was the outcome of the Master's regard for men and women and of his deep concern for the welfare of children.

QUESTIONS AND DISCUSSION TOPICS

1. What was the penalty of marital infidelity under the Mosaic Law? Why did Jesus refuse to apply this law to the woman caught in adultery?

2. What is the fundamental law of Jesus concerning adultery? Which is the more severe punishment, that inflicted from without or that which is registered in the deterioration of personality?

3. What was the teaching of the followers of Hillel concerning marriage? What was the teaching of the followers of Shammai?

4. Describe the attitude of the Jews toward marriage at the time of Christ. What were the effects of this attitude in the life of the nation?

5. Why did the Law of Moses permit divorce? How did Jesus justify his extension of the Law of Moses regarding marriage?

6. What is the responsibility of the third party in marital discord? What was the teaching of Paul in this connection?

7. At what points can marriage best be safeguarded? Which of the following factors are most significant in protecting the home: education, social pressure, ecclesiastical restraints, spiritual vigor?

8. What considerations make the blessing of children important? In what way does this ordinance tend to stabilize the home?

WHAT THE LESSON MEANS FOR TODAY

The safeguards of stable marriage are still spiritual. They cannot be developed overnight; they must be built into the very nature of the contracting parties. Education for marriage must include specialized knowledges, but the fundamental requirement is not greater knowledge; it is greater self-discipline motivated by love. Education for marriage to be adequate, must be education for life.

Chapter 31

THE DISCIPLE AND HIS POSSESSIONS

Jesus said he came that people might have life and have it more abundantly.[1] He was not concerned with things except in their relation to life. Nor was he concerned with just any kind of life but with life that promotes richness and deep satisfaction among individuals. This life, he taught, is a life of discipleship.[2] It calls for undivided loyalty:

> If ye keep my commandments, ye shall abide in my love; even as I have kept my Father's commandments, and abide in his love. These things have I spoken unto you, that my joy might remain in you, and that your joy might be full.[3]

> Where your treasure is, there will your heart be also. . . . No man can serve two masters, for either he will hate the one and love the other; or else he will hold to the one and despise the other. Ye cannot serve God and Mammon.[4]

The demand for undivided loyalty comes under constant challenge in all our relationships with who and what we regard as our own—our relatives, our friends, our reputations, our possessions, even life itself:

> He who loveth father and mother more than me, is not worthy of me; and he who loveth son or daughter more than me, is not worthy of me. And he who taketh not his cross and followeth after me, is not worthy of me. He who seeketh to save his life shall lose it; and he that loseth his life for my sake shall find it.[5]

In his eagerness to win people for God and the kingdom, Jesus was confronted by many enemies. Of these one of the greatest was the love of possessions. Because of this he counseled his apostles at the beginning of their ministry:

> Store up no treasure for yourself on earth, where moth and rust corrode, where thieves break in and steal: store up treasures for yourselves in heaven, where neither moth nor rust corrode, where thieves do not break in and steal. For where your treasure lies, your heart will lie there too.

> The eye is the lamp of the body: so, if your Eye is generous, the whole of your body will be illuminated, but if your Eye is selfish, the whole of your body will be darkened. And if your very light turns dark, then—what a darkness it is![6]

There is no suggestion here that wealth is in itself evil. In its right place, it is a very valuable tool; but it is hard to keep in its place. It is easy to persuade ourselves that our desire to do good safeguards us in seeking riches. This is true only when this desire is itself safeguarded at numerous points along the way. Our difficulty lies in the fact that the acquisition of power of any sort changes our point of view and wealth gives power which can easily blind us to our obligations as disciples. However well-intentioned we are, we cannot be trusted to decide for ourselves, apart from any social or spiritual controls, whether or not it is better for us to be rich. Our interests and our affections warp our judgment in such matters, and it is not difficult to justify compromises which impoverish the kingdom even while they multiply riches.

On several occasions Jesus found it necessary to remind his apostles of the threat of riches. One of these occasions occurred during the last journey to Jerusalem. Jesus was talking with the disciples regarding the unpardonable sin of blasphemy against the Holy Ghost[7] when a man in the crowd interrupted him, saying: "Master, speak to my brother, that he divide the inheritance with me." Replying to this man, Jesus said, "Take heed, and beware of covetousness; for a man's life consisteth not in the abundance of the things which he possesseth."[8] Evidently the Master was more concerned about the spirit the man was exhibiting than he was about the inheritance involved. Taking advantage of the interruption to impress a lesson, as he so often did, Jesus then told the multitude the story of a rich farmer who decided to build bigger barns to hold his grain but was still totally unprepared for the larger needs of the future.[9]

There was no suggestion in this parable that the farmer had gained his riches by unfair practices or that he was given to riotous living. Indeed, according to the standards of the world, he was a wise and farsighted businessman who was making reasonable and prudent arrangements for the future. With his reserve well cared for, the rich farmer planned to "eat, drink, and be merry." Jesus called this man a fool because he was to die that night. He had made provision for a future he was never to enjoy and yet had made no provision whatever for the future he could not escape.

There was another reason why Jesus called this farmer a fool. The man was doomed, even though he had not died that night. He had worked hard, for such success as he had won does not come easily. He had found scant happiness in his work as such, daydreaming rather of a time when, having amassed wealth, he would be able to retire. His whole philosophy of life was summed up in the phrase "eat, drink, and be merry." What a heartbreaking tragedy, and how frequently it is repeated today. How few of us are able to find the reward of our labor in the joy of laboring and our true wealth in work which challenges us and at the same time enriches humanity. How many of us are looking forward to some future time when we can retire. And how many of us may easily be lost and broken a few months after this retirement has taken us away from the tasks which gave life meaning and purpose!

A problem that is not quite identical, but which is directly related, is the problem of those good women who are so completely devoted to their children that when these children marry they suddenly find themselves without any real reason for living. To all such persons Jesus comes with this parable which teaches that work is a high privilege; that it should be its own justification and should yield its own satisfactions; and that any resultant wealth, any capital accretions, are of value only when they minister to further life. Beyond this point, wealth is an illusion and not a reality.

While the company continued on the way to Jerusalem, the perils of riches were further dramatized for the disciples in an incident none of those in the inner circle ever forgot. A rich young man saw Jesus coming and, running to the Master eagerly, "kneeled to him, and asked him, Good Master, what shall I do that I may inherit eternal life?"[10] The heart of Jesus warmed to him, and yet the young ruler's question was itself evidence that he was on the wrong track. He evidently thought of eternal life as a reward, in much the same way the rich man of the parable thought of his retirement as the goal of life's endeavor. The young ruler was satisfied with his life as he was living it—honorable, clean, and comfortable. He was not asking any more of this present life. He wanted the best possible guarantees for the life to come, however, and was willing to make what he considered reasonable sacrifices to merit such guarantees. The last thing in the world the young man wanted was to forego completely the privileged place in this present life which his wealth guaranteed him.

From the information given us, it is easy to see that this young man had much to commend him. He was a good citizen—conservative, saving, yet generous and friendly and wholesome. If he could have been won, he would have made a fine addition to the little band of disciples; it is small wonder that the heart of the Master went out to him. Difficult though it was for this young man to see the truth, his wealth was his great enemy; it came between him and life, sheltering him in a way which also stunted him. A young man, he needed to feel the zest of life lived adventurously. Knowing the decisive choice he was setting before his questioner, Jesus nevertheless recognized that the situation was desperate and said:

One thing thou lackest; go thy way, sell whatosever thou hast, and give to the poor, and thou shalt have treasure in heaven; and come, take up thy cross, and follow me.[11]

The young man knew that if he gave his substance to the poor, he would become one with them, sharing their life without. That was indeed a cross. His love of wealth had sapped his strength; he could not lift his cross and for this reason "went away sorrowful."

One of life's greatest tragedies is to be able to see more than one has the courage to do. Certainly this young man had seen enough in Jesus to make him come eagerly to the Master for help in solving his only major problem. Yet Jesus could not bargain with him. It simply is not possible to love the privileges of wealth as this man loved them and still be kingdom of God material. It is life that counts—not possessions or luxury or social preference or power over lives of others. Jesus did not come that people might have secondary things but that they might have an abundance of the one thing which is primary—life with zest and glory.

The twelve looked on with deep concern during the dialogue between Jesus and the young ruler. They heard with amazement the terms of discipleship which Jesus set forth; and their surprise was not lessened in any degree when the Master continued:

> How hard is it for them who trust in riches to enter into the kingdom of God! It is easier for a camel to go through the eye of a needle, than for a rich man to enter into the kingdom of God.[12]

The Master was telling them once again that kingdom standards are not the same as worldly standards. Character counts infinitely more than cash. Their thoughts turned inward. *If there is no place in the kingdom for this young man,* they thought, *what about us!* So Peter said to Jesus clearly, "Behold, we have forsaken all, and followed thee; what shall we have therefore?"[13]

At first the question of Peter seems selfish and calculating, as if he were estimating whether the investment of his life was financially worthwhile. There may have been some such feeling, but it is more likely that the sobering experience with the rich young ruler had brought clearly to his mind the whole question of what the Master was seeking to teach. Evidently wealth was but an incidental consideration in kingdom affairs. He brought the whole situation into focus with his question. What he wanted to know was: "Just what are the goals of the kingdom? What are its rewards? What shall we have in return for what we have sacrificed?"

Jesus did not resent Peter's question. Instead, he reverted for the moment to the form in which they had thought of the kingdom before he came into their lives. He promised them special responsibility in that kingdom. Then, continuing, Jesus promised that their sacrifices would be blessed to their good, that those who gave up home would find many homes open to them, that those who forgot their lives in service would find the eternal life about which the young man had been so concerned. Then, clinching his argument by a story as was his custom, Jesus told about the owner of a vineyard who hired men at various times during the day but when evening came gave them all the same wages. When those who had worked from early morning complained that they had received no greater reward than those who had worked only an hour, the employer told them quite clearly that that was his business. He had done what he had agreed to do for those employed early in the day; he would do what pleased him for those employed late in the day. So also will God reward those who serve him, dealing justly with all people but adding generosity to justice wherever the circumstances may so require.

It is quite likely that when the apostles listened to this story of the householder and his vineyard, they caught the primary point: If people work honestly through the heat and burden of the day they can trust the Good Householder to see to their needs when evening comes. But the parable goes much further than this, although we must dig for its richer ore. This householder, obviously, was not seeking to get as much as possible done for his money or he would have bargained with those hired late in the day for a small remuneration. Instead, it is apparent that he felt some obligation to those who had been idle in the marketplace and who were destitute because no one had hired them. This obligation he discharged generously, reasoning that these men must live and that if they had served according to their ability they had a right to live.

It is not too much to say that in this parable Jesus pointed out a new and creative way to solve our economic problems. People who regard their wealth as a sacred trust and who therefore consider the needs of others as their responsibility can help as no lesser persons can possibly help. The rich young man needed to sell what he had and then distribute his wealth to the poor so that he would be free to follow Jesus. But the wealthy householder could perhaps serve God better by continuing to employ laborers in his vineyard, for he had the glimmerings of social conscience. He believed in a living wage for all.[14]

NOTES

1. John 10:10.
2. John 17:6-11.
3. John 15:10, 11, in the setting of John 15:5-11.
4. Matthew 6:21, 24.
5. Matthew 10:32-34.
6. Matthew 6:19-23, Moffatt.
7. Luke 12:10, KJ; 12, IV.

8. Luke 12:17, IV.
9. Luke 12:16-21, KJ; 18-23, IV.
10. Mark 10:15; Luke 18:18.
11. Mark 10:19, 20.
12. Mark 10:23, 24.
13. Matthew 19:27.
14. Admirably discussed in *The Social Teachings of the Prophets and Jesus* by Charles Foster Kent, pp. 228-238.

Study Helps for

Chapter 31

LESSON PURPOSE

To show the attitude of Jesus toward wealth and to impress the essential rightness of this attitude and its importance in our time

SCRIPTURE REFERENCES

Matthew 19:16-30; Mark 10:17-31, KJ; 15-30 IV; Luke 18:18-30; Doctrine and Covenants 56:5, 6; Mosiah 9:59-64.

HIGH POINTS OF THE LESSON

- "A man's life consisteth not in the abundance of the things which he possesseth."
- Major rewards of the labor of people of the kingdom are in their labor, and in the develpment which that labor brings in them.
- Wealth which promotes life is a great blessing; wealth which thwarts life is a major tragedy.

QUESTIONS AND DISCUSSION TOPICS

1. What is Mammon? Under what circumstances is wealth evil?

2. How does the acquisition of power and prestige change our point of view? What safeguards are available for a righteous use of prestige?

3. Explore the meaning of *covetousness.* How is it possible to covet one's own possessions? (See Doctrine and Covenants 18:3.) What does this mean?

4. If workers cannot readily change jobs, what other solutions might they find in the personal challenge of Saints? Discuss the importance of the nature of the work and their attitude toward that work.

5. What do we mean by eternal life? When do we begin to reap its benefits?

6. Why did Jesus tell the rich young man to sell his goods and give to the poor? What is the principle involved here?

7. Consider the statement of Jesus that "a rich man shall hardly enter into the kingdom of heaven" (Matthew 19:23). But note that "with men this is impossible, but with God all things are possible" (Matthew 19:26). What is the root of the problem? (Matthew 13:22).

8. What is the teaching of the parable concerning laborers in the vineyard? Relate this to the doctrine of stewardship.

WHAT THE LESSON MEANS FOR TODAY

Such qualities as industry and thrift are essential to kingdom building. So are craftsmanship, organization, management, sympathy, fraternity, patience, and other elements of good business. These personal characteristics are wealth of a high order, and have spiritual signficance of great importance.

Chapter 32

THE MIRACLES OF JESUS

Matthew tells us that soon after the experience in the wilderness, where Jesus thought through his problems with God, the Master began his public ministry and

> went about all Galilee teaching in their synagogues, and preaching the gospel of the kingdom; and healing all manner of sickness, and all manner of diseases among the people which believed in his name. And his fame went throughout all Syria; and they brought unto him all sick people that were taken with divers diseases, and torments, and those who were possessed with devils, and those who were lunatic, and those that had the palsy; and he healed them.[1]

We cannot construct a consistent picture of the life of Jesus from the Gospels if we do not take into account his miraculous powers. The narration of the miracles of Jesus is not a veneer. Miracles are included because, in the minds of the writers, they teach something of Jesus and his message. We might find some of the miracle stories hard to understand, but there can be no question of their importance to the writers of the synoptic gospels.

It is difficult to say exactly what is meant in the scriptures when reference is made to miracles. In the minds of many they refer to unusual happenings. But the distinctive nature and quality of the gospel miracles show that the saints reserved this term more and more exclusively for use in reference to happenings which are beyond the ordinary understanding of people but which are brought to pass by the power of God.

There is a theory abroad that belief in miracles is a superstition which grew up after the death of Jesus. It found place in the New Testament, according to the theory, because that was an unscientific age and people had not yet learned to distinguish between facts and fancies. As a matter of fact, nothing could be further from the truth. The most authentic record we have regarding the character of Christianity at the beginning of the Christian Era is contained in the Gospel of Mark and Mark records more miracles than any of the other Gospels. All the evidence of the Gospels themselves shows that the miraculous element in them is there because of the compelling conviction of the writers that if they told the life of Jesus as it truly was it would bear its own witness. Far from the miracles being an addition to the gospel story, they form an inseparable part of what God revealed to the world in his Son Jesus Christ; and when they are properly understood, they help us to see into the heart of that revelation. They show God at work in this world, not handicapped by the laws he has set in operation but helped by them; not a prisoner in the universe of his own creation but free to do his will just because that universe is orderly. In such a universe, life on a lower plane is responsive to life on a higher plane.[2]

Belief in God necessarily involves the expectation of miracles. Isaiah wrote:

> My thoughts are not your thoughts, neither are your ways my ways, saith the Lord. For as the heavens are higher than the earth, so are my ways higher than your ways, and my thoughts than your thoughts.[3]

By his grace the Lord leads us in ways of expanding understanding. Happenings which our forebears considered miraculous we can now duplicate. What we call "laws of nature" do not limit the power of God to act according to his wisdom, for the laws of nature are his laws. What we may call miracles are his ways of acting. As we study them, we may learn of him—of his love, his wisdom, his power. This takes time and dedication. Our full understanding may be delayed, but it is not the divine intention that the ways of God shall forever be "past finding out."[4]

Jesus appears to have regarded miracles as a normal part of his life. According to John he may have had them in mind, in part at least, when he talked of his "works."[5] Matthew regarded them as evidences of power.[6] They were often spontaneous and seemed to have no purpose beyond the situation of which they were a part. But this was not always so. Jesus said that the raising of Lazarus was "for the glory of God,"[7] and this, of course, was noised abroad. But when the telling of his miracles might distract attention from the more important aspects of the ministry of the Lord Jesus, those blessed were told not to publish what had transpired.[8]

The miracle stories in the New Testament are usually so brief that, unless we consider them carefully, we miss such deeper meanings as they may have had for the discerning. Sometimes, however, the related importance of a miracle is quite clear.

On one occasion, for example, a man who was suffering from palsy was very anxious to get to the Master in order to be healed. The press of the crowd around the house where Jesus was teaching made it impossible for anyone to enter by the doorway. The sick man had four of his friends carry him in his bed up the outer stairway and then let him down through the roof into the room with the Master. Seeing the man's faith and, as we may well presume, sensing his pentitence, the Lord said, "Son, thy sins be forgiven thee." And when one of the scribes accused him of blasphemy, Jesus continued:

> That ye may know that the Son of man hath power on earth to forgive sins (he said to the sick of the palsy), I say unto thee, Arise, and take up thy bed, and go thy way into thy house.

Here faith and healing and divine forgiveness were shown to be related to each other. To many the dramatic recital was such that they "were all amazed, and many glorified God, saying, We never saw the power of God after this manner."[9]

During the entire course of his ministry, Jesus was surrounded by disease. The vice both of the East and of the West flowed into Palestine, and the many physical ills which always accompany such conditions were apparent on every side. Insanity and demon possession, palsy, leprosy, blindness, and other diseases are mentioned in the Gospels as casually as the other commonplace incidents of the background of the times. They are taken for granted. Then, too, the widespread poverty, poor housing, primitive sanitary conditions, almost complete lack of medical knowledge, and a thousand allied factors added to the ever present burden of sickness. In such a world it was not possible for Jesus to remain aloof, and he did not attempt to do so. Instead, he went to the heart of the problem and became the greatest constructive force in the history of the healing arts.

The healing ministry of Jesus grew naturally out of his great compassion. This is illustrated by an incident that occurred soon after Jesus had completed an important preaching tour which had so impressed the Jews that many of them sought to make him their king. He wanted to be alone either for rest or meditation or for intimate personal communion with his disciples. He therefore left Galilee for Phoenicia, where he was entirely outside Jewish territory. Here one of the native women came to him with an earnest plea for her sick daughter. The solution seemed simple to one of his powers, but it was not as simple as at first appeared. His mission was to his own people, and he did not want to begin a new mission here. Besides that, he knew that if he healed the girl, other sick people of the vicinity would crowd around him with similar pleas and might defeat the whole purpose of the trip. Yet he could not withstand the appeal of the mother's great need, and her daughter was healed.[10]

One often remembered occasion when Jesus used his miraculous powers to satisfy the physical needs of people centered in the territory of Bethsaida Julias, just east of the Jordan, where the people had crowded to hear him. Giving up the rest he had sought, he preached to them until the day was far spent and they were hungry. Then he, who would not turn stones into bread to satisfy his own hunger, took five loaves and two fishes and blessed and broke and distributed them so that there was sufficient to satisfy the hunger of five thousand people.[11] There was immediate and obvious value here: the people were fed. But behind this lay much greater value, for the incident dramatized the providential love of God in a way people never forgot. The disciples were especially enlightened. They could not provide the needed food; but they could distribute that which Jesus had blessed to the multitude, and they could conserve the fragments against future needs. This Jesus allowed them to do, letting each share the tasks as fully as his strength would permit. Here, as well as years later, "he was known of them in breaking of bread."[12]

It was like the Master to use occasional situations to dramatize and impress the great lessons he had to teach. This is apparently what he did when he "rebuked the wind, and said unto the sea, Peace; be still."[13] Here again the need for his help was immediate; and for the moment the disciples saw no further than the safety they enjoyed and the power which secured it for them, saying, "What manner of man is this, that even the wind and the sea obey him?"[14] But after a time they grew in understanding and learned the inner secrets of the peace that passeth all understanding, peace that can be shared by those who put their trust in the Lord whether death is certain or is just threatening.[15]

The resolve of the Master that nothing should interfere with the perception of his true mission led him to disparage signs for their own sake. He said to the nobleman who requested that he come from Cana to Capernaum: "Except ye see signs and wonders, ye will not believe."[16] When the priests demanded a sign after the cleansing of the Temple, the only sign he would give them was the assurance of his power to restore the religion they were destroying by their secular policies.[17] When the same demand was pressed upon him in Galilee by the scribes and Pharisees, he showed his indignation at the request by describing those who made it as "an evil and adulterous generation," and by telling them that the only sign he offered was "the sign of the prophet Jonas," the call to repentance, and the threat of judgment.[18]

On the other hand, when Jesus sent his apostles into the world, he promised: "These signs shall follow them that believe."[19] The explanation for this apparent contradiction seems to be clear. When the power to do a wonderful work arises out of the rich quality of a person's ministry and is a sign of that quality, it is a very helpful confirmation of that person's acceptance with God and affiliation with divine forces.[20] But when people seek signs of a spectacular nature apart from the spiritual life which should give birth to these signs, they are separating the fruit from the root, confusing the temporary with the eternal, and falling victims to a temptation which is a constant menace against the coming of the kingdom.

Concern lest his healing ministry should become a hindrance rather than an aid caused the Master to avoid undue publicity. We have already seen this in connection with the Syrophoenician woman's daughter. He had thought this through at the time of his temptation in the wilderness; now he followed out the principle established at that time. After his fame as a healer had spread through all the regions round about Galilee and he had "healed many that were sick of divers diseases, and cast out many devils" and "suffered not the devils to speak, because they knew him," he left early in the morning for another place.[21] His compassion for their need would not let him refuse to use his great powers; neither could he permit his healing ministry to deflect him from his main purpose.

It has been said that he was like an army surgeon entrusted with an urgent and important message, who, on his way to deliver his message, was halted by the need of a man in mortal agony which he could relieve if he would take the time. In just such a situation, Jesus sought to solve his problem by urging those whom he healed to keep the good news to themselves, so that other needy ones would not crowd in to be healed and so consume the time and the energy which he desired to give to even more important work. But many were like the leper whom Jesus told:

> See thou say nothing to any man; but go thy way, show thyself to the priest [so that the man would be quite sure that he really was cleansed of leprosy], and offer for thy cleansing, those things which Moses commanded, for a testimony unto them. But he went out, and began to publish it much, and to blaze abroad the matter, insomuch that Jesus could no more openly enter into the city, but was without in solitary places.[22]

On another occasion Jesus apparently reversed this procedure; but here the situation is readily understandable. Jesus had healed a man who had been possessed and who now wished to follow him. The man could apparently be trusted to tell his friends without losing his perspective. Moreover, Jesus was about to cross to the other side of the sea and so would not be hampered by any publicity which might ensue. He therefore told the man to rejoice with his friends in the compassion of his heavenly Father.[23]

In the mind of Jesus the healing of the body was important, but it must not take precedence over the healing of the soul. The apostles were given "power and authority over all devils, and to cure diseases"; but there was specific purpose in the order of their commission which put the preaching of the kingdom of God first and the healing of the sick second.[24] Physical healing was a demonstration of the power and loving-kindness of their Father in heaven and an important preparation that the poor might have the gospel preached to them. Harassed by insanity, set apart from their fellows by leprosy, crippled by paralysis, tortured by fear and pain, these people had little reason to be receptive to the gospel of joy and peace and power until they had been restored to health and quietness. Jesus was therefore willing and glad to heal and bless them, even though he was troubled lest their joy in the lesser blessings should blind them to their need of spiritual healings. He feared that some might so rejoice in their strength that they would forget all else in their joy. It is more important to love one's neighbor than it is to be physically well.

The ministry of healing was not easy. Rather, it made demands of those called to exercise it and also on those for whom it was exercised. Jesus himself was not always able to heal. When he was in his own country he was prevented from doing many mighty works because of the unbelief of those who knew him and who perhaps because of this, could not understand either his purpose or the reality of his powers.[25] Again, Jesus healed a lunatic whom his disciples lacked faith to heal. Later he explained to them that the power to heal in critical situations such as this would require much "prayer and fasting."[26]

The saints of the apostolic age—after the resurrection—found that two miracles were basic to their own spiritual life and to their expectation of miraculous endowments for their own ministries—the miracle of the resurrection and the resulting miracle of their own faith. So Paul wrote to the Corinthians: "Now is Christ risen from the dead, and become the firstfruits of them that slept."[27] To the Ephesians he wrote: "By grace are ye saved through faith; and that not of yourselves; but it is the gift of God."[28]

When we study the New Testament record of the miracles of Jesus, there comes a time when we begin to see them as closely related to the preaching of the kingdom which, as we know, was his basic concern. The miracles and the words of the Savior centered in the kingdom of God. His words and his works are a unity. The command to preach the kingdom was never separated from the command to cast out demons and to heal the sick.

And he called the twelve, and began to send them forth two by two; and gave them power over unclean spirits. . . . And they went out, and preached that men should repent. And they cast out many devils, and anointed with oil many that were sick, and they were healed.[29]

He sent them to preach the kingdom of God, and to heal the sick. . . . And they departed, and went through the towns, preaching the gospel, and healing everywhere.[30]

Much of the ministry of the associates of the Lord Jesus was individual or by members of the seventy who traveled two by two. It is not difficult to see, however, that the basic command to heal as part of the proclamation of the kingdom is consistent with organized endeavors which were not then possible but which are now evident in the teaching missions of the Christian churches and people.

The miraculous healing powers of Jesus were inseparably connected with his remarkable personality. His own obvious physical well-being, his deep-rooted sanity, his broad interests, his joy in living were all factors bearing testimony to an underlying spiritual health which sprang from his absolute confidence in God. He did his utmost to pass on these healing powers[31] and even promised his disciples that they should surpass him in the work they should do,[32] but his most effective method of continuing these miraculous gifts was in creating people like himself in their love of God and of the common people.

NOTES

1. Matthew 4:22, 23.
2. In his *Introduction to New Testament Thought* (Abingdon-Cokesbury, 1950), p. 157, Dr. Fredrick C. Grant points out that the attempt to explain away the miraculous element in the gospels is "a hopeless one," and that this is clear from the failure of the 200 years of effort pointed in this direction. Miracles are the warp and woof of the Gospels. There the supernatural is the truly natural.
3. Isaiah 55:8, 9.
4. Romans 3:11-31.
5. John 5:37; 10:25, 38.
6. Matthew 11:21, KJ; 23, IV.
7. John 11:4.
8. Matthew 8:4; Mark 8:26, 30, KJ; Luke 5:14.
9. Mark 2:3-9.
10. Mark 7:22-28.
11. Mark 6:34-44.
12. Luke 24:34.
13. Mark 4:31.
14. Mark 4:33.
15. II Timothy 2:6-8.
16. John 4:50.
17. John 2:19.
18. Matthew 12:39-41, KJ.
19. Mark 16:16.
20. Mark 16:17-19.
21. Mark 1:25-31.
22. Mark 1:39, 40.
23. Mark 5:19, 20, KJ; 16, 17, IV.
24. Luke 9:1, 2.
25. Deuteronomy 18:15; Mark 6:6-8.
26. Matthew 17:21.
27. I Corinthians 15:20.
28. Ephesians 2:8.
29. Mark 6:9, 13, 14.
30. Luke 9:2, 6.
31. Mark 16:16-19.
32. John 14:12.

Study Helps for

Chapter 32

LESSON PURPOSE

To teach the importance of miracles in the gospel of Christ

SCRIPTURE REFERENCES

Mark 2:1-12, KJ; 1-9, IV; 6:34-46, KJ; 35-48, IV; John 4:46-53, KJ; 48-55, IV; Mormon 4:75-84.

HIGH POINTS OF THE LESSON

- The most authentic records we have of the ministry of Jesus show him working miracles out of his deep love for people and his close communion with God, but the satisfaction of physical needs, while important, was secondary to the preaching of the gospel.
- Concern lest this satisfaction of physical needs should overshadow his richer ministry was a constant factor in the public life of Jesus.
- Jesus was anxious for people to love and live the gospel so that they could enjoy eternal life and not merely immediate but temporary blessings.

QUESTIONS AND DISCUSSION TOPICS

1. What is a miracle? Is miracle-working power a unique evidence of divine favor? Name some miracles known among the Saints but often taken for granted, e.g., the miracles of understanding and of love.
2. Consider the time factor in healing. Is healing miraculous because it is quick? Name some of the lessons learned best in prolonged periods of recovery.
3. What factors were important in the healing ministry of Jesus? Are they still important in the Christian ministries of today?
4. Jesus both preached the gospel of the kingdom and healed the sick. How were these related, if at all? What values accrued to those who were healed and—in addition—were grateful?
5. What factors in our modern world make the gift of healing especially important? Consider, for example, the disruptive impact of noise and speed and labor and international strife and the preventive and healing values of the gospel.
6. The friends who brought the sick to Jesus had a minor but important part in their healing. Consider the obligation highly privileged believers have to be generous and faithful in support of healing and educational ministries among the needy.
7. There were occasions when Jesus healed a sinner and then admonished him to "sin no more, lest a worse thing come unto thee" (John 5:14). Consider this in relation to modern drug and alcoholic abuses.
8. What is the relation between faith and spiritual power? Between repentance and spiritual power? Between carrying one's share of the burdens of the needy and spiritual power? (Galatians 6:2).

WHAT THE LESSON MEANS FOR TODAY

God has wonderfully blessed us in leading the way to that conquest over ignorance which has given us power to perform many onetime miracles for ourselves. Today we witness many more creative miracles than ever before; we have become so accustomed to them that we tend to take them for granted. But there is one field still comparatively undeveloped—the field of creative spiritual achievement. Here more than anywhere we need divine guidance wedded to miraculous spiritual powers. To make ungodly persons love God and each other is still the challenge of the ages. We must experience miracles in this field or civilization is doomed.

Chapter 33

THE JUSTICE AND JUDGMENT OF JESUS

Early in his ministry Jesus laid down the revolutionary principle that people are to be judged in terms of the motives behind their deeds. Murder and adultery he made matters of desire and attitude of mind.[1] Jesus was always willing, moreover, to weigh any particular deed against the total purpose of the person involved. When the woman taken in the act of adultery was brought before him for judgment he took into account her current attitude as well as her past sins. He knew she could not escape punishment. If she continued in her old way of life, punishment was swift and sure on a purely physical plane. On the other hand, if she should become a follower of Jesus, her own remorse would be punishment in itself. So when Jesus passed judgment on this woman, he took into account the finer moral possibilities which he could quicken in her. By refusing to condemn her, he not only saved her from being stoned to death but also saved her for a better life.

This type of justice involves much more than the enumeration of failures and the measuring out of exact penalties. It involves instead an understanding helpfulness, a creative love, and an eye to future possibilities. The judgment of Jesus took into account both the individual and the act, ignoring neither but recognizing both. Because it was so comprehensive, going to the wellsprings of action in the lives of those he judged, the judgment and justice of Jesus were creative, remaking persons instead of condemning them.

This attitude brought Jesus into immediate conflict with those who thought in terms of law to be administered rather than in terms of people to be helped. The old rule of "an eye for an eye, and a tooth for a tooth" looked backward. It made no provision for helping an evil person and provided no recompense for society. In the very fact of punishing the wrongdoer, it limited that person's power to make restitution. It acted on the principle that one who had been caught doing wrong would probably do wrong again and that his or her power to do wrong should therefore be limited, even though this required limitation of the power to do right.

The Spirit of Jesus does more than maintain justice; it creates justice. It looks to the future. If present forgiveness makes for future willing justice through the awakening of spiritual responsiveness, then forgiveness becomes a part of this justice. This is difficult for many of us to understand, for we have been schooled in the idea that the evildoers must pay for their ill-doing. "Almost all things are by the law purged with blood; and without shedding of blood is no remission."[2] We have failed to realize that the remorse good persons feel because of their past sins is a much more salutary punishment than an outraged society can ever impose without their consent. When Jesus won Saul on the road to Damascus, he knew that whatever the saints might come to feel about this man, Saul, or Paul, would never forgive himself for the way in which he had persecuted the Christians, and that the desire to atone would drive Paul forward in a life of ministry enriched at every point by his appreciation of the forgiveness he had received so freely.

An age which was concerned about punishing evil-doers on the basis of retribution was also concerned about rewarding well-doers as though righteousness was a matter of bargaining with God. Peter and the disciples were concerned on at least one occasion about what their reward would be in view of their sacrifice of lesser things for the sake of the kingdom,[3] and on another occasion they quarreled concerning the places they could occupy in the kingdom.[4] It took them a long time to realize that "God so loved the world, that he gave. . ."[5] and that the first requirement laid on a true disciple is that he shall deny himself.[6] These things did not at first seem any more just than the failure to punish the woman caught in sin had seemed.

The basis of the difficulty of the contemporaries of Jesus was failure to understand the true nature of reward and punishment. These people thought of rewards and punishments as something tacked on to certain acts rather than as consequences of these acts. They had not yet realized that the most severe punishment for sin is the fact that the persons who commit sin become sinners; their wrongdoings warp their judgment, corrode their finer natures, and sear their souls. The essential reward of the righteous, on the other hand, is a clearer understanding, a finer nature, and the growth of the soul. The good way of life is its own reward. In serving God we grow like him. The idea of reward and punishment is valid only in that the advance made in either direction proceeds with constantly increasing tempo. Life builds upon itself until it is sometimes difficult to realize how directly the consequences we can observe are related to the causes which produce them. God is always eager to bless his children. When we are in touch with him the channels of divine blessing are open, and these blessings fill our lives. When we are not in touch with him these channels are closed, and every part of our life is impoverished.

Jesus taught those nearest to him that the only reward our heavenly Father desires is the love of his children. Modern revelation says: "This is my work and my glory, to bring to pass the immortality, and eternal life of man."[7] In the same spirit of sacrificial dedication, the Master prayed at the end of his life for the glory he had before the world was,[8] asking no further reward than the joy of having served humankind. It was to this kind of life and the expectation of this kind of reward that Jesus called his disciples. He taught that the greatest possible happiness could not come through possessions but through being—through growing kinship with Divinity.

Jesus promised his disciples sufficient of the material things needed for life to enable them to discharge their spiritual obligations. Other material gains come, but Jesus did not promise these rewards to the ones making the sacrifices. This might seem unjust, but it is not. It is the nature of life itself. We are so inseparably connected that every generation lives on the sacrifices of the generations which preceded it. If there is to be any progress, it must come through the sacrifice of some who build things which they can never hope to enjoy. The reward of such persons does not lie in the praise of the multitude either here or hereafter but in the fact that they become like God in living after his pattern. The treasures of eternal life which these persons build up within themselves do not corrupt and cannot be stolen.[9] All people are safe when their investments are of this type, for they cannot be robbed of the distinctive quality of their souls.

The great and inclusive reward of the righteous person is eternal life. Many of us have thought of eternal life in terms of duration—life which does not end. Jesus did not think of it this way. He thought of it in terms of quality—life lived toward God. Such life will extend into eternity, but it does not wait until death to begin. Rather it is a life of eternal quality, in which the vision and purposes of the ages are brought to bear on the problems and the opportunities of the eternal now. Most of all, eternal life is life characterized by right relationships such as Jesus lived toward God and toward people. It is a just life, the life of creative justice. In understanding the nature of eternal life we must look to Jesus, whose life has always been the light of Christians.[10] Jesus is "the way, the truth, and the life."[11] He in whom the life of Christ abides "hath life; and he that hath not the Son of God hath not life."[12]

Eternal life is redeemed from pettiness and inconclusiveness by being directed toward great and worthy ends. Such life as this cannot be hastened or pressed forward unduly. Our finest virtues are rooted deep; they spring up gradually after many days and nights and have to be watered, in all likelihood, with many tears. The fruits of the Spirit ripen slowly and come to perfection almost unaware. The judgment of Him who is eternal is part of the life of Him who is eternal; and we do not learn to exercise this judgment in relation to ourselves or in relation to others in a moment. But just because the foundations are so well laid, and the superstructure is reared under the direction of One who loves us, and for that reason works with infinite patience, there is every reason to believe that the temple of our lives will be completed—if not in time, then in eternity.

Eternal life begins here and now. It is the life of God shared by the faithful and expanding with the years, the life of the kingdom. Our first timid adventures on the higher levels of this life merge into the assurance of confidence as we learn to trust God more readily. Then we turn from careful contemplation of every step and walk boldly because we walk toward our Lord. The inner turmoil of life is quieted. Distractions lose their power. The stern demands of duty are warmed by the fellowship of love. The stiff awkwardness of spiritual adolescence passes away, and we "walk in newness of life," alert, sure, and free. Thus in time we come to pass through the doorway of death under the guidance of our great Elder Brother. Eternity has already cast its shadow before, and we are prepared and happy.

NOTES

1. Matthew 5:21-28, KJ; 23-30, IV.
2. Hebrews 9:22.
3. Luke 18:28.
4. Luke 22:24.
5. John 3:16.
6. Matthew 16:24, KJ; 25, IV.
7. Doctrine and Covenants 22:23b.
8. John 17:5.
9. Matthew 6:19, 20.
10. John 1:4.
11. John 14:6.
12. I John 5:12.

Study Helps for

Chapter 33

LESSON PURPOSE

To show that the justice and judgment of Jesus are related to persons and their possibilities rather than to arbitrary administration of the letter of the law. Jesus is more concerned about causing people to be just than about punishing them for past injustice.

SCRIPTURE REFERENCES

Matthew 5:21-28, KJ; 23-30, IV; John 8:1-11.

HIGH POINTS OF THE LESSON

- The judgment passed by Jesus took into account both the individual and the act, ignoring neither but recognizing both.
- The Spirit of Jesus does more than maintain justice; it creates justice.
- The great reward of righteous people is eternal life, which is essentially life patterned after the life of Jesus, and into this way of life people enter as they learn to do the will of God.

QUESTIONS AND DISCUSSION TOPICS

1. Why did Jesus place emphasis on motives rather than on deeds? Why was this teaching resented by the leaders of the Jews?

2. Discuss the reasons for the attitude taken by Jesus in relation to the woman accused of adultery. What are the principles involved?

3. Can sinners escape the consequences of their sins? Under what circumstances is it possible that those who are forgiven may feel worse about their sins than those who did not even ask forgiveness?

4. Consider the qualities which believers must cultivate to be just. Note the bearing of our own guilt on our judgment of others (Luke 6:41-42).

5. Read the story of the talents (Matthew 15:14-30). Note that the rewards given the faithful servants were opportunities for which these servants had prepared themselves. Consider the principle involved here and in the judgment on the unfaithful servant.

6. Eternal life has been defined as the life of God in the souls of persons. It is primarily a matter of quality, but of its own nature it points toward eternity. Comment on this.

7. Discuss the meaning of the promise of Jesus: "He that endureth to the end shall be saved." Why is no salvation promised to the person who runs well for two-thirds of the race?

8. Discuss briefly the relation between the justice of Jesus and the spirit of discernment, the practice of brother- and sisterhood, the building of the kingdom.

WHAT THE LESSON MEANS FOR TODAY

In our own inner lives we must beware the sinful thought and the unloving attitude, passing judgment on them long before they are manifest in overt acts. Moreover, we who hope for forgiveness must ourselves be forgiving. In intelligent forgiveness, free of any feeling of vindictiveness or of spiritual superiority, we shall persuade people to atone for their past injustices and to live lives of future justice. On this level we are the inheritors of the best in time and eternity.

Chapter 34

THE RAISING OF LAZARUS

Jesus went from Pera to Jerusalem to attend the Feast of Dedication, but he soon returned to resume his Perean ministry. Here a messenger from Mary and Martha reached him stating that Lazarus of Bethany, their brother, was sick. Jesus either did not understand how ill Lazarus really was or he stayed away from Bethany for some other reason. It may have been that if he had gone back with the messenger he would have been stoned,[1] and that he delayed in order to make the Jews think that he was not returning to Judea at present. Whatever the reason, the Master waited for two days. Then he overrode the objections of his disciples and set out for Bethany. By that time Lazarus was dead.

John's narrative of these events seems at first to indicate that Jesus waited deliberately in order that the death of Lazarus would create a better opportunity to show forth the power and glory of God.[2] It is a little difficult to accept this interpretation of the delay. Such a course was directly contrary to the usual procedure of Jesus, and there were plenty of other opportunities for him to demonstrate his power if he so desired. It is more likely that since other circumstances made it wise for Jesus to wait before going to Bethany he did so without undue concern, knowing that he could meet any situation which might arise.

Those nearest the Master had no doubt about what the rulers of the Jews would do to Jesus if he fell into their power. They would stone him. Now that Lazarus was dead, the journey to Bethany, therefore, seemed foolish. They tried to dissuade Jesus from going, but when he persisted Thomas found a ready response among the twelve, saying, "Let us also go, that we may die with him."[3] Afterward, when these men failed to stand by him in his hour of greatest need, Jesus must have taken a great deal of satisfaction in remembering that the disciples went with him to Bethany in spite of their fears.

Bethany was only about two miles from Jerusalem, and many of their friends had come to the home of Mary and Martha to comfort the sisters in their bereavement. When Martha heard that Jesus was near the village, she left Mary to look after the needs of these guests and went to meet him. Both she and Mary, who later joined her, had seen him heal others, and they thought that if only he could have been with them in time Lazarus need not have died. Some of the believing Jews also felt this way. Jesus was touched by their confidence in him and evidently sympathized with them. After a short delay he led the way to the sepulcher, and when he and the friends of the family had arrived he asked some of them to move the stone from the entrance. Then, lifting up his eyes, he thanked God for the power which had always attended his ministry and called Lazarus to come forth. And Lazarus, still wearing the grave clothes, came forth.

The raising of Lazarus is thought by many to be the greatest miracle performed by Jesus during his earthly ministry. It is of special interest, therefore, to note this experience in some detail. From the very beginning, when the messenger came to him in Perea, Jesus seems to have taken it for granted that Lazarus would be raised by the power of God. With this in mind, it is at first a little difficult to understand why the Master "groaned in the spirit, and was troubled" and "wept."[4] It may be that Jesus wept because he shared the deep grief of those who loved Lazarus, even though he knew this grief would soon be turned to joy. Perhaps also the tender heart of the compassionate Jesus was touched by a grief which was symbolic of the grief of many millions who were living and dying without hope because they did not know of the promise of life in Christ Jesus.

There are no words in the scripture more beautiful and more reassuring than the words of Jesus to Martha when she had confessed her belief in the "resurrection at the last day":

> Jesus said unto her, I am the resurrection, and the life; he that believeth in me, though he were dead, yet shall he live; and whosoever liveth and believeth in me shall never die.[5]

Life is not primarily a matter of time, nor even of earthly habitation, but of relationship to Christ. In him even the dead have life. To know him and to live in him is to live on a plane where death has lost its sting, the grave has lost its victory, and life is triumphant. To know Christ and to love him is to walk now in newness of life and to face all the tomorrows unafraid.

Lazarus had been dead four days. Although he was dead to this world and to his sisters and his friends, he must have lived somewhere. Otherwise his coming forth would have been in fact a new creation. The Lazarus who came forth from the tomb was not a new man but was the brother Mary and Martha had known and loved, the dear friend of Jesus. He had been away, but even though body and spirit had been separated they had not been blotted out in extinction. When the spirit and the body were reunited, Lazarus came forth to pick up the threads of life where they had been laid down—a living testimony to the fact that life goes on elsewhere after it has ceased here.

Although Lazarus had been raised from the dead, he was still subject to the threat of death. The return of Lazarus from the grave was a visible demonstration of the power of Jesus in the realm of the departed, but he had not been resurrected in the sense in which the

Master was to be resurrected a short time later. Lazarus needed to be called forth, since he had no power of life within himself. When the Lord Jesus came forth, he did so of himself, saying: "I lay down my life, that I might take it again."[6] Jesus, our Lord, is the only one strong enough to go into the house of death and there bind the master of the house and liberate those held prisoner.[7]

Many sages have recognized the raising of Lazarus as a parable as well as a miracle, for here is a living illustration of the power of Christ in the lives of people. Only that power can call forth the higher self which is buried within every one of us.

Rigid I lie in a winding-sheet
  Which my own hands did weave;
My narrow cell is my self—my self,
  Whose wall I may not cleave.

But in the dawn of the early morn
  A clear Voice seems to say:
"I am the Lord of the final word—
  Ye may not say me nay.

"Unfold your hands, that your brother's need
  May ever find them free.
Unbind your feet from their winding-sheet,
  Henceforth they walk with me."

And lo, I hear! I am blind no more!
  I am no longer dumb!
Out from the doom of a self-wrought tomb
  Pulsate with life I come!*

Such a miracle as the raising of Lazarus could not be ignored. "Many of the Jews which came to Mary, and had seen the things which Jesus did, believed on him. But some of them went their ways to the Pharisees, and told them what things Jesus had done."[8] The Pharisees recognized the situation as critical, more critical than it had ever been before. It is possible that if Jesus had been willing to use force to win national independence for the Jews, many of these leaders might have followed him. This Jesus would not do, and so the

*Author unknown.

politically minded Sadducees and the bigoted and worldly Pharisees decided against him. They were afraid that the adoration of the crowd would lead them to start a messianic movement which could not succeed, and that this would give the Romans an excuse for despoiling the country and removing the Jewish leaders from their places of authority. "If we let him thus alone," they said, "all men will believe on him; and the Romans shall come and take away both our place and nation."[9] Caiaphas, the ruthless high priest, was determined there should be no revolt. Refusing to take any risks, and undeterred by the injustice involved, he stated that it was better than one man should die for the people rather than that the whole nation should perish.[10] By such specious reasoning he became the leader of those who were determined Jesus must die.

Jesus was keenly aware of the fate which lay ahead of him. He was quite willing to seal his testimony with his life's blood when the time for doing so should come. But he was determined to select the time and place to suit his own purposes so that his sacrifice would mean all that it could possibly mean to this people. Driven by this determination, and by his eagerness to make every available moment count in the further instruction of his disciples, Jesus retired from Jerusalem to Ephraim, about four miles northeast of Bethel, and "walked no more openly among the Jews."[11] He was about twenty miles from Jerusalem, but the secret of his hiding place was so well kept that Jesus remained unmolested until the time for the Passover drew near, notwithstanding the fact that the chief priests and the Pharisees had virtually set a price on his head and on that of Lazarus.[12]

NOTES

1. John 11:8.
2. John 11:1-45.
3. John 11:16.
4. John 11:33-35.
5. John 11:25, 26.
6. John 10:17.
7. Matthew 12:29, KJ; 24, IV.
8. John 11:45, 46.
9. John 11:48.
10. John 11:50.
11. John 11:54.
12. John 11:57.

Study Helps for

Chapter 34

LESSON PURPOSE

To show that the hope of resurrection centers in Jesus

SCRIPTURE REFERENCES

John 11.

HIGH POINTS OF THE LESSON

- The faithfulness of the disciples in following Jesus into danger at Bethany.
- The present significance of the Resurrection.
- The power of God manifest in the resurrection of Lazarus.
- The wicked determination of the rulers of the Jews in spite of this miracle.
- The prudent retreat of Jesus until his own plans were mature.

QUESTIONS AND DISCUSSION TOPICS

1. What are the possible reasons why Jesus did not at once go to Bethany so as to be near Lazarus in his sickness?

2. What was the attitude of the twelve at this time? With what later attitude is this in striking contrast? Why were the twelve faithful at Bethany and less faithful at Jerusalem?

3. Why did Jesus weep at the news of the death of Lazarus? Note Doctrine and Covenants 36:6-8 in this connection.

4. What is the meaning of the statement of Jesus; "I am the resurrection, and the life"?

5. What is the significance of the resurrection of Lazarus in relation to life beyond the grave?

6. What was the reaction of the Pharisees and Sadducees to the raising of Lazarus? Why did they take this attitude? What light does this throw on their request for a sign of the divine authority of Jesus?

7. What did Jesus do under these circumstances? Why? What lesson is there here for us?

8. It is probable that many of the friends of Jesus died during his lifetime. Why did he not raise more of them?

WHAT THE LESSON MEANS FOR TODAY

There are times when all of us feel that it is useless for us to struggle longer to overcome the habits which seem to kill all hope of higher life. We need the help of a power greater than our own which makes for righteousness. Such power is available for us much as it was available for Lazarus. The voice of God is calling today. It is for us to decide whether or not we will respond.

Chapter 35

THE TRIUMPHAL ENTRY

When the time for the Passover drew near, Jesus went toward the Holy City by way of Jericho and Bethany. The steep highway was crowded with pilgrims going to the feast. A feeling of crisis was in the air. The news of the raising of Lazarus was being told everywhere and so was the reaction of the chief priests and the Pharisees. Would Jesus come to the feast? If he did come, what would he do? What would the chief priests do?

Prior to this time Jesus had avoided public proclamation of his messiahship, since the people did not realize what kind of deliverer he was. It was quite likely that if they believed him to be the Messiah they would add to his difficulties by trying to crowd him into doing what their preconceived notions of the Messiah led them to expect him to do. Nevertheless, he had prepared the way for them to understand, if they would, by three years of patient, affectionate, and soul-searching ministry. When he had healed their minds and their bodies, he had sought to make these things serve as a prelude to even deeper and more significant healing. At this time, therefore, when to go forward meant death and to go backward meant the defeat of his purpose, Jesus determined to announce his messiahship publicly, but to do so in such a way that those with eyes to see should see and those with ears to hear should understand.

When Jesus and his disciples came near to Bethany, he sent Peter and John to borrow a colt. The animal was secured. Since no saddle was available, the disciples spread their cloaks upon it and seated Jesus there. In this way the Master rode into Jerusalem, not richly caparisoned as an earthly king would have been but nevertheless deliberately fulfilling the prophecies of Isaiah and of Zechariah:

> Rejoice greatly, O daughter of Zion; shout, O daughter of Jerusalem; behold, thy King cometh unto thee; he is just, and having salvation; lowly, and riding upon an ass, and upon a colt the foal of an ass.[1]

No Jew versed in the scriptures of his race could possibly misunderstand. Nor did they. Jesus was taking his life in his hands by announcing for all who looked on that he was indeed the expected Messiah, entering his capital city as the Prince of Peace.

The word that Jesus was coming was passed ahead along the road. As the Master and his small company came down the steep highway toward the city, the pilgrims spread their garments in the road and cut palm branches and spread them in the way. At this display of enthusiasm, certain of the Pharisees asked Jesus to rebuke the people, but "he answered and said unto them, If these should hold their peace, the stones would immediately cry out."[2] What a condemnation of their own lack of response.

In his story of the triumphal entry, John tells us that "these things understood not his disciples at the first."[3] By "these things" John may have meant the Master's decision to make a clear statement of his messiahship, which was unmistakable even though it was symbolic. Or he may have been alluding to the present inability of the disciples to understand fully why Jesus would not lead the Jews in their fight for political freedom. Or, again, it may have been the whole rapidly changing situation. At least it is not difficult to see that events were moving so quickly that it was hard for even the disciples to fully appreciate what was taking place. Only when they looked back from the other side of the Resurrection, when additional evidence plus the ministry of the Spirit had laid more sure foundations for insight, did they see truly. For the present, they did not realize that

Jesus could do nothing as a political or social liberator that would be enough. It was his business to lead the fight against oppressors but not merely against Roman oppressors. To enter Jerusalem as a conqueror might dethrone Caesar, but Jesus' task was to do much more than this. He must lay such a claim on the hearts of people that they would enthrone him of their own free will as the Lord of righteousness. Of course they did not understand these things at first. That kind of insight takes time and inspiration.

After Jesus had ridden into the city amid the acclamations of the crowd, he went to the Temple that he might complete the symbolism of his living parable. He was a king, but since he was not an earthly king he was not going to a king's palace. His place was in the Temple, the center of the spiritual life of his people. The Roman soldiers who were looking on must have accepted this as a further evidence that what was happening was of religious significance and no concern of theirs; apparently they made no attempt to molest Jesus. From their worldly point of view, the picture of a king coming into his capital city as Jesus had done evoked amusement and ridicule rather than a call to punitive action.

When evening drew near the Master returned to Bethany where he could stay overnight with his friends and be reasonably secure from molestation. On the next day he came again to the Temple. There was a strange contrast between the two visits. On Palm Sunday he came as the Prince of Peace, but on the day following he came in hot indignation to cleanse the Temple of those who made it a place of merchandise instead of a house of prayer.[4] The money changers and the sellers of doves had been operating by direct connivance of the rulers of the Temple and by virtue of this support were becoming rich by plundering the poor. It was the worst type of public graft—graft made effective through religion. The two visits seemed entirely different, yet there was a definite relation between them. Now that Jesus had publicly announced himself as the Messiah, and had thereby proclaimed his moral right to direct the worship of the Temple, it was imperative that he should disassociate himself forever from the graft flourishing there. It was especially important that he take his stand with the prophets in proclaiming the unfailing concern of God with righteousness, justice, and equity, without which sacrifice is meaningless.

There was another reason also why Jesus must act. His repeated proclamation that he came as the Prince of Peace must not be understood to mean that in renouncing political power he was renouncing spiritual authority.

While many have seen in this cleansing of the Temple an abandonment by Jesus of his principle of moral suasion, the force which he used was moral rather than physical. The fire of his indignation was made powerful by the rightness of his cause rather than by any physical strength he himself might put forth. He gave voice to the conscience of the nation and thereby denounced all religion which condones injustice and all spiritual authority which neglects its social obligations. It is hardly to be wondered at that the Sadducees, who were directly involved in this temple traffic, afterwards joined with the Pharisees to see that this man who threatened their vested interests should be put out of the way.

The period which followed the cleansing of the Temple was one of intense activity in the life of the Master and was reported in greater detail than any similar period. This may be attributed to the fact that the events took place in Jerusalem, the home of Mark, who is our chief source of information regarding them. It is evident that during this week Jesus made no attempt to compromise; he recognized that the chief priests and scribes and Pharisees were determined to "reject the counsel of God against themselves" and acted accordingly. Teaching every day in the Temple, he indicated that his rejection by the official leaders of the Jews would not stop his work but would cause God to turn from those who had rejected his Son. The kingdom would be taken from them "and given to a nation bringing forth the fruits thereof."[5] The stone which was rejected by the "builders" (those who were supposed to know all about stones and building) was to be made the very cornerstone of the new temple.[6]

The Jewish rulers, meanwhile, were doing their utmost to trap Jesus into some act or statement which would undermine his popularity with the people. First, they questioned his authority. In an adroit rebuttal Jesus challenged them concerning the authority of John the Baptist. When they refused to meet this challenge, he refused to present his own credentials. Yet his very challenge allied him in the minds of the people with John, whom they knew was sent from God and had authority from heaven.[7]

Returning to the attack, the Pharisees asked, "Is it lawful to give tribute unto Caesar, or not?"[8] The Master saw immediately that this was but a ruse to force him to take sides in the conflict between Romans and Jews, and again he met their adroitness with a genius which outdid them, saying, "Render therefore unto Caesar the things which are Caesar's; and unto God the things that are God's."

Still undaunted, the Sadducees came to him with an involved question about marriage in the resurrection, and once again Jesus was equal to their sophistry. Without becoming entangled in the trick question, he laid down a principle which is of vital importance in meeting abstruse questions of theology. He said, "God is not the God of the dead, but of the living."[9] This is equivalent to saying that our heavenly Father will guide us wherever we are, in this life or in the next, leading us in ways appropriate to the life we are living and to be understood and justified on that plane of life rather than any other.

Yet once more the Pharisees sought to undermine him. This time one of them, a lawyer, asked him, "Master, which is the great commandment in the law?" And once again Jesus used their question to make the truth stand out in vivid clarity: "Thou shalt love the Lord thy God with all thy heart, and with all thy soul, and with all thy mind. This is the first and great commandment. And the second is like unto it; Thou shalt love thy neighbor as thyself."[10] Nothing could have emphasized more effectively how far the Pharisees had fallen short by insisting on the minutiae of the law and forgetting the "weightier matters" of righteousness and justice and equity. It is small wonder that "no man after that durst ask him any question."[11]

NOTES

1. Zechariah 9:9; see also Isaiah 62:11 and Matthew 21:4, 5.
2. Luke 19:39.
3. John 12:16.
4. Matthew 21:12-17, KJ; 10-15, IV; Mark 11:15-19, KJ; 17-21, IV; Luke 19:45-48, KJ; 44-47, IV.
5. Matthew 21:43, KJ.
6. Psalm 118:22; Mark 12:11; Acts 4:11.
7. Matthew 21:23-27, KJ; 21-25, IV; Luke 20:1-8.
8. Matthew 22:17; Mark 12:16; Luke 20:22.
9. Matthew 22:31.
10. Matthew 22:35-38.
11. Mark 12:34, KJ; 40, IV.

Study Helps for

Chapter 35

LESSON PURPOSE

To emphasize the primary importance of Jesus' work as Messiah. He had to minister to the deepest needs of people. He could do this as Prince of Peace but not as the conqueror whom his people expected.

SCRIPTURE REFERENCES

Matthew 21:1-9; Mark 11:1-12; Luke 19:28-43; John 12:12-19.

HIGH POINTS OF THE LESSON

- The dramatic announcement of his messiahship conveyed in Jesus' deliberate fulfillment of the prophecies of Isaiah and Zechariah.
- The impossibility of ending oppression by killing the oppressors.
- The moral passion of Jesus shown in his cleansing of the Temple.
- The great commandment.

QUESTIONS AND DISCUSSION TOPICS

1. Why had Jesus avoided clear public proclamation of his messiahship prior to this time? What preparation had he made for this proclamation? Why did he now make the clear announcement?

2. Why did Jesus ride into Jerusalem as he did? Why did the Jews welcome him so tumultuously?

3. Describe the cleansing of the Temple. Why did Jesus do this at this time? How effective do you think he was in ending the graft he denounced? What permanent effects did his action have?

4. What is the meaning of the statement, "The stone which the builders rejected, the same is become the head of the corner"? On what occasion was this quotation from the Psalms used to confound the leaders of the Jews?

5. What is the meaning of the statement of Jesus, "Render therefore unto Caesar the things which are Caesar's; and unto God the things that are God's"? Does this leave anything for Caesar? What?

6. Discuss, briefly, the statement of Jesus that "God is not the God of the dead, but of the living."

7. What is the great commandment of the law? How had the life and teachings of Jesus made this a new commandment? (John 13:34).

WHAT THE LESSON MEANS FOR TODAY

The practice of Christianity calls for such self-discipline as was exemplified in the life of the Master. The conflict with evil must be pursued adroitly and persistently, with the campaign plan for personal life and for the life of the church carefully and prayerfully mapped out. But the weapons of our warfare are not carnal. They center in the revelations of God, taught with intelligence and administered in love. The Prince of Peace, our leader, is not ineffective because he believes in the way of love. He is strong to teach, to endure, and to win. Though we accept him at first for lesser personal reasons it is our faith and hope that we will come in time to accept him for himself.

Chapter 36

THE REJECTION OF THE JEWS

In the century preceding the birth of Jesus the Pharisees were the most powerful religious group among the Jews. The word "Pharisee" means "separatist," and these men sought to keep themselves separate from everything which did not conform to the Law of Moses and the oral law which had been developed in connection with it. Under them the Law of Moses had been interpreted in detailed statutes. It governed every aspect of life and set up standards which the common people could never expect to attain. There were many admirable men among the Pharisees; but as a group they were narrow, bigoted, and intolerant. Although they did not lack genuine religious sentiment, they laid heavy burdens on the shoulders of the common people and gave them no help in carrying these burdens. They conformed to the requirements of the law but did so to be seen publicly rather than out of zeal for the truth; they coveted places of honor but had made a graft of religion.[1]

The position of the Pharisees was such that if they had welcomed the Master, the common people would have followed their example. Jesus knew this, and sought to win them both for their own sakes and for the sake of the people, avoiding public clashes with them as long as he possibly could. When Jesus came to Jerusalem for his last Passover, all hope of cooperation had vanished. Indeed, by this time the Pharisees were convinced that Jesus was a public menace, and they were openly seeking to destroy him and the work he was doing. During the Passion Week this conflict became evident to all who came to the Temple.

The criticism passed by Jesus upon the Pharisees

centered in their attitude toward God and religion.[2] Jesus taught that God was the Father, to be obeyed through love. The Pharisees[3] taught that God was primarily the Lawgiver, to be obeyed through fear.

The public denunciation of the Pharisees by Jesus came to a climax in his pronouncement of seven "woes" or statements of disapproval directed against their character and conduct. This denunciation is important to us today since it indicates those things which the Lord hates in any society, ancient or modern. These are as follows:

Supposedly spiritual leadership which actually obstructs the way into the kingdom[4]

Proselyting which converts people to an institution but not to God[5]

Rationalization which obscures the truth[6]

Obedience to part of the law as an excuse for disobeying the remainder of the law[7]

Emphasis on ceremonial cleanness as a substitute for inner rightness[8]

Hypocrisy under the guise of religion[9]

Worship of the past to distract attention from the inquities of the present[10]

Because they had forgotten the word of the prophet that mercy is greater than sacrifice, the Pharisees had turned religion into a sham. They were hypocrites, play actors deceived by their own mummery, blind leaders of the blind.

If we can catch the mood of the Master as he so scathingly denounced the leaders of his own people, we shall find that his indignation is associated with a deep regret. He was not upbraiding these men because of what they had done to him, nor because of what they were about to do. His concern was that they who might have led others into the full sunlight of truth had loved darkness rather than light, and so had condemned a nation to darkness at the same time they condemned themselves. After these denunciations Jesus turned his back on the Pharisees, but in that same mood of deep regret he looked over Jerusalem and cried out:

> O Jerusalem! Jerusalem! Ye who will kill the prophets, and will stone them who are sent unto you; how often would I have gathered your children together, even as a hen gathers her chickens under her wings, and ye would not. Behold, your house is left unto you desolate! For I say unto you, that ye shall not see me henceforth, and know that I am he of whom it is written by the prophets, until ye shall say, Blessed is he that cometh in the name of the Lord.[11]

It was probably later in the day on which the foregoing incidents had occurred, and while Jesus was still in the temple enclosure, that certain Greeks came to Philip and asked him to introduce them to Jesus.[12] It is known that the Prince of Egessa sent an emissary to Jesus asking him to come to Egessa; it is probable that it was for this purpose that these Greeks now wished to see Jesus. Certainly this situation involved much more than a passing interest, for when Philip and Andrew came to Jesus to ask him to see the Greeks, Jesus answered, as if in protest,

> The hour is come, that the Son of man should be glorified. . . . Now is my soul troubled; and what shall I say? Father, save me from this hour; but for this cause came I unto this hour. Father, glorify thy name.[13]

It is not unlikely that the disquietude of the Master lay in his knowledge that these men were offering him a way out, that they came with an invitation to abandon the Jews who as a people had never caught the real import of his message and whose leaders had rejected him. Dr. Stanley Jones says:

> The Greeks were asking him to love his life and save it, and thus save others; they were asking him to bless without believing. But he knew it could not be done. It is small wonder that, when Jesus refused to see these men, in order that he might complete his testimony in his martyrdom, a voice from heaven recognized his offering and strengthened him for what lay ahead.[14]

This day in the Temple was significant in that it marked an important stage in the transition from acclamation to condemnation which occurred between the triumphal entry of Jesus into Jerusalem and his arrest. This transition took place, fundamentally, because Jesus refused to accept the leadership of the nation on the terms proposed and expected by the people. It was this which brought him into his final conflict with the rulers of the Jews. His denunciation of these leaders of the religious life of his people was not an outburst of passionate resentment; it was a proclamation of eternal judgment. Judaism had been weighed in the balance and was found wanting. Although some of the rulers and some of the Pharisees believed in him, the nation as a whole had rejected him as it had been prophesied that they would.[15] In rejecting Jesus they had rejected God and the life eternal which he was eager to share with them. They could not escape the judgment which involved such a rejection.[16]

As Jesus left the temple enclosure, sad at heart because of what had transpired there, some of his disciples commented on the marvelous beauty of the temple building.[17] The Temple was indeed a structure of unparalleled external splendor. At the time of Jesus it had been forty-six years in rebuilding, and it was still unfinished.[18] The stones of which it was constructed were notable for their size and their beauty. All the cloisters of the Temple were double, and each of the pillars of the cloisters was one stone of white marble, twenty-five cubits in height.[19] Notwithstanding all this splendor, the beauty of the Temple was intended only to symbolize the beauty and grandeur of the overshadowing presence of God. Without this divine presence the Temple was just a building of imposing appearance, not essentially different from any other building. But if the glory of God did indeed rest upon this house, then it was unique—of far greater value than any other building, no matter how beautiful or how well situated it might be.

Throughout his lifetime Jesus had loved the Temple. It is not unlikely that as he left its sacred courts for this last time he remembered with poignant emotion the visit he had paid to it twenty years before and the happy days spent in conversation with the doctors and learned men. Since then Jesus had taken advantage of many opportunities to visit the Temple and to share with others the sense of the immediate presence of Divnity which the devout Jews found there. Now the rulers of the Jews had rejected him and were seeking to kill him. They still offered sacrifices in the Temple, but now these sacrifices no longer pointed to the truth they had been instituted to symbolize.

All this was in the background of his consciousness as the Master replied to the comments of his disciples concerning the beauty of the Temple. The Temple had served its spiritual purpose, and it had no other reason for existence. The Master said, "Seest thou these great buildings? There shall not be left one stone upon another, that shall not be thrown down."[20] Those who heard were dumbfounded. The Temple was the center of their national life and the symbol of their national genius. They believed that it was divinely protected and that its destruction could have no significance except that it had been rejected by God. Truly, Jesus was leaving no room for misunderstanding or for compromise. For the moment, however, what he had said was but a prediction which was particularly hard to believe. It was nearly forty years later that the prophecy was literally fulfilled in the complete destruction of the Temple by the Roman legions under Titus. By that time many of the leaders and the people who had rejected Jesus were dead.

The Jews of the generation of Jesus had inherited a great destiny. Their children inherited a barren hope.

NOTES

1. Matthew 23:1-7, KJ; 1-4, IV; Mark 12:38-40, KJ; 45, 46, IV; Luke 20:45-47.
2. See *New Standard Bible Dictionary,* p. 703.
3. Galatians 2:3-5; 5:1; 6:13; Romans 8:14-15; II John 1:7.
4. Matthew 23:13, KJ; 10, IV.
5. Matthew 23:15, KJ; 12, IV.
6. Matthew 23:16, KJ; 13, IV.
7. Matthew 23:23, KJ; 20, IV.
8. Matthew 23:25, KJ; 22, IV.
9. Matthew 23:27, KJ; 24, IV.
10. Matthew 23:29-31, KJ; 26-28, IV.
11. Matthew 23:37-40.
12. John 12:21.
13. John 12:23, 27, 28.
14. See John 12:28.
15. John 12:37-40.
16. John 12:44-50.
17. Matthew 24:1; Mark 13:1; Luke 21:5.
18. John 2:20.
19. Josephus, *Jewish Wall V,* chapter 5.
20. Mark 13:2, KJ.

Study Helps for

Chapter 36

LESSON PURPOSE

To make clear the spiritual lack which forced the Master to turn from the Jews

SCRIPTURE REFERENCES

Matthew 21:12-17; Mark 11:15-19, KJ; 17-21, IV; Luke 19:45-48, KJ; 44-47, IV; 21:37, 38; John 2:13-22.

Matthew 23; Mark 12:38-40, KJ; 45, 46, IV; Luke 20:45-47; John 12:37, 38.

II Nephi 11:20-25; Jacob 3:26-28; IV Nephi 1:34.

HIGH POINTS OF THE LESSON

- The failure of the leaders of the Jews because of their inadequate understanding of the nature of God.
- The woes pronounced against the Pharisees by Jesus.
- The refusal of Jesus to go with the Greeks
- The destruction of the Temple and its significance.

QUESTIONS AND DISCUSSION TOPICS

1. Who were the Pharisees? What were their good points? Why were they found in opposition to Jesus?

2. In your own words restate each of the "woes" pronounced by Jesus on the Pharisees. Relate each of them to modern conditions.

3. What was the mood of the Master as he pronounced these woes on the Pharisees? Why did he turn from doing so to lament over Jerusalem?

4. Why was Jesus so disquieted by the visit of the Greeks at this time? Why was it not possible for him to go with them and leave the Jews to their fate?

5. Why did the Jews abandon their earlier enthusiasm for Jesus? What was the effect of their changed attitude on the life of the nation? What was its effect on the future of the Jews?

6. What was the distinctive glory of the Temple at Jerusalem? Why did Jesus utter his prophecy of the destruction of this Temple at this time? What was the significance of this destruction?

7. In what sense were the Jews rejected? For a time practically all the members of the church were Jews. Consider Pentecost in this connection (Acts 2:36-41).

WHAT THE LESSON MEANS FOR TODAY

Although the rejection of the religious leaders of the Jews became more and more evident with the passing of the years, the lessons of her history and the words of the prophets and psalmists were treasured in the apostolic church. But they were now seen in light of the continuing purpose of God in Christ.

Chapter 37

SIGNS OF THE END

Toward evening on Tuesday of Passion Week after Jesus had foretold the destruction of the Temple he and the twelve set out for Bethany. The Master must have been worn with the strain of his crowded days in the Holy City, and as the little party crossed the Valley of Kidron and began the ascent of the Mount of Olives Jesus sat down to rest, looking back toward the Temple which was so clearly visible a short distance away. While he was resting, Peter, James, John, and Andrew came to him privately and asked him when the destruction of the Temple would come to pass and what would be the sign of his coming and of the end of the world.[1]

These days had been difficult for the disciples as well as for their Master, and the prophecy concerning the Temple had been the most amazing declaration of an astonishing week. Could it be true, they wondered, that the Temple would actually be destroyed? And if it was true, what would this mean? They were still very human and resented the opposition of the leaders of the Jews; they felt very much as had James and John when these two wished to call fire from heaven on the Samaritans who refused to receive Jesus.[2] One thing seemed certain to them: The destruction of the Temple would be an incontrovertible sign of the wrath of God against the people who had rejected the Messiah. The disciples thought that such a sign, naturally would be followed by the coming of Jesus in triumph, and that this would end the age.

Jesus did not answer the questions of his disciples immediately. Instead he sought to lift them above any desire for vengeance on the Jews and to open their understanding concerning the future and the part they were to play in it. To this end he pleaded with them to build toward a stable faith, saying, "Take heed that no man deceive you."[3] Their hour of triumph was not as near as they had supposed. Before that day was to come, many imposters were to rise and deceive many; there were to be wars and rumors of wars; there were to be famines and earthquakes and pestilences. Moreover, the apostles themselves would be hated and persecuted and killed.[4] Many weaker disciples would stumble, and with the increase of iniquity the love of many would wax cold. Yet, regardless of these many trials, the Master promised that those who remained faithful would have great power in their personal ministry; they would stand before governors and kings without fear;[5] through them the gospel would be preached in all the world, and those who endured to the end would be saved.[6]

The predictions of the Master were fulfilled in surprising detail. Within a few years the emperor Caligula issued a decree requiring that his statue be set up and worshiped in the Temple. The Jews protested so vehemently that war was declared against them, although actual hostilities were averted by the death of the emperor. Threats of war were renewed by both Claudius and Nero.[7] There were many local enmities. Famine and pestilence stalked abroad and were particularly deadly in Palestine.[8] Earthquakes occurred with alarming frequency and unusual severity, particularly in Syria, Macedonia, Campania, and Achaia.[9]

In commenting on the persecutions which Jesus prophesied would overtake the apostles and other disciples, Dr. Adam Clark says: "We need go no further than the Acts of the Apostles for the completion of these particulars." Some were delivered to councils, as were Peter and John.[10] Some were brought before rulers and kings, as was Paul before Gallio,[11] before

Felix,[12] before Festus and Agrippa.[13] Some had utterance and wisdom which their adversaries were not able to resist, such as Stephen[14] and Paul, who made even Felix himself tremble.[15] Some were imprisoned, as were Peter and John.[16] Some were beaten, as were Paul and Silas.[17] Some were put to death, as were Stephen[18] and James, the brother of John.[19]

The prophecy concerning the coming of false prophets was also fulfilled in great detail. Prominent among these false prophets were Simon Magus, who drew many people after him;[20] Menander, Dositheus, Theudas, Hymenaeus, Philetus, the false apostles referred to by Paul;[21] and others. Under these conditions the love of many did, in fact, wax cold, and the great apostasy had set in before the last of the apostles ceased his earthly ministry.

Jesus said that the gospel of the kingdom should be preached "in all the world" and, according to Mark, this was to precede the destruction of Jerusalem.[22] The Inspired Version of the scriptures renders Mark's account so that it harmonizes with the account given by Matthew, and in both the order of events is so rearranged that the preaching of the gospel of the kingdom is predicted as one of the signs of the end of the world. As a matter of fact, the gospel of the kingdom was preached throughout the then known world before the destruction of Jerusalem. Paul, writing about thirty years after the ascension of Jesus, affirmed that the gospel had already been carried to every nation, and "preached to every creature which is under heaven."[23] In the present widespread proclamation of the gospel, this prophecy of the Lord Jesus is having a second fulfillment.

Continuing with his answer to the question of the four apostles, Jesus told them that after the wars and persecutions which lay immediately ahead of them would come "the abomination of desolation, spoken of by Daniel the prophet."[24] Daniel's phrase means literally, "that which maketh desolate." In the connection in which it was used by the prophet the word which is translated *abomination* strictly means "image of a false god." What the author of Daniel had in mind was that the Temple would be desecrated by setting up a heathen idol, or by the worship of false gods there, and that this desecration would make Israel desolate. In the day of Jesus Daniel's phrase had come to mean the major spiritual catastrophe of an age. When Jesus said that the "abomination of desolation" should come to pass, the Jews understood him perfectly. In reporting him, both Matthew and Mark used this phrase and knew that the Jews would understand. Luke could not be sure that his Gentile hearers would know what the phrase meant, and he substituted for it the clear-cut warning, "When ye shall see Jerusalem compassed with armies, then know that the desolation thereof is nigh."[25] Jerusalem was taken by the Romans in September, A.D. 70. Before the Temple was destroyed the Roman ensign was set up inside the temple court, and the Roman soldiers offered sacrifices there.

It is obvious from the question of the apostles that they thought the destruction of the Temple would be quickly succeeded by the triumph of the Lord Jesus and the end of the era. In the answers of the Master which we have so far studied, Jesus made it clear that the scepter should "depart from Judah" now that the Messiah (Shiloh) had come and had been rejected.[26] The end of the period of Jewish preeminence would be clearly marked by the destruction of the Temple. But destruction of a temple or of a people cannot establish the kingdom of God which is born of righteousness.

The Master, therefore, continued his answer to their question beyond the "abomination of desolation. . .concerning the destruction of Jerusalem,"[27] and showed that many of the things which he had said would come to pass before this great national calamity would be duplicated thereafter on a much larger scale. False christs and false prophets were again to arise and show great signs and wonders;[28] wars and rumors of wars were again to multiply; nations were again to raise against each other; famines, pestilences and earthquakes would yet again carry the universal unrest into the realm of nature; and because iniquity would again be rife, the love of many would wax cold. But there is an affirmative note to the prophecy concerning this later period: In that day shall the Lord send forth "his angels, and shall gather together his elect from the four winds, from the uttermost part of the earth, to the uttermost part of heaven."[29] In that day—when worldly people are eating and drinking and marrying and giving in marriage but when others have heard the preaching of the gospel in all the world and have been gathered together under the guidance of Divinity—then shall the Lord come indeed, and the end of the age shall be ushered in.

The surprising forecast of events which the Master gave in reply to the question of his disciples immediately gave rise to a further question which, although unspoken, was nevertheless very important: If the day of their triumph was to be so long delayed, what should be the attitude of believers? Jesus had already indicated his answer in part, saying, "He that shall endure unto the end, the same shall be saved."[30] Now the Master went on to elaborate by pointing out that the specific date of the culmination of all things is not revealed.[31] The end will come unexpectedly and will find people busy with the ordinary affairs of life and unconcerned regarding the approach of the day of culmination.[32] Under the circumstances the faithful must watch for the end and must live in full expectancy of its coming no matter how long it may be delayed. The keynote was "What I say unto you, I say unto all, Watch."[33]

In order to emphasize the importance of unwavering diligence, the Master reinforced his teaching with the story of the ten virgins, five of whom were wise and five foolish. It is to be noted that these were all persons who anticipated the coming of the "bridegroom," yet half of them were shut out from the wedding feast because they had been lulled to sleep by the postponement of the great event and so had not made adequate preparation. Later Jesus gave them another parable addressed to the same basic problem. While the parable of the ten virgins had emphasized the need for watchfulness, the parable of the talents emphasized the need for intelligent activity on the part of the faithful.[34]

Jesus concluded his teaching at this time by emphasizing the absolute certainty of judgment when the end of the age shall come.[35] He had already taught them much about the importance of clear thought and sound belief. He had permitted them to serve him in the ordinances of the gospel. Now, in picturing the judgment, he showed that clear thought and sound belief and obedience to the ordinances have as their end a new way of life whose keynote is brotherhood and sisterhood under God. In the judgment, he said, the sheep shall be divided from the goats according to the measure of their conformity to those standards. Those who serve Jesus, serve others; those who serve others in his way serve Jesus. Thus from the far reaches of his prophetic vision, in which he bridged the centuries from that day to the end of time, the Master returned to the essence of his message for his disciples in every age: "Inasmuch as ye have done it unto one of the least of these my brethren, ye have done it unto me."[36]

NOTES

1. Matthew 24:3, KJ; 4, IV; Mark 13:3, 4, KJ; 7, 8, IV; Luke 21:7.
2. Luke 9:54.
3. Matthew 24:4, KJ; 5, IV.
4. Matthew 24:5-12, KJ; 6-10, IV; Mark 13:5-9, KJ; 9-11, IV; Luke 21:8-11.
5. Mark 13:9, KJ; Luke 21:12-15, KJ.
6. Mark 13:13; Matthew 24:13, KJ; 11, IV.
7. See Josephus, *Wars,* II, Ch. 10.
8. Josephus, *Antiquities,* XX, ch. 2; see also Acts 11:29.
9. See Tacitus, *Annals,* Books XII and IV; Josephus, *Wars,* IV, ch. 4.
10. Acts 3:1; 4:1-7.
11. Acts 18:12.
12. Acts 24.
13. Acts 25.
14. Acts 6:10.
15. Acts 24:25.
16. Acts 4:3.
17. Acts 16:23.
18. Acts 7:59.
19. Acts 12:2.
20. Acts 8:9, 13, 18-24.
21. II Corinthians 11:13.
22. Mark 13:6. See Mark 13:10, KJ.
23. Colossians 1:23.
24. Matthew 24:15, KJ; see also Daniel 9:27; 11:31; 12:11.
25. Luke 21:20, KJ, 19, IV.
26. Genesis 49:10.
27. Mark 13:14, IV.
28. Matthew 24:24, KJ; 23, IV; Mark 13:22, KJ; 25, IV.
29. Mark 13:27, KJ; see also Mark 13:44, IV.
30. Matthew 24:13, KJ; Mark 13:13.
31. Matthew 24:36, KJ; 43, IV; Mark 13:32, KJ; 53, IV.
32. Matthew 24:38-44; Mark 13:33-37, KJ.
33. Mark 13:37, KJ; Luke 21:36.
34. Matthew 25:14-30.

35. Matthew 25:31-46.

36. Matthew 25:40, KJ; 41, IV.

Study Helps for

Chapter 37

LESSON PURPOSE

To show that the major signs of the culmination of our age will be the preaching of the gospel and the gathering of the people of God, and to emphasize the obligations which these facts impose

SCRIPTURE REFERENCES

Matthew 23; 24; Mark 13; Luke 21:5-8.

HIGH POINTS OF THE LESSON

- The exact nature of the prophecy of the Master concerning the coming of the end.
- The early fulfillment of this prophecy in many details.
- The more complete fulfillment of the prophecy in the latter days, including the emphasis on worldwide preaching of the gospel and the gathering of the people of God.
- The certainty of judgment
- The intervening period of preparation and of expectation.

QUESTIONS AND DISCUSSION TOPICS

1. What did the apostles anticipate would happen very shortly after the destruction of the Temple at Jerusalem? What spiritual factors had they failed to consider in thinking of the future?

2. What immediate safeguards did Jesus attempt to build into the lives of the apostles? What evidence do we have that some of the disciples anticipated an earlier return of the Lord than was justified by his counsel?

3. What were the major events prophesied for the future? Around what two events was the fulfillment of these prophecies centered?

4. Which of these prophecies were fulfilled prior to the destruction of Jerusalem?

5. What was meant by the "abomination of desolation"? What additional light is thrown on this phrase by its use in the Inspired Version of the Bible?

6. Which of the prophecies of Jesus were to be fulfilled at a later date than the destruction of Jerusalem? What are the distinctive signs of the coming of this latter day?

7. What is the central teaching of the parable of the ten virgins? How should this parable be applied to our present spiritual needs?

8. What is the central teaching of the parable of the sheep and the goats?

WHAT THE LESSON MEANS FOR TODAY

Jesus answered the question of his disciples concerning the signs of his coming and of the end of the world in a way which was intended to prepare them to play their parts in the drama of early church life which was to unfold in the near future. They were to be stable and yet expectant, doing what they could without fear or doubt no matter what might happen, and yet confidently looking forward for the Lord to do his part. We have been warned of the crucial nature of our own age for the same reason. History is repeating itself on a larger scale than heretofore. We have every inducement to be faithful to our commitment.

Chapter 38

JUDAS

When Jesus entered Jerusalem in triumph, the twelve seemed to feel that at last their mission was beginning to be successful. Then, as the implacable opposition of the chief priests and the scribes and Pharisees became more and more apparent, the hearts of these friends of the Master again grew troubled. The rejection of Israel and the prophecy of the destruction of the Temple and of the coming days of woe probably affected each one of them differently, but all of them were sad.

One of the twelve appears to have been more distressed than any of the others. This was Judas, a Judean even more aggressively eager for the deliverance of his people than the rest of them who were all Galileans.

Judas was treasurer of the little group and probably something of a businessman. As we meet him in the Gospels, we have the feeling that he was a man of the world without being especially worldly; that he was practical, hardheaded, impatient with idle dreaming, and yet something of a dreamer himself. Separated a little from the others, Judas meditated on the events of the Passover week. He knew that the chief priests and scribes were eager to arrest Jesus and to execute him but afraid that the people might rise in his defense. He pondered this, too. Then he agreed to deliver Jesus to the chief priests.[1]

We do not know, of course, why Judas betrayed Jesus. Nevertheless, it is almost impossible to avoid conjecture about an act which ever since has been the symbol of the blackest treachery. The very name of Judas is a byword for treachery.

The most obvious and most widely accepted explanation of the treachery of Judas is that he was greedy. Some of the twelve thought this was at least a contributory cause. In telling the story of the anointing of Jesus in the house of Simon the leper in Bethany, Mark said:

> There were some that had indignation within themselves, and said, Why was this waste of the ointment made? For it might have been sold for more than three hundred pence, and have been given to the poor.[2]

John, who loved Jesus, did not report the matter in this general fashion. John said,

> Then saith one of his disciples, Judas Iscariot, Simon's son, which should betray him, Why was not this ointment sold for three hundred pence, and given to the poor? This he said, not that he cared for the poor; but because he was a thief, and had the bag, and bare what was put therein.[3]

If greed was indeed the reason for the betrayal, how significant the many warnings Jesus had uttered against covetousness must have seemed when considered with Judas as an example. It was probably the experience of the Master watching as Judas weighed the contents of the bag he carried as treasurer which prompted him to say,

> Provide yourselves bags which wax not old, a treasure in the heavens that faileth not, where no thief approacheth, neither moth corrupteth. For where your treasure is, there will your heart be also.[4]

It has also been suggested that a major cause for the treachery of Judas was jealousy. Coming from Judea, which was the stronghold of the purer and stricter influences in the religious life of the Jews, he naturally did not always see eye to eye with the Galileans who came from an area which was notoriously liberal in religious thought and therefore less highly regarded by the strict Jews. We have a hint of the weight of such matters in the minds of these men when we remember that Nathanael, whom Jesus described as "an Israelite indeed, in whom is no guile," said to Philip, "Can there any good thing come out of Nazareth?"[5] Against this background it does not seem unlikely that Judas, the man of affairs, entrusted with the business concerns of the group, was deeply resentful over the preference given to Peter, James, and John and, at times, to Andrew and Philip. If this conjecture has any foundation, then Judas was probably especially hurt when Jesus rebuked him at the time of the anointing by Mary at Bethany. Even so great a betrayal might well have been occasioned by a mild rebuke added to buildup of resentment. We have a parallel in modern times. High in the arches of the great hall at West Point there are shields bearing the names and records of men who have defended the United States with special distinction. Only one shield lacks an inscription, the shield which once bore the name of Benedict Arnold. It is said that Arnold became a traitor at heart on the day Washington was forced to discipline him for some minor infraction of military rules. Arnold was wrong and the reprimand was mild, but he went away bitterly resentful. In time this resentment became his master and dominated him, until one day he who had once stood with the notables of his generation woke up to find himself a traitor.

A third possible cause for the disloyalty of Judas might have been his disillusionment. Even at the close of his earthly ministry, the disciples nearest the Master were only beginning to awaken to the fact that the kingdom Jesus intended to inaugurate was in truth the kingdom of God and not just a refinement of the kingdoms of this world; that it was different in quality and not just in power. It is suggested that Judas may have followed the Master in the hope that the kingdom of God would prove to be a kingdom imposed by the power of God but not essentially different from the other kingdoms of that day; and that in this kingdom important places would be available for those who had been with Jesus from the beginning. If this is so, then it is probable that Judas, who was still keenly aware of the marvelous qualities of leadership Jesus possessed, sought to precipitate a situation which would force Jesus to take a public stand before the opportunities of the Passover gathering had been lost. One writer says:

> It was this apparently that Judas did. His mind may still have been drawn between disappointment and a tempestuous hope. There was still a chance that he might not have been wrong, still the chance that Jesus had the power to call such forces to his side as would rout his enemies. The only way to prove that was to force Jesus' hand; to put him into a position where, if he could act, he would have to act. Then if he did not deliver himself and vindicate his leadership, he deserved whatever happened. He had been a false claimant of messiahship, and those who had followed him had been deceived. What wrong was it then to let him die?[6]

Any of these reasons may have been the true one, but it is much more likely that the cause prompting Judas to treason was a combination of several or all of them. Certainly no one of them by itself seems to explain his moral decline and debacle. Greed, for example, is not a complete explanation, for Judas could have absconded with the treasury at any time. Or, if money was his chief concern, he could have bargained with the chief priests for much more than the thirty pieces of silver usually paid for a common slave. Whatever the reason, explanations may help us to understand but they must not lead us to condone. Judas was a man of ability who was capable of responding to the highest challenge. Notwithstanding this, he permitted the spirit of evil to possess him even when his Lord was depending on him.[7] If we are ever to believe in the freedom of the will, then we must believe that at some point during the period of his apostleship Judas chose to nourish in his own inner life those forbidden things which came in time to possess him. He did not start out to be a traitor; he merely started out to have his own way. His inner life was such that he had betrayed his Lord in spirit long before he did so in fact.

The compact between Caiaphas and Judas by which

Jesus was betrayed was utterly inexcusable on both sides. Caiaphas promoted the lowest type of disloyalty in the name of the public good: He was a grafting politician who happened to hold a position of spiritual authority. Judas took money to betray his Master with a kiss and was even more to be condemned than Caiaphas, for his intimacy with Jesus increased his responsibility. The height to which Judas had climbed determined the depth to which he fell.

The heart of the Master must have been very sore as he watched Judas losing his battle for his own honor, but the only thing Jesus could do was to keep on trying to deflect Judas from his wicked purpose. In the final analysis he must leave the right of self-determination with each individual. So the traitor chose to betray his Lord, and Judas "went immediately out; and it was night."[8]

NOTES

1. Matthew 26:1-5, KJ; 1-4, IV; Mark 14:1, 2, 10, 11, KJ; 1-3, 31, 32, IV; Luke 22:1-6.
2. Mark 14:4, 5, KJ.
3. John 12:4, 5.
4. Luke 12:33, 34. See also 12:36, 37.
5. John 1:46, 47.
6. Walter Russell Bowie, *The Master,* p. 269.
7. Luke 22:3.
8. John 13:30.

Study Helps for

Chapter 38

LESSON PURPOSE

To analyze the temptations which betray people and lead them to betray the Lord Jesus. To build defenses against these insidious evils.

SCRIPTURE REFERENCES

Matthew 26:1-5, 14-16; Mark 14:1, 2, 10, 11, KJ; 1-3, 31, 32, IV; Luke 22:11-23.

HIGH POINTS OF THE LESSON

- The wickedness of covetousness.
- The high cost of pride and jealousy.
- The sin of holding resentment.
- The responsibility which comes with opportunity.

QUESTIONS AND DISCUSSION TOPICS

1. Why did the disciples follow Jesus at first? How did their reasons for following him change as they came to know him better?
2. As Judas became better acquainted with Jesus, how did his changing concepts lead to tragedy?
3. Discuss greed as a possible cause of the betrayal of Jesus by Judas. Note the bearing of the doctrine of stewardship on the sin of covetousness. Why does Paul call covetousness idolatry?
4. What evidence is there that Judas may have been jealous? If jealousy is evidence of insecurity, what factors might have caused Judas to feel insecure? How may pride and jealousy be overcome?
5. It may be that Judas did not want the kingdom of God when he found what it would be like. What is the difference between wanting the kingdom and wanting only the benefits of the kingdom? What is the difference between wanting to live on the basis of sacrificial love and wanting merely to enjoy the pleasant fruits of fellowship?
6. Jesus said that one who is unclean in thought is an adulterer. In view of this principle, when did Judas betray his Lord? Discuss the statement that no one starts out deliberately to betray; he or she merely starts out on the road which leads to that betrayal.
7. Why was Judas particularly wicked in betraying Jesus? Discuss the principle that opportunity increases responsibility.
8. Since Jesus understood Judas, why did he not restrain him? Why could he not pray for Judas to be forgiven?

WHAT THE LESSON MEANS FOR TODAY

We betray the Master whenever we are untrue to the best that we know. None of us can afford the luxury of excusing ourselves in "small" sins. Now is the time for all to judge themselves as God judges them and to eliminate all taint of evil. Spiritual surgery is sometimes essential to spiritual lifesaving.

Chapter 39

THE LAST SUPPER

Celebration of the Passover was essentially a family affair. The association between Jesus and the twelve was so close, however, that it seems to have been taken for granted that they would eat the Passover together in Jerusalem. When the time for the feast approached, Peter and John asked Jesus where they were to eat the meal. It seems a little strange that this detail had not been arranged and communicated to the group before this time. This may be explained by the desire of Jesus to keep the information from reaching his enemies by way of Judas. Now that the time had come, Jesus instructed his two disciples that when they reached the city they would meet a man bearing a pitcher of water. On the way they probably would pass several women with pitchers, but to see a man with a pitcher was sufficiently unusual to be a means of identification. This man they were to follow until he led them to the place appointed. Christian tradition has it that the house was the home of Mary, mother of John Mark.

As a rule preparations for the Passover were quite elaborate and were governed by tradition. Having arranged for the place of meeting in harmony with the instructions of Jesus, Peter and John secured the lamb for the evening meal. They took it to the priests within the temple courts where it was killed and flayed and the blood poured at the foot of the altar of sacrifice. Then the lamb was roasted and the bitter herbs, the sauce, and the unleavened bread prepared and taken to the room for the meal.

On Thursday evening, as we reckon time, but after sunset and therefore at the beginning of Friday according to the Jewish calendar, the little company came together in the upper room. For Jesus, particularly, the occasion must have been one of deep emotion. Throughout the centuries since its institution, the Passover had looked backward to the deliverance of the children of Israel from Egypt and forward, in a dramatic prophecy, to the sacrifice of the Son of God for the redemption of all people. It is probable that not many realized this double significance of the meal, but certainly Jesus did. He knew that before the time for the annual feast came round again, the prophecies of the Passover would be fulfilled and he would have become in fact "the Lamb of God, who taketh away the sin of the world."[1]

His deep emotion found expression in his statement, "With desire I have desired to eat this passover with you before I suffer: For I say unto you, I will not any more eat thereof, until it be fulfilled in the kingdom of God."[2]

Luke indicates the beginning of the Passover meal, when he tells us that Jesus received the cup and gave thanks and divided among his disciples.[3] This implies that the Passover meal took the usual course, but no details are given. From nonbiblical sources we are told that this course was about as follows:

The blessing of the first cup of wine.
Hand washing and prayer.
Bitter herbs, dipped in a mixture of fruit and vinegar, passed and eaten.
The second cup of wine with the question, "What mean ye by this service?" and the answer, "It is the sacrifice of the Lord's passover, who passed over the houses of the children of Israel in Egypt, when he smote the Egyptians, and delivered our houses."[4]
Singing of the first part of the hallel.[5]
The "sop" dipped in vinegar and eaten.[6]
The eating of the paschal lamb.
The eating of a piece of unleaven bread.
A third cup of wine with a prayer of blessing.
The fourth cup of wine.
The blessing in song.[7]

At some point in the meal—we do not know just when—some contention arose among the disciples as to which of them was the greatest.[8] Jesus joined in the conversation to point out that, as he had taught them so many times before, earthly leaders exercise dominion over those under them, but the great ones of the kingdom of God are the servants of all.[9] Jesus now gave force to his lesson of humility by girding himself with a towel, washing his disciples' feet, and wiping them on a towel. Most of the disciples received this ministry in abashed silence, but when the Master came to Peter, that disciple felt so utterly unworthy that for a time he refused this service from the Lord. Then, when Jesus insisted, Peter swung from one extreme to the other, welcoming both the washing of his feet and the admonition of Jesus that the disciples, who were surely no greater than their Master, should serve each other in similar humility and goodwill.

The Passover meal was usually eaten in quiet solemnity, but there was a feeling of more than usual sadness during this particular meal. It was occasioned in part by the kindly rebuke of the Master who had just acted as their servant when they had contended with each other for the chief place. Even more significant was the presence of Judas, whose heart must have been filled with forebodings. Jesus knew Judas; he looked into his heart and read his wicked purpose. If Jesus had said outright what was happening, it is highly probable that Peter and the others would have restrained Judas from carrying out his contract with the chief priests. The Master preferred not to do this. While Judas sought to hide his true intention, the Master pleaded with him, in a way which was clear to the traitor even though it was not understood by the twelve, to abandon the course he had set for himself before it was too late.

Paul has given us the oldest account of the Last Supper.[10] From this and from the Gospel narratives it seems that the Passover meal and Jesus' washing of the disciples' feet were before Jesus instituted what has come to be known as the Lord's Supper. Paul says that

> the Lord Jesus, the same night in which he was betrayed, took bread; and when he had given thanks, he brake it, and said, Take, eat; this is my body, which is broken for you; this do in remembrance of me.[11]

Our Roman Catholic friends have laid great stress on the fact that the Master said, "This *is* my body." On this foundation has been built the doctrine of transubstantiation according to which the sacramental emblems, when properly blessed by the priest, become in fact the broken body and the spilled blood of the Lord Jesus. This hardly seems to be required by the record. Jesus was still with them, and his body was not yet broken nor was his blood spilled. The bread and the wine were emblems. They were eaten in a simple but deeply impressive dramatization of what was actually taking place that night. They were to be eaten through the years that were yet to come in solemn remembrance of an offering far more costly and far more significant than the Passover.

Paul states that the Master asked his disciples to partake of the bread and wine in remembrance of his self-sacrifice on behalf of those he loved. The bread and the wine were readily available and commonplace food, yet now they were to be forever charged with new and significant meaning. The thought of communion, which is derived from sharing in a common meal and of participating together in the blessings which flow from discipleship, is an important part of this remembrance, but it is not the most important part. The most significant aspects of the memorial are typified in the breaking of the bread, the pouring of the wine, and the giving of these emblems to the disciples. In the early church this was so clearly realized that the breaking and the pouring were given special prominence.

While the supper partaken of under such solemn circumstances initiated a great memorial feast, it also typified the consummation of a great covenant. The wine, in particular, was a symbol of the blood which hitherto had been sprinkled on the Book of the Law and on the people to be a witness of the covenant between God and them.[12] The whole figure of the new covenant established between God and people and written in their hearts had been foreseen in the prophecy of Jeremiah:

> Behold, the days come, saith the Lord, that I will make a new covenant with the house of Israel, and with the house of Judah; not according to the covenant that I made with their fathers, in the day that I took them by the hand to bring them out of the land of Egypt; which my covenant they brake, although I was a husband unto them, saith the Lord; but this shall be the covenant that I will make with the house of Israel; After those days, saith the Lord, I will put my law in their inward parts, and write it in their hearts; and will be their God, and they shall be my people. And they shall teach no more every man his neighbor, and every man his brother, saying, Know the Lord; for they shall all know me, from the least of them unto the greatest of them, saith the Lord; for I will forgive their iniquity, and I will remember their sin no more.[13]

With such a background as this, a meal instituted in the atmosphere of tragedy and betrayal has nevertheless come to suggest triumph through heroic self-sacrifice and discipleship made strong through the love of God.

When the meal was over, Judas slipped quietly away; with his retirement the prevailing gloom was lifted a little and Jesus talked more freely. At last the disciples were beginning to understand, and the Master was able to discuss what was nearest his heart. "Let not your heart be troubled," he said. "Ye believe in God, believe also in me."[14] Here the Master completely identified himself with his Father and continued by telling his disciples that he was going ahead of them to prepare the way for them in a world which lies beyond this present earthly life. He described himself as the way, the truth, and the life, saying, "No man cometh unto the Father, but by me."[15] No man ever made such claims and then supported his claims with such credentials as Jesus brought. Dimly the disciples sensed this. If their hearts had recognized the truth of what Jesus said they would not have been so utterly desolate when, later, his word seemed to be contradicted by his crucifixion.

With the horrors of his humiliation and crucifixion looming large in the immediate future, Jesus still concerned himself about these poor, weak men and the maturing of their understanding. He told them they must live in such intimate relationship with him that they would derive their life from him as the branches derive their life from the vine. He told them for the first time that they must pray the Father in his name.[16] He called them friend rather than servants.[17] He promised them that in the days to come they would do even greater things than he had done, being inspired and directed and strengthened by another Comforter who should be to them all that he had been in his visible bodily presence. Even while he reminded them of his great love, he announced also the certainty of judgment.[18]

And so, speaking plainly at last, Jesus led the disciples forth into the night, deeply concerned and yet strangely comforted.

NOTES

1. John 1:29.
2. Luke 22:15, 16, KJ; note the different rendering in the Inspired Version.
3. Luke 22:17.
4. Exodus 12:26, 27.
5. Psalms 113, 114.
6. The "sop" was a piece of paschal lamb and bitter herb in bread.
7. Psalms 115, 118. This is reproduced from *The Life of Christ,* by I. B. Burgess, p. 249. Used by permission of University of Chicago Press.
8. Luke 22:24.
9. Luke 22:25-27.

10. I Corinthians 11:23-30.
11. I Corinthians 11:23, 24.
12. Exodus 24:6-8.
13. Jeremiah 31:31-34.
14. John 14:1.
15. John 14:6.
16. John 14:14.
17. John 15:13-15.
18. John 15:19-25.

Study Helps for

Chapter 39

LESSON PURPOSE

To indicate the nature of the Lord's Supper and its place in the history and practice of the church.

SCRIPTURE REFERENCES

Mark 14:12-26, KJ; 10-27, IV; Luke 22:14-30; John 13:1-30; 14-17.

HIGH POINTS OF THE LESSON

- The Passover meal as a prelude to the Lord's Supper.
- The washing of the disciples' feet by Jesus.
- The institution of the memorial supper.
- Subsequent conversation with the disciples.

QUESTIONS AND DISCUSSION TOPICS

1. Who made the preparation for the Passover? What were the preparations? Why were these preparations kept secret?
2. What event did the Passover commemorate? To what event did it look forward? Why did Jesus approach this meal with such deep emotion?
3. Describe the course of the Passover meal. What do we mean by "unleavened bread"? What was the prevailing tone at this Passover?
4. Over what point did contention arise during the meal? How did Jesus meet this problem? What was the reaction of Peter? What was the significance of this ceremony?
5. What is the essential Roman Catholic doctrine concerning the Eucharist (Communion)? Discuss this briefly.
6. What is the primary significance of the sacrament of the Lord's Supper? What is the relation of the idea of communion to this primary significance? What is the purpose of the breaking of bread and the pouring of wine in this service?
7. Discuss the sacrament in relation to the new covenant. What is the "new covenant"?

8. What important teaching was communicated to the disciples after they had partaken of the Lord's Supper? What great promise did Jesus give to them? What illustration did he use to indicate the relationship of the disciples to himself?

WHAT THE LESSON MEANS FOR TODAY

The sacrament of the Lord's Supper is still our central act of worship. Its effectiveness depends on the qualities of heart and mind of those who participate. The requirement that we shall not partake of this sacrament unworthily, however, is not a requirement that those who have lost the spirit of loving shall not partake. It is a requirement that they shall regain the spirit of loving in order that they might partake.

Chapter 40

THE ARREST AND TRIAL OF JESUS

When Jesus and the eleven crossed over the brook called Kidron and began the ascent of the Mount of Olives it was quite late, and the strain of the evening's activities superimposed upon those of the preceding week was beginning to tell on every one of them. After a while they came to the Garden of Gethsemane. Leaving eight of the disciples there, Jesus went farther among the olive trees with Peter, James, and John and asked them to wait for him. Then he went still farther into the garden, fell on his face, and sought his Father for the strength he so much needed. Meanwhile the disciples dozed fitfully, but John caught the words of the prayer of the Master and preserved them for us.[1]

Jesus prayed that he might not be required to drink the bitter cup being prepared for him. This prayer was not primarily a petition but an exploration of the mind of God regarding the demands of the situation. His trial and crucifixion would involve a long and horrible experience for Jesus and one almost as horrible for those who loved and trusted him. He shrank from this experience for his own sake and for theirs. Yet he wanted to do the will of the Father even more than he wanted to escape the agony of Calvary. So he prayed that if there was any way of escape which did not involve betrayal of his trust it should be made clear to him. If there was no other way, he was ready to go forward to mockery and to death.

We must not think of Jesus during these crucial hours as an actor, waiting for his cue and knowing both the lines he was to say and the climax toward which the drama was tending. It is true that he knew much of what lay before him. There was not much doubt that if he did not escape at this time, he would be sacrificed to the malignant hatred of the rulers of the Jews. He knew also of the resurrection and of the life beyond; he had discussed these things with Moses and Elias on the mount of transfiguration[2] and with his disciples. But there must have been some element of faith in his response to the challenge of this crisis. Otherwise his prayer in Gethsemane would have been without meaning. He was still a man; as a man he faced the future with assured faith but without that certain knowledge which would have made him an automaton.

There was still a chance for Jesus to save his life. He must not delay long, however, for Judas had been gone for some time and would soon come back with the emissaries of the high priest. Three of the Master's friends were within a few feet, and eight more were near the gate of the garden. These could be relied on for help. But if Jesus saved himself his cause would be lost. If he saved his life now, no matter where he went he would have to abandon his crusade or start afresh. He could not abandon his cause, and to start afresh, with another people, was unthinkable. That would mean giving up all that God had prepared among the Jews in forty generations—their passionate monotheism, their scriptures, their hope of the kingdom, their expectation of the Messiah. The Jews had not received him, in spite of what God had done by way of preparation; but the other nations had nothing. The Jews were of Israel, and any new Israel which was to be brought into being must have a historic and spiritual connection with the Israel of the past, which had been blessed of God through so many centuries.

All this, and infinitely more than we can imagine, must have been in the heart and mind of Jesus as he faced with his Father the unalterable facts of his situation. He was in agony, but surely his agony was not primarily because of the physical pain that confronted him; it lay rather on what was gathered up in this moment. Repudiated by the Pharisees, unwanted by the people, betrayed by one of his disciples and followed hesitantly by the others, Jesus was confronted by the most cruel death that human barbarity could devise. The situation, nevertheless, did hold promise at one point: His death might speak to people with a commanding authority which they had been quite unwilling to recognize in his life. It was because of this that he was able to pray, "Not what I will, but what thou wilt." In so doing Jesus was no mere teacher; he was the Master and Savior.

It was not far from the place where Jesus and the apostles had partaken of the Lord's Supper to the palace of the high priest and from there to Gethsemane. Much time had already been consumed in conversation and in prayer since Judas had left the upper room. Jesus could not have been long in the garden, therefore, when Judas arrived. He was accompanied by a group of the servants and dependents of the high priest and of the temple police, carrying torches and armed with swords and staves.[3] Judas had already agreed with these that he would point out Jesus by kissing him. This he did. The use of a kiss as the means of betrayal seems to have shocked Jesus,[4] but he made little protest save to remind the officers that he had been in the Temple daily and that there was no need for them to come after him as though he were a thief.[5] "Then all the disciples forsook him, and fled."[6]

Jesus was first led to the house of Annas, the ex-high priest and the father-in-law of Caiaphas. This man was still one of the most influential men in the Jewish heirarchy; and since Annas was directly involved in the public graft which Jesus had condemned, he was personally interested in seeing that the plot against the life of Jesus was carried through successfully.[7] The inquisition in the house of Annas had no legal warrant; it was resorted to as a preliminary which might reveal the line of defense Jesus would follow. The conspirators knew that the hearing before the Sanhedrin would have to be managed adroitly. Public sympathy could easily be swung once more in favor of Jesus; if this should happen, the corrupt rulers would be in a worse situation than before. Now that the investigation had begun, it must succeed at all cost.

John seems to have had ready access to the home of the high priest, and his influence probably admitted Peter. But there was no doubt of the attitude of those gathered inside. In such an atmosphere the braggadocio of the stormy fisherman soon evaporated. He was out of his element, bewildered and afraid. He would have been glad to fight for Jesus, but the air of legality in what the chief priests were doing unmanned him. Questioned by the doorkeeper and by the officers, he first blustered and then finally denied his Lord. Reminded by the cock's crow that even his denial had been anticipated by Jesus, he "went out, and wept bitterly."[8]

While all this was going on, Jesus was being mocked and derided by the soldiers who had him in their custody.[9] Then, when daylight was fully come, he was taken before the assembly of the "elders of the people and the chief priests, and the scribes."[10] It is possible that some members of the Sanhedrin, such as Nicodemus, still strongly favored Jesus. On the other hand, the leaders and most of the members of the council were bitterly antagonistic. These were already convinced of the guilt of the Master, and because of their influence and their determination to make a case the proceedings were highly irregular. Lacking witnesses sufficient to secure an indictment, they sought to have Jesus incriminate himself.

The Master remained silent as long as he could, but when they demanded to know whether or not he was the Christ he could not keep silent any longer. His silence would be interpreted as cowardice or as an admission of the charges. He was not the Christ of their expectations and might have answered their questions to this effect, but if he had done so his statement would have been published abroad as a complete repudiation of his ministry and teachings. An affirmative answer would leave him open to a charge of blasphemy and, what was more important in the eyes of the Romans to whom Jesus would be sent for sentence, it could be construed as a prelude to nationalistic revolt. So Jesus answered to the effect that he was indeed the Christ but that his vindication would have to come at the hands of God. This was enough. It gave his accusers a basis on which they could take him before Pilate, the Roman governor, and this they did.[11]

When Jesus entered the judgment hall of Pilate, there was little to indicate the crucial nature of the moment. To Pilate it seemed that here was just another trivial case brought before him by these troublesome Jews; he would have laughed aloud had someone hinted that he, even more than the "pale Galilean," was awaiting judgment. There *was* something of nobility in the quiet dignity of the man who stood accused, but that Jesus was indeed what he claimed to be seemed incredible.

The first charge, an obviously false one, was that Jesus had perverted the Jewish nation.[12] The next—and much more important from the viewpoint of the Romans—was that he had commanded the Jews not to pay tribute to Caesar. This was a deliberate distortion of the facts; Jesus had taught them to "render therefore unto Caesar, the things which are Caesar's; and unto God the things which are God's."[13] The third charge—

well calculated to arouse the suspicion of Pilate and one which his superiors would expect him to investigate carefully in the interests of Rome—was that Jesus claimed to be a king. Before the Sanhedrin this charge had been blasphemy. Before Pilate it was insurrection. It was this third charge to which Pilate gave attention.[14] Jesus did not look like a zealous nationalist who would stir up the people against Rome, and his quiet answers to the questioning of Pilate confirmed this impression. Jesus did not deny that he was a king, but he went on to explain that whereas other kings were born to exercise dominion he had been born to bear witness of the truth. His kingdom was in the realm of the spirit. The Romans had a philosophic interest in such matters, but they did not take them seriously. Pilate therefore acquitted Jesus of the charge of insurrection, saying, "I find no fault in this man."[15]

Like most Roman officials, Pilate probably preferred to act justly. He was determined to succeed, however, and ruthless as to the manner of his success. When he saw that his decision was displeasing to the Jews and gathered from their outcries that Jesus was from Galilee, he therefore sought to shift the responsibility for decision from his own shoulders by sending Jesus to Herod. This was an adroit political move. Herod was pleased to have this opportunity to see Jesus and to have his own authority recognized at the same time,[16] but he was too wily to accept responsibility. After some questioning, which Jesus knew to be pointless and to which he did not deign to reply, Herod and his soldiers "set him at naught, and mocked him, and arrayed him in a gorgeous robe, and sent him again to Pilate."[17]

The charges brought against Jesus were so flagrantly unjust that even now Pilate was reluctant to condemn him. Thinking to satisfy the rulers of the Jews, he offered to have Jesus scourged and then release him.[18]

Finding that this would not satisfy them, he remembered the tradition according to which the governor was accustomed to release one prisoner a year at the time of the great feast, at the request of the Jews, and he offered to release Jesus. This would have been equivalent to finding the Master guilty and then giving him a pardon. But the Jews were implacable. Stirring up the people, they refused Pilate's offer and instead cried out for Barabbas, who was awaiting execution for sedition and murder. Left with the clear choice between dealing fairly with Jesus and being unfavorably reported to Rome, Pilate hesitated no longer. He washed his hands publicly as a token that he disclaimed responsibility and delivered Jesus to be crucified. So, repeating the age-old alliance between politics and the venal administration of justice, Pilate gave sentence. Jesus was condemned, robed in purple garments, mocked, and led away to be executed.[19]

NOTES

1. Matthew 26:36-44, KJ; 33-41, IV; Mark 14:35-39, KJ; 39-44, IV; Luke 22:41-44; John 17.
2. Luke 9:30, 31.
3. Matthew 26:47-56, KJ; 44-54, IV; Mark 14:43-52, KJ; 48-57, IV; Luke 22:47-53; John 18:1-12.
4. Luke 22:48.
5. Matthew 26:55, 56, KJ; 53, 54, IV; Mark 14:48, 49, KJ; 54, 55, IV; Luke 22:52, 53.
6. Matthew 26:56, KJ; 54, IV; Mark 14:50, KJ; 56, IV.
7. John 18:12-14.
8. Luke 22:54-62; John 18:15-18, 25-27; Matthew 26:69-76; Mark 14:66-72.
9. Luke 22:63, 64.
10. Luke 22:66.
11. Luke 22:67-71.
12. Luke 23:2.

13. Luke 23:2; Matthew 22:21.
14. Matthew 27:11; Mark 15:2, KJ; 3, IV; Luke 23:2, 3.
15. Luke 23:4; John 18:37, 38.
16. Luke 23:12.
17. Luke 23:11.
18. Luke 23:16.
19. Matthew 27:26-31, KJ; 28-33, IV; Mark 15:15-20, KJ; 18-23, IV; Luke 23:25; John 19:16.

Study Helps for

Chapter 40

LESSON PURPOSE

To narrate the circumstances of the arrest and trial of Jesus in such a way as to remind us that public graft induced by blindness and prejudice still crucifies the Christ

SCRIPTURE REFERENCES

Matthew 26:36-65; 27:11-14; Mark 14:33-64; Luke 22:39-71; 23:1-16; John 18; 19:1-16.

HIGH POINTS OF THE LESSON

- The prayer of Jesus in the garden.
- Why Jesus refused to escape.
- The attitude of the apostles.
- The charges in the trial before Pilate.
- Pilate's impossible attempt to be neutral.

QUESTIONS AND DISCUSSION TOPICS

1. Where was the Garden of Gethsemane? Which of the disciples went there with Jesus? What positions did they take up in the garden at the suggestion of Jesus? What did they then do?

2. What were the main characteristics of Jesus' prayer in the Garden? Enumerate these and note the significance of each of them.

3. If Jesus could have escaped at this time, why did he not do so? What great opportunity did his death provide for Jesus?

4. Where did Jesus have his first hearing? Why was he taken to this place? Which of the apostles were most intimately connected with this hearing? What happened to Jesus here?

5. What was the Sanhedrin? How was opinion divided? What irregular proceedings prevailed at this trial? What was the purpose of this hearing and how far was this purpose accomplished?

6. What were the charges made against Jesus before Pilate? Which of these was regarded as the most serious? What was the verdict of Pilate?

7. How did Jesus come to have a hearing before Herod? What happened at this hearing? What attempt did Pilate then make to free Jesus? How did the Jews defeat this attempt? What was the final action of Pilate?

8. Enumerate the antisocial forces which led to the conviction and execution of Jesus.

WHAT THE LESSON MEANS FOR TODAY

Corrupt public officials prefer to conduct the business of government within the framework of the law if possible, but when their rule is threatened they take a conventional course to meet this threat. It involves such an alliance between graft and politics as was old when Rome was young. It was such an alliance which crucified Jesus. The Jews incurred responsibility for the murder of Jesus when they listened to the appeals to self-interest made by their rulers and joined them in their demand for the death penalty. We incur similar responsibility today when we listen to self-serving appeals and give support to wickedness in high places.

Chapter 41

THE CRUCIFIXION

Ever since that black Friday morning when Jesus was taken outside the Holy City and crucified between two thieves, good and thoughtful people have been trying to understand and explain what happened there. Apparently it would have been easy for Jesus to avoid Gethsemane and Calvary. He might have compromised with the Jews, he might have accepted the invitation of the Greeks and abandoned the Jews, or he might have called to his aid those heavenly powers he had so far refused to use for his own purposes. Yet as we come to know the Master revealed to us in the Gospels, we can find no point at which he might have stepped aside from the path he had chosen to follow. Jesus chose the way of the cross because that was the way in which his ministry led him. He could appeal to people from a cross as he could from no other vantage place. Millions have been born again because Jesus died on Calvary.

Jesus avoided death as long as there was nothing to be gained by letting sinful men have their way with him.[1] But after his disciples had been trained, and he and they had preached the gospel in the major centers of the land, Jesus quietly chose the time and place so that what was done could never again be hidden. Then he let his enemies have their way. They caused his death but they did not gain their end. The cross tells his message, not theirs.

Those who actually participated in the crucifixion of Jesus were either greedy for money and power, as were the witnesses against him, or heartlessly cruel like the Roman soldiers. Yet when their task was finished and they looked back on it, they could not feel easy about what they had done. Neither those who had shared in the crucifixion nor the many others who had cried out, "Release unto us Barabbas," could forget the pitiful, lonely figure on the cross. It was as though Jesus had said to them, "I want you to see sin as it really is; not when you are hot with passion, nor when your fear for your property rights has blinded you to the truth, but in its final consequences. I have never sinned, and yet for that very reason you can see in me here on the cross the picture of what sin really does to humanity. If this will not stop you from sinning, nothing will. In the hope that it will stop you, I die gladly." Insofar as a deep consciousness of the meaning of sin is a first step toward salvation from sin, the cross of Christ has been the most effective instrument of redemption ever known. Not even the life of Christ quickened the sensitivities of persons to such a horror of sin as his death has done.

The sin which killed Jesus on Calvary had its roots in the pride, self-will and rebellion of ordinary people. The sin of that day was related to and typical of the sin of every other time and place. And the sin of every other time and place, like the sin of that day, always condemns the innocent to death. The sin of our day is condemning those who are not yet born just as the sins of our fathers have condemned us to suffer. Sin, which thus destroys the highest creation of God, has been God's problem as well as ours from the dawn of creation. Because God loves us, he has never been able to disassociate himself from us and from the problems created by our sinfulness. Because our willful rebellion kills his finest hopes for us, it has broken his heart from the beginning. The crucifixion of the Son of God at Calvary was therefore but a momentary and visible illustration of the crucifixion endured by Divinity ever since sin first came into the world.

Sin was God's problem even before people were created. If he was to make people fit for companionship with himself, then they had to be free. But if they were to be free, there was every probability that they would want their own way before they had matured enough to know which way was best; that they would set their puny understanding against the larger understanding of Divinity; that they would rebel against the commands of God and would go their own way even though this way would lead to destruction. So God had to choose among three alternatives: (1) to fashion creatures lacking the capacity for choice and self-direction, who would therefore be less than persons; (2) to make persons capable of choice, and therefore of sin, and to leave them to themselves, which meant leaving them to die; or (3) to make persons capable of choice, and therefore of sin, but to take on himself the burden of their redemption.

People cannot save themselves from their own sin. Sin has so blinded them that they do not recognize it, and this blindness has become part of their very nature. When our first parents sinned they did so as individuals, but they were also the forerunners of our race. No matter how eager they may have been to accept responsibility for their own sins themselves, it was impossible for them to do so. By the simple fact of their parenthood, they were knit to all future generations. Their rebellion tainted the heritage they passed on to their children, and to their children's children; it has even reached to us. That taint is now inescapable, crowding in on us with every impact of the social order. It was inescapable in the time of Jesus. When our first parents sinned, the law which ties the generations together began to tie us together for evil. It was not the will of God that this should be so. It was his will that the very reverse should happen, and that the generations should be united for good; but Adam and Eve chose otherwise, and the law which was designed to work for our good began to work for our detriment also.[2] By our first sinning, sin has become a habit too strong for us to break. We have put ourselves in a place where we cannot help ourselves. God must help us or we are doomed.

The principle of the salvation of the lower by the higher runs all through nature. If I hurt my foot it is lost unless the blood of life flows to it, taking on itself the pain of that injury and achieving a restoration which my foot alone cannot achieve. God in the universe is like the spirit of life in the body. "In him we live, and move, and have our being."[3] Knowing from the beginning of time that we would be rebellious and that death would enter into the world through our sins, our heavenly Father provided, before the beginning of time, for the flowing of his life into ours. Because we were wicked, and the powers of evil—which are the powers of death—were loosed in our individual and social lives, the God who created us determined also to redeem us. He would give his life for us and save us from our blind helplessness. He did not begin to do this at Calvary. He has been doing it from the beginning. But at Calvary people saw for the first time what sin costs God and at the same time saw sin as it really is. Then it was that they became more deeply concerned about sin than ever before.

Calvary is a frank appeal to the emotions, but it is the emotional appeal at its very best. Here Jesus did for humanity what no amount of logical exposition or mere arguing could ever do. The tragedy of Calvary has become the seed of more triumphant life than any other event in history. There was no other way to appeal to people of all time, to move humanity so deeply and to such worthy ends. All understand the language of sacrifice and pain.

Because the revelation of the cross appeals to the best that is in us, no matter how deeply this best is covered up, it has become the heart of our message. It is not the intellectual validity of his message, nor the sublime beauty of his life and his teachings, but the unutterable devotion of his sacrifice that has won people in every age—the rich and the poor, the wise and the foolish, the learned and the illiterate, all those who will give themselves time to listen and understand the message of Calvary.

Water becomes steam only at a certain heat—and apparently there had to be an intense experience to set free the great religious forces available. Calvary has provided such an experience, and all who can be persuaded to listen to the message of the cross find that it takes hold of them and remakes them. Listen to what it meant to the headstrong Peter, and note how this experience belongs to every age:

> For even hereunto were ye called; because Christ also suffered for us, leaving us an example, that ye should follow his steps; who did no sin, neither was guile found in his mouth; who, when he was reviled, reviled not again; when he suffered, he threatened not; but committed himself to him that judgeth righteously; who his own self bare our sins in his own body on the tree, that we, being dead to sins, should live unto righteousness; by whose stripes ye were healed. For ye were as sheep going astray; but are now returned unto the Shepherd and Bishop of your souls.[4]

Jesus was not punished for us although he did suffer for us. There is a vast difference between the two. Our Father does not punish the innocent. He did not demand that his Son should be punished for us. What happened was that our blindness made it imperative that he should show us in the body of Jesus just what sin is and does. The pain Christ bore was the price paid for our understanding.

To accept the atonement wrought by Jesus Christ means to be at one with God through making our own the lessons which Jesus died to teach. This is much more than just acknowledging that Jesus died for us. In the end it means that we, who could not help ourselves because we were too blind to know our true condition, must now help Christ to do for others what he did for us.

We must love people, and because we love them we must make willing sacrifices that they might come to the way of life. Jesus did not come that we might be saved the necessity of sacrifice. Sacrifice is life. He came that we might be awakened to the need for sacrifice in his cause and that we might respond to the need with glad surrender and so be like him.

The Sermon on the Mount is an excellent statement of Christian ethics for a person who is already won to Christianity. No ethical statement, however, has power enough to take hold of persons who are degrading themselves below the beasts and transform them into ministers of God to their fellows. Only the love found at Calvary can do this. When we really see what happened there, we echo with glad hearts the words of Paul:

> Therefore if any man live in Christ, he is a new creature; old things are passed away; behold, all things are become new. And receiveth all the things of God, who hath reconciled us to himself by Jesus Christ, and hath given to us the ministry of reconciliation: To wit, that God is in Christ, reconciling the world unto himself, not imputing their trespasses unto them; and hath committed unto us the word of reconcilation. Now then we are ambassadors for Christ, as though God did beseech you by us; we pray you in Christ's stead, be ye reconciled to God. For he that made him to be sin for us, who knew no sin; that we might be made the righteousness of God in him.[5]

NOTES

1. John 8:59.
2. Romans 5:12, 16, 19; Ephesians 2:3; Mosiah 1:119; Helaman 5:70.
3. Acts 17:28.
4. I Peter 2:21-25.
5. II Corinthians 5:17-21.

Study Helps for

Chapter 41

LESSON PURPOSE

To consider together the meaning for the human race of the sacrifice of Christ at Calvary

SCRIPTURE REFERENCES

John 3:14-21; Isaiah 53:2-8; Romans 5:6-21.

HIGH POINTS OF THE LESSON

- Jesus avoided the cross until he could make it tell his story and not the story of his enemies.
- The sin which killed Jesus at Calvary had its roots in the pride, self-will and rebellion of humankind.
- God made our sin his problem from before the beginning of time, because God loves us. He took on himself the burden of our redemption as the natural sequence of our creation.
- Calvary reveals the true nature of sin, which kills the innocent.
- Calvary also reveals the price God will pay for our redemption and the way we must go for the redemption of our fellows.

QUESTIONS AND DISCUSSION TOPICS

1. How might Jesus have avoided Gethsemane and Calvary? Why did he not do so? In what sense did he *choose* the way of the cross?

2. Why did Jesus avoid Calvary until the Passover season? What important work did he have to complete before that time? What difference did the time and place of his crucifixon make to the effectiveness of his message?

3. What were the roots of the sin which killed Jesus at Calvary? How did the crucifixion of Jesus contribute to human awareness of the real signficance of sin?

4. Why did God make sin his problem? When did he do so? What other methods could he use to reveal the true nature of sin?

5. Why can't people save themselves from their own sin? Discuss the principle of the salvation of the lower by the higher in this connection.

6. Why has the sacrifice of Jesus at Calvary become the heart of the Christian message? What has it taught us about God and his love? What has it taught us about sin? Why is this demonstration so much more effective than any sermons?

7. Discuss the statement that "Jesus was not punished for us although he did suffer for us."

8. What requirement does the atonement lay on us? How does it become effective for us?

WHAT THE LESSON MEANS FOR TODAY

Before we can really understand the story of the atonement we must read it with our hearts. When we do this, we realize that Jesus has here epitomized his way of life for us. Out of his great love for us, he died gladly that we might have life. The atonement becomes effective in our lives when we gladly pattern our own lives after his life.

Chapter 42

THE RESURRECTION

Jesus died at about three o'clock on Friday afternoon. The Jews were anxious that his body and the bodies of the two thieves crucified with him should not remain exposed on their crosses after that evening, when the Sabbath began, and asked that these might be taken away.[1] Before this could be done, Joseph of Arimathea begged the body of Jesus from Pilate. He was joined by Nicodemus, who brought spices.[2] Together they took the body, wrapped it in a clean linen cloth, and laid it in a tomb which Joseph had recently had hewn out of the rock.[3]

On the morrow, the morning of the Sabbath, the rulers of the Jews went to Pilate and told him that Jesus had publicly prophesied that he would rise again after three days. They had no belief in this but were afraid that the disiples might come and steal the body. At their request, therefore, they were given guards who were to remain on duty until after the three days had elapsed. Then, having sealed the stone and being content that they had provided against every adverse possibility, they went away.[4]

When the disciples knew that Jesus was actually dead and buried and that a guard had been set at the tomb, they lost hope. Their despair was deepened by the feeling that not only was Jesus dead but that, in their opinion, his death was itself an evidence that God had deserted him. Both Jews and Gentiles shared the common belief that disaster was a punishment for evil. Jesus had denied this superstition specifically when he had been questioned regarding the slaughter of the Galileans by Pilate, and he had also denied at that time that the fall of the tower of Siloam was a punishment visited upon the eighteen persons who were killed in its collapse.[5] Notwithstanding his teaching, however, the idea had persisted. Sharing this conviction almost against their own wishes, the disciples felt that in spite of the winsome personality of Jesus, his overflowing kindness, and his transparent sincerity, he must have been deceived or he could never have been killed.

When the morning of the resurrection was fully come, Jesus made himself known to Mary Magdalene[6] and later to Peter[7] and the remaining apostles.[8] The disciples, who might have been expected to accept the news readily, did not do so. When Mary Magdalene brought word that Jesus had indeed risen they "believed not," and when Cleopas and his companion of Emmaus road added their testimony, "neither believed they them."[9] Luke wrote that the apostles heard the stories of the women who had been to the sepulcher as "idle tales."[10] Nevertheless, Peter and John were impressed enough to go to the grave themselves. When Peter saw the empty tomb, with the grave clothes laid to one side, he was not fully convinced but nevertheless left "wondering in himself at that which was come to pass."[11] At first only John, the beloved disciple, "believed."[12] When the news first reached Thomas his reaction was: "Except I shall see in his hands the print of the nails, and put my finger into the print of the nails, and thrust my hand into his side, I will not believe."[13]

The New Testament references are not always clear as to the details of these appearances, but they give substantial evidence that in this respect the elder disciples did not follow "cunningly devised fables."[14] Here is a list of these appearances:

To two women returning from the sepulcher[15]

To Mary Magdalene on the same day[16]

To Peter, on the day of the resurrection, in Jerusalem[17]

To two disciples on the same day, on the way to Emmaus[18]

To the ten apostles on the same day in Jerusalem[19]

To the eleven, a week later in Jerusalem[20]

To several disciples, including at least four apostles, at the Sea of Galilee[21]

To five hundred brethren[22]

To James[23]

To the apostles at Jerusalem before the Ascension[24]

To Paul[25]

Latter Day Saints have additional testimony of the resurrection and of the post-resurrection ministry of the Lord Jesus in the Book of Mormon and in modern revelation.[26]

Even as the appearances of the Lord Jesus multiplied, "some doubted."[27] But the reasons for their doubt changed. At first it was amazement and fear—possibly, for some, the fear of being deceived.[28] Then as they lived with the mounting evidences they gradually came to see in the Lord more than they had ever seen before. When he was crucified, wicked men had done the worst they could do to him. But, as Peter was to say at Pentecost, Jesus "hath God raised up, having loosed the pains of death; because it was not possible that he should be holden of it."[29] Jesus was not just a great and beloved leader. He was the Son of God, and spoke with such authority as people had never truly heard before. So it was that they came to wrestle with what this meant and—knowing themselves—believed, amazingly, for joy. It seemed to good to be true.[30]

Some who do not believe have urged as a reason for their disbelief that the risen Lord did not appear to his enemies, notwithstanding the fact that these were the ones who most needed to be convinced. This is true. It is also in complete harmony with the ministry of Jesus from the beginning. He steadfastly refused to coerce people into faith. As far as was possible, those who believed must follow him because of the goodness of God even more than because of the power of God. Peter sensed this when he told Cornelius later that "him God raised up the third day, and showed him openly; not to all the people, but unto witnesses chosen before of God."[31]

Dr. W. R. Maltby has said:

> For the same reason that not an angel stirred before the crucifixion to stay it and scatter his murderers, for that same reason our Lord did not show himself to his enemies now. It is strange to think that he may have brushed the sleeve of Caiaphas in the streets of Jerusalem that Easter Day, or watched Pilate on the steps of his own court, looked on them with pity and desire, and out of love for them went no further, nor forced a conviction where there would be no consent. All those methods of violence were alien to him, and, though none of his disciples understood at the time, we can see why he forced no unwilling door, and went only to the hearts that were waiting for him.[32]

Down the years there have been repeated attempts to explain away the fact of the Resurrection, but ever since Pentecost it has been too late for doubt. The church leaders we meet in the Acts of the Apostles are not the same people we met in the Gospels. They are different in faith, in the temper of their minds, in spirit, in courage, in the power to endure. At Calvary they had had all the facts of the Christian message except one. After Easter, the addition of the fact of the Resurrection had opened the way to understanding, and all other facts had been fused into one great assurance. This transformation is a matter of history, and it has no adequate explanation except the one given by those in whose lives it took place. All that was best in the disciples of Jesus was jeopardized when they lost hope at Calvary. Now all that was best in them was resurrected and augmented, and they found themselves heirs to such power as had never before been wielded. The only explanation which truly explains is that the Christ thought dead had risen again; because of this, these disciples had been reborn.

The testimony of the disciples and the records in the Gospels and Epistles are by no means the only evidences of the power of the Resurrection in the lives of people. The testimony that Jesus had risen from the dead soon became a bond of union in the fellowship of the believers and the chief reason for the amazing growth of their fellowship. For the early Christians one fact was paramount; it was beyond argument and was adequate answer to all questions. Christ was risen; people had seen him after his rising, had heard him, and spoken with him, and had touched him. It became their exultant and inspiring salutation: "Christ is risen."

As the days passed, and they drew away from the immediate experience of the resurrection of Jesus, those who loved him realized that the true victory of the Resurrection had really been won a long time before Easter. It gradually dawned on their understanding that every triumph over temptation and every creative act of righteousness throughout the life of the Master had served to make more sure the resurrection which should ultimately come. Great as the fact of the resurrection was, and important as it was to become as the center of their experience and hope, it could not be separated from the Christian way of living.

Before raising Lazarus from the dead, Jesus had said to Martha, "I am the resurrection, and the life; he that believeth in me, though he were dead, yet shall he live; and whosoever liveth and believeth in me shall never die."[33] His disciples had never really understood what this statement of the Master meant; now they realized that Jesus conquered death because he had always lived above sin. We do not know just how this conquest of death was achieved, but the facts are beyond dispute. Because he was without sin he had power to lay down his life and power to take it again.[34] The Resurrection had shown that the wrath of enemies, no matter how powerful, cannot finally destroy a righteous person. In the strength of this conviction the early Christians moved forward into new life, and their insight was confirmed in experience. When they lost the fear of death and became afraid only of the sin which flouts the love of God, they became the outstanding people of their generation, the front rank of a great army raised with Christ to a new and continuing life.

While evidence supporting the Resurrection is overwhelming, we do not arrive at a vital belief in it just by adding up the testimonies of the witnesses. This vital belief comes, rather, in the experience of doing the will of God. As we give attention to the evidence in the scriptures, we know that if we are ever to believe in resurrection from the dead as a principle we must believe first in the resurrection of Jesus. As we study the life of Jesus, we become convinced that if ever a man deserved to live again, Jesus did. As we share the life of the great heroes of Christianity, we know that if ever a miracle transformed the lives of people, this miracle has done so. But the final conviction comes as the testimony of the Spirit of God is granted to us, illuminating our minds, cheering our hearts, and giving us new life in the service of our Master. Like the tree which draws nourishment equally from the soil and from the air, so faith rooted in the historic fact of the Resurrection and in the personal experience of new life gathers color and individuality as it matures. The Resurrection tells us that pain and death are incidental and that the guarantee of victory does not lie on the other side of the grave but here, where we make our decisions for life and not for death.

Throughout history people have been "subject to bondage" through fear of death.[35] Jesus has shown us that there is no need for this fear, for death is an event and not an end, a gateway and not a blank wall. We may therefore reasonably begin here tasks which will require eternity for their fulfillment, and we may love our dear ones without fear of eternal separation. Death awaits all of us, separating us for a time; but the resurrection also awaits us. If we live worthily we may thereafter be united in fellowship with the great company of those who have lived in the light of God from the dawn of time.

NOTES

1. John 19:31-33.
2. John 19:38, 39.
3. Matthew 27:59, 60, KJ; 62, IV; Mark 15:45, 46, KJ; 49, 50, IV; Luke 23:52-54; John 19:40-42.
4. Matthew 27:62-66, KJ; 64-67, IV.
5. Luke 13:1-5.
6. Mark 16:9, KJ; 8, IV; John 20:14-18.
7. Luke 24:34.
8. John 20:19-29; Acts 1:1-9.
9. Mark 16:12, 13, KJ; 11, 12, IV; Luke 24:13-35, KJ; 12-34, IV.
10. Luke 24:10.
11. Luke 24:11.
12. John 20:8.
13. John 20:25.
14. II Peter 1:16. This has primary reference to the transfiguration, but reaches out to include the whole life and ministry of Jesus.
15. Matthew 28:8-10, KJ; 6-9, IV.
16. John 20:11-18.
17. Luke 24:34, KJ; 33, IV.
18. Luke 24:13-35, KJ; 12-34, IV; Mark 16:12, 13, KJ; 11, 12, IV.
19. Luke 24:36-49, KJ; 35-48, IV; John 20:19-23; I Corinthians 15:5.
20. John 20:26-29.
21. John 21:1-23.
22. I Corinthians 15:6.

23. I Corinthians 15:7.

24. Luke 24:50-52; Acts 1:3-8. Note also Mark 16:19, KJ; 20, IV.

25. Acts 9:3-7; I Corinthians 15:8.

26. III Nephi 5, 6-7, 8, 9:16; Ether 1:76 f.; 5:40, 41; D. and C. 76:3g.

27. Matthew 28:16, IV.

28. Mark 16:9-13, KJ; 8-10, IV; Luke 24:11, KJ; 10, IV.

29. Acts 2:24.

30. Luke 24:41. See also I Peter 1:8.

31. Acts 10:40, 41.

32. W. R. Maltby, *The Meaning of the Resurrection,* p. 11. Used by permission of the Epworth Press, London, England.

33. John 11:25, 26.

34. John 10:17, 18.

35. Hebrews 2:15.

Study Helps for

Chapter 42

LESSON PURPOSE

To sense the signficance of the Resurrection in the lives of the early saints and in the lives of godly people today

SCRIPTURE REFERENCES

John 5:24-29; 11:23-27; I Corinthians 15:12-23, 51-58.

HIGH POINTS OF THE LESSON

- The despair of the disciples after the crucifixion.
- The indisputable fact of the Resurrection.
- The restraint of Jesus in appearing to his disciples.
- The significance of the Resurrection in the life of the early disciples.

QUESTIONS AND DISCUSSION TOPICS

1. Why was the body of Jesus removed from the cross so soon? Where was it placed? Why was the tomb guarded?

2. Why was the despair of the disciples especially acute? What do you think of the belief then current that calamity is always the result of wickedness?

3. List the resurrection appearances of Jesus. Why did the Master appear on each of these occasions? Why did he not appear to his enemies and try to convince them?

4. Give illustrations of the restraint of Jesus in appearing to his disciples. Why was Jesus so restrained?

5. What are the evidences attesting the fact of the Resurrection? In what way is the Christian church an evidence of the Resurrection?

6. What is the relation between the life and the resurrection of Jesus? Why was it easier for those who loved Jesus to believe in his resurrection than to believe in the resurrection of anyone else?

7. What were the deepest spiritual results of the Resurrection in the lives of the disciples? What was its effect in the life of the early church?

8. What is the present practical significance of the Resurrection? What assurances does it give?

WHAT THE LESSON MEANS FOR TODAY

Our heavenly Father has many times acted in history with a clear demonstration of the power of godliness, but nowhere more significantly than in the fact of the Resurrection. Here people did to his Son the worst that they could possibly do. Here Jesus met the great enemy of all humankind. Here Jesus showed once and for all that the power of God is able to overcome in every situation, great or small. The fact of the Resurrection is a guarantee of power available to meet every need. Jesus who conquered death conquers the sin which breeds death, if we will but trust and cooperate with him.

Chapter 43

THE FORTY DAYS

Between the time of his Resurrection and his ascension the Lord Jesus gave himself to the further instruction of his apostles. This continued as he

> through the Holy Ghost had given commandments unto the apostles whom he had chosen; to whom also he showed himself alive after his sufferings by many infallible proofs, being seen of them forty days, and speaking of the things pertaining to the kingdom of God.[1]

Early in the post-resurrection experience the apostles and those gathered with them were trying to grasp the signficance of the resurrection when Jesus came quietly into their midst, although the doors were shut.[2] Greeting them, the Master showed that he knew what had been going on by immediately answering the questions which had been in their minds and on their lips. He showed them his hands, his feet, and his side, "and while they yet wondered and believed not for joy, he said unto them, Have ye here any meat? And they gave him a piece of a broiled fish, and a honeycomb. And he took it and did eat before them."[3] There is a wealth of meaning in the comment of John: "Then were the disciples glad, when they *saw* the Lord."[4] They saw Jesus then with eyes newly opened and hearts newly understanding. The Master renewed their commission, sending them forth as his Father had sent him, clothing them with authority to represent him among all people and to preach repentance and remission of sins in his name.[5]

For some reason Thomas was not with his fellow apostles when the Master appeared to the group in Jerusalem, and he found it particularly difficult to believe their story. The Master left him with his doubts for a week. As far as we know he did not appear to any of the others either during this period. Then the Lord again appeared to the apostolic group. Thomas, despite all his prior doubts, found the evidence of the Resurrection more than enough.[6]

By this time the others had had opportunity to become accustomed to the triumph of the Master and had already begun to realize what it could mean in their own lives and in the lives of others. Moreover, the lapse of time had specifically ruled out any possibility that these appearances could have been the result of post-crucifixion hysteria. The appearances were too widely spaced and they had been observed by too many persons under too wide a variety of conditions for such an attempted explanation to satisfy.

Renan, the French skeptic, once said that we owe the Resurrection story to Mary Magdalene, "a highly emotional woman." Let us be grateful that we do have the testimony of Mary, but let us also be grateful that we have the testimony of some others who did not find belief as easy as Mary did. Thomas was one of these, but he was not the only one. Saul, who became the great apostle to the Gentiles, was another. When Thomas saw the risen Lord he fell down and worshiped. And when Paul became convinced he thereafter rated the Resurrection above every other evidence of the divinity of Jesus Christ, and wrote that Jesus was declared to be "the Son of God with power, by the Spirit according to the truth through the resurrection from the dead."[7]

The angel at the sepulcher had sent word to the disciples that Jesus would go before them into Galilee. For some reason the apostles delayed their departure for a week. It is not unlikely that they were held in Jerusalem by the inquiries of the believers who wanted to hear their testimony concerning Jesus.

When they could get away the apostles went northward, and before long they were back in their native province. Here, at the suggestion of Peter, seven of them went fishing.[8] They worked all night but caught nothing. About daybreak when they came near to land, tired and dispirited, Jesus stood on the beach and asked what success they had had. When they told him, he suggested that they cast a net on the right side of the boat. They did so, and soon the net was full of fish, "and for all there were so many, yet the net was not broken."

This third appearance to the twelve as a group would never be forgotten. Every man there recognized his experience on the lake as a parable of his relationship to the Lord. Henceforth, the disciples knew that without Jesus they could do nothing, but that under his guidance they could be able "fishers of men."[9] In the day of their success, those who loved him would recognize the guidance of the Lord,[10] but others not quite so clear-sighted could nevertheless help with the common task.[11] Even the unbroken net had its message, for had not Jesus himself told them that the kingdom is like a net cast into the sea?[12] Did not the strength of this net give promise of the strength of the kingdom?

It was probably soon after this experience that the eleven apostles went to the mountain where Jesus had asked them to meet him.[13] It may be that some others, in addition to the apostles, were also present, for Matthew reports that "when they saw him they worshiped him, but some doubted."[14] Since all of the apostles had had personal contact with the resurrected Lord prior to this time, it does not seem likely that any of these were among the doubters. Quite possibly it was to this occasion that Paul referred twenty-five years later when he wrote that Jesus "was seen of about five hundred brethren at once."[15] To this group on the mount, many of whom may have doubted when they were too far away to see clearly but whose faith would be strong when they were in close touch with Jesus, the

Master declared, "All power is given unto me in heaven and in earth."[16] Under this authority the Master commissioned his ministry to go into all the world and preach the gospel, making disciples, baptizing them in the name of the Father and of the Son and of the Holy Ghost, and teaching them to observe all things he had taught and commanded. Those who would do this in faith were promised that the signs of his presence would accompany them in all their work. They would cast out evil spirits, and speak with new tongues; they would be protected against harm; they would heal the sick.

This appearance to the eleven is narrated by both Matthew and Mark. It may have been on the same occasion, or it may have been after the expiration of several days or a few weeks, that Jesus again appeared and instructed the brethren regarding the scripture reference to his coming and to his ministry.[17] Continuing, he said, "Ye are witnesses of these things." Other people might philosophize, but these men knew. Nevertheless, it would not be sufficient for them to go abroad with a mere statement of the facts involved. They must also be endowed with power from on high in order that their testimony would pierce the hearts of their hearers. Then, instructed and endowed, they were to carry the message of repentance and remission of sins in the name of Jesus from the city where Jesus had been crucified and raised again to the far corners of the earth.

John tells us that during this period Jesus did many things which are not recorded.[18] Many of these things were known among the disciples and are hinted rather than stated in the Gospels. The fact that the Master talked with Peter so frequently certainly seems to indicate that Peter held some responsibility distinct from that of his brethren in the apostolic group. On the other hand, the fact that Matthias was chosen to complete the Twelve[19] seems to indicate that Peter retained his place in this group. If this is so, it would appear that the Twelve with Peter at their head directed the growth of the infant church, at least for a time. Later James, the Lord's brother, occupied a position of special prominence which may even have superseded that of Peter.[20]

After Cleopas and his companion on the Emmaus road recognized Jesus, "he vanished out of their sight";[21] yet when they took their good news to their brethren in Jerusalem, the Master came into their midst and showed that he was well aware of what had transpired. This type of appearance was repeated again and again. The disciples did not know where to find Jesus, but he evidently knew where to find them; always, when he found them, he knew what had transpired, understood the situation, said the needed word, and quietly assumed control.[22] When this had happened once or twice, how could the disciples help asking themselves whether their friend and Master was ever really absent at all? They became aware, in a way which would not have been possible had he not died and risen again, that he is always present and always available, whether he is visible or not. Because they loved him and wanted him near, it was not long until they came to take it for granted that he was near and that he knew exactly what was taking place—and they began to govern their acts and their very thoughts accordingly.

This habit of acknowledging the presence of Jesus would never have evolved had Jesus never appeared to his disciples after his death; neither would it have become a habit had the Master always stayed with them. It involved a fundamental and important growth in their spiritual understanding. They were learning to think of Jesus as always present and always understanding. While he had been visible, he had been available only to as many as could see him, comforting and strengthening individuals or comparatively small groups. Now those who knew him and loved him realized that he did not need to be visible in order to bless them; they could be blessed by the sense of his presence without regard to time, place, or numbers.

For forty days Jesus ministered among his believing disciples, "speaking of the things pertaining to the kingdom of God."[23] During that time, whether they thought through what was happening among them or not, they gradually became aware that they could always rely on the guidance and companionship of their Lord if they would take his presence for granted and act accordingly. Since death could not take him from them, nothing else could. It was no longer necessary for them to apprehend him with their bodily senses. He was present to their spiritual vision.

When they had come this far, the disciples were ready for fulfillment of the promise of Jesus:

> If ye love me, keep my commandments. And I will pray the Father, and he shall give you another Comforter, that he may abide with you forever; even the Spirit of truth; whom the world cannot receive, because it seeth him not, neither knoweth him; but ye know him; for he dwelleth with you, and shall be in you. I will not leave you comfortless; I will come to you. Yet a little while, and the world seeth me no more; but ye see me; because I live, ye shall live also. At that day ye shall know that I am in my Father, and ye in me, and I in you. . . . These things have I spoken unto you, being yet present with you. But the Comforter, which is the Holy Ghost, whom the Father will send in my name, he shall teach you all things, and bring all things to your remembrance, whatsoever I have said unto you. Peace I leave with you, my peace I give unto you; not as the world giveth, give I unto you. Let not your heart be troubled, neither let it be afraid. . . . And now I have told you before it come to pass, that, when it is come to pass, ye might believe.[24]

Only one thing more was needed, and that was some convincing experience that this Comforter was actually available, that Jesus was actually present for the many even as he had been present among the few. In order that they should have this experience, it was imperative that he leave them and return to his place in the heavens. When the time was ripe he did this,[25] but not until he had explained: "It is expedient for you that I go away; for if I go not away, the Comforter will not come unto you; but if I depart, I will send him unto you."[26] His last promise to his disciples was that he would send them his Spirit,[27] whose guidance and power would make them his effectual witnesses.

NOTES

1. Acts 1:2, 3.
2. John 20:19.
3. Luke 24:40-42.
4. John 20:20.
5. John 20:21-23; Luke 24:45-49, KJ; 44-48, IV.
6. John 20:24-29.
7. Romans 1:4.
8. John 21:1-24.
9. Matthew 4:19, KJ; 18, IV.
10. John 21:7.
11. John 21:8.
12. Matthew 13:47, KJ; 48, IV.
13. Matthew 28:16-20, KJ; 15-19, IV; Mark 16:15-18, KJ; 14-19, IV.
14. Matthew 28:17, KJ; 16, IV.
15. I Corinthians 15:6.
16. Matthew 28:18, KJ; 17, IV.
17. Luke 24:44-49, KJ; 43-48, IV.
18. John 20:30, 31; 21:25.
19. Acts 1:20-26.
20. Acts 12:17; 15:13; 21:18; Galatians 1:18, 19; 2:9, 12.
21. Luke 24:31, KJ.
22. Admirably discussed in *The Meaning of the Resurrection* by W. R. Maltby, Epworth Press, London, England.
23. Acts 1:3, KJ.
24. John 14:15-20, 25-27, 29.
25. Acts 1:9-11.

26. John 16:7.

27. Acts 1:8.

Study Helps for

Chapter 43

LESSON PURPOSE

To impress the reality of the presence of Jesus by tracing the growth of this presence in the hearts and minds of the disciples after the resurrection

SCRIPTURE REFERENCES

Mark 16:12-14, KJ; 11-13, IV; John 20:19-31; I Corinthians 15:5-8.

HIGH POINTS OF THE LESSON

- Many of the disciples found it hard to believe that Jesus was actually risen from the dead. They had to be convinced.
- Jesus not only appeared to many and convinced them but he also made them realize that he did not need to be visible to them in order to know what was transpiring. He was made ultimately convincing by his actual appearance, disappearance, and reappearance. These paved the way for the bestowal of the Holy Spirit and its confirming power.

QUESTIONS AND DISCUSSION TOPICS

1. Describe the appearance of Jesus to Cleopas and his companion. Why did Jesus explain the scriptures to them before he made himself known?

2. Why did Jesus appear to Peter? What did this do for Peter?

3. What happened at the appearance in the upper room? What was the significance of Jesus' eating with the apostles? What was the significance of his appearance while the door was barred against the Jews? Why did Jesus recommission the apostles at this time?

4. Describe the appearance to Thomas. To what other doubter did he appear later? What is the signficance of these appearances?

5. What happened when Jesus appeared to the seven apostles at the lake? Why did this seem to be especially important? What happened to Peter?

6. What were the circumstances of Jesus' appearance at the mount in Galilee? Who was there? What was accomplished?

7. What was accomplished by the fact that when Jesus apppeared to his disciples he showed them that he knew what had happened before he appeared?

8. What was the chief topic of conversation between Jesus and the disciples during the forty days?

9. What was the relation of the Comforter to the Master in the minds of the disciples? What was his relation to the realization of their kingdom hopes?

10. Summarize the values gained during the resurrection period. How were these forty days related to the growth which came later?

WHAT THE LESSON MEANS FOR TODAY

One of the most fruitful topics of meditation is the actual availability of the Lord Jesus by his Spirit today. We who build God's kingdom must do so under his guidance, and this guidance must be sufficiently real to make a definite difference in the spiritual quality of the building done.

Chapter 44

THE ASCENSION

The Lord Jesus ministered among his disciples during the forty days following his resurrection, recalling what he had taught prior to his crucifixion but illuminating it by his presence as the significance of his resurrection became clearer in their hearts and minds.

This could not continue forever. Nor was it necessary. Henceforth they would be guided by their memories of him and the light and power of the Holy Spirit. The time had come when it was "expedient" that he should go away.[1]

Luke has left us the most complete account of what happened. He wrote that Jesus "led them out as far as to Bethany, and he lifted up his hands and blessed them. And it came to pass, while he blessed them, he was taken from them, and carried up into heaven."[2]

> And when he had spoken these things, while they beheld, he was taken up; and a cloud received him out of their sight. And while they looked steadfastly toward heaven as he went up, behold, two men stood by them in white apparel; which also said, Ye men of Galilee, why stand ye gazing up into heaven? this same Jesus, which is taken up from you into heaven, shall so come in like manner as ye have seen him go into heaven.[3]

The testimony of Mark agrees with this: "So then, after the Lord had spoken unto them, he was received up into heaven, and sat on the right hand of God."[4]

It should be noted that those present were not mere onlookers. Luke says that as the Lord left them, they "worshiped him," and then "returned to Jerusalem with great joy; and were continually in the temple, praising and blessing God."[5]

Many students of the New Testament have felt that some such dramatic means as the visible ascent of the Lord had to be adopted in order to convince the disciples that the period of his post-resurrection glory was now coming to an end. Without such an experience many would have continued in hope that the resurrection appearances might go on indefinitely. Or, without such a climactic experience, their unaided expectations would have yielded place to all kinds of doubts as to what had become of their Lord.

When we think about the ascension of our Lord, we soon recognize it as the natural completion of the resurrection. Dr. William Barclay wrote, "There would have been something quite wrong with the resurrection appearances had they just slowly faded out."[6]

Although the fact of the resurrection was now confirmed to those who were nearest the Master, recognition of these facts was not enough by itself. It was a necessary prelude to the testimony they were called to bear. But they still needed guidance in understanding what the resurrection implied in terms of the divinity of the Lord Jesus, of what the new knowledge required of them, and of their need for a total rearrangement of their standards of value. Jesus had promised that the Comforter would guide his disciples into all truth, saying: "He shall glorify me; for he shall receive of mine, and shall show it unto you."[7] But it would take time for this to be accomplished. The disciples must be convinced, not just informed. Preparing for this, Jesus blessed them and renewed their apostolic commission but told them to go into Jerusalem and there tarry until they were endowed with further power from on high. So the eleven, and Mary, the mother of Jesus, with his brethren and the believing women, "returned to Jerusalem with great joy; and were continually in the temple, praising and blessing God."[8]

The waiting, which was now commanded, was of major importance. It is often so. "It was by the response of imagination and will as well as of the intellect that they begin to grasp what the Spirit may do for us."[9]

Jesus himself waited for thirty years before he began his public ministry, growing, in the meantime, "in wisdom and stature, and in favor with God and man."[10] The apostle Paul probably left for Arabia soon after his conversion and stayed there for three years where he assessed the meaning of his life and his calling as a special witness in light of his vision on the Damascus Road.[11] Joseph Smith waited and matured during the years between 1820 and 1830 before the church was organized.[12] To quote Dr. William Barclay again, "There can never be a foreground of effective activity without a background of passive receptivity."[13]

So the disciples waited. But this was not idle waiting. Rather it was filled with anticipation of the endowment which had been promised them. In their waiting under shared concern, the atmosphere was created in which the Spirit of God which they had known in the ministry of Jesus fortified their affections, quickened their understanding, and confirmed them in their steadily enriched hope.

The Ascension proclaims that the Lord Jesus not only lives but reigns. This was in a very real sense the completion of the resurrection message. It was one thing to assert that Jesus was no longer held fast by death. It was quite another thing to confess that he shares in the eternity, omnipresence, and omnipotence of God. But the early saints said just this. They pictured Jesus at the right hand of God. In the scriptures this phrase is always concerned with the omnipotent energy of God. To sit down at the right hand of God means to be clothed with all of the energy and power of omnipotence. One who sits at the right hand of God shares with God in the government of the universe. Paul wrote that

> [God] raised him [Christ] from the dead, and set him at his own right hand in the heavenly places, far above all principality, and power, and might, and

dominion, and every name that is named, not only in this world, but also in that which is to come; and hath put all things under his feet.[14]

The Apostle Peter shared this insight of his fellow witness, writing in his first epistle that "Jesus Christ. . . is gone into heaven, and is on the right hand of God; angels and authorities and powers being made subject unto him."[15] The book of Hebrews shares the testimony of the continuing concern of the Lord for all people:

> God, who at sundry times and divers manners spake in times past unto the fathers by the prophets, hath in these last days spoken unto us by his Son, whom he hath appointed heir of all things, by whom also he made the worlds, who being the brightness of his glory, and the express image of his person, and upholding all things by the word of his power, when he had by himself purged our sins, sat down on the right hand of the Majesty on high; being made so much better than the angels, as he hath by inheritance obtained a more excellent name than they.[16]

The first apostles had known Jesus as a man before they knew him as the Lord. They remembered his understanding and his compassion and believed that the characteristics which they had loved in him were now manifest by him in the realms of glory. They found here enduring resources of faith, strength, and courage. To the Roman saints Paul wrote: "It is Christ that died, yea rather, that is risen again, who is even at the right hand of God, who also maketh intercession for us."[17] To those in Ephesus he wrote:

> If ye then be risen with Christ, seek those things which are above, where Christ sitteth on the right hand of God. Set your affection on things above, not on things on the earth.[18]

The death, resurrection, ascension, and continued ministry of our Lord from the very presence of the Father belong together. Each event makes its contribution to the story of our redemption. No one aspect of the culmination of the mission of Christ can be fully understood without reference to the others.

As Dr. Joseph Haroutunian wrote a few years ago, "If Christ died but did not rise again, our faith is vain. If he rose but did not ascend, he is not gone to God the

Father Almighty. If he is not on the right hand of God the Father, he does not reign, and we have no king."[19]

NOTES

1. John 16:7.
2. Luke 24:49, 50.
3. Acts 1:9-11.
4. Mark 16:20.
5. Luke 24:51, 52.
6. *Daily Study Bible,* "The Acts of the Apostles," p. 6.
7. John 16:14.
8. Luke 24:52.
9. See *The Resurrection of Christ,* A. M. Ramsey, Geffrey Bles, 52 Daughtery St., London, W. C I (1945).
10. Luke 2:52.
11. Galatians 1:16-18.
12. D. and C. 17:1a.
13. *The Promise of the Holy Spirit,* Epworth Press (1960), p. 46.
14. Ephesians 1:20-22. See also Hebrews 1:1-4; Acts 2:32-36; 7:55, 56.
15. I Peter 3:21, 22.
16. Hebrews 1:1-4.
17. Romans 8:34.
18. Colossians 3:1, 2.
19. See article on the "Ascension," *Interpretation,* July 1956.

Study Helps for

Chapter 44

LESSON PURPOSE

To understand better the effect of the crucifixion, resurrection, and ascension on the disciples who witnessed these events or accepted their testimony.

SCRIPTURE REFERENCES

Acts 1:9-11; Mark 16:20

HIGH POINTS OF THE LESSON

- The resurrection of Christ put the crucifixion into an entirely new perspective. The disciples saw that Jesus was the victor rather than the victim.
- The ascension of our Lord was the natural completion of the resurrection. It limited ill-founded conjecture.
- The total resurrection-ascension experience was permeated by the power of the Holy Spirit, guiding the disciples into understanding.

QUESTIONS AND DISCUSSION TOPICS

1. How did the resurrection of Christ give meaning to the crucifixion?

2. Matthew reports that after the resurrection Jesus met with the disciples "and when they saw him they worshiped him; but some doubted (Matthew 28:16). But Luke says that at the ascension the disciples "worshiped him." Luke does not mention any doubters (Luke 24:52). What had the disciples come to believe about Jesus that had changed their doubt to worship?

3. In what sense did the ascension round out crucifixion-resurrection-instruction sequence?

4. Note the bearing of the post-resurrection experience of the apostles on the boldness with which they now proclaimed their faith. Comment on their changed attitude toward persecution and death.

5. Consider the maturing of understanding which occurs when people of exploring faith share their high expectations in fellowship, prayer, and love.

6. The early disciples thought of Jesus as "seated at the right hand of God. What did they mean by this?

7. Some of the disciples had known Jesus as a man before they knew him to be the Son of God. Now, as they worshiped and served, they came to know him more and more truly. What effect did this have on their understanding of "the God and Father of our Lord Jesus Christ"?

8. In Gethsemane Jesus had prayed that his Father would grant him the glory which he had shared with the Father before the world was (John 17:5). The greatest glory which could come to him was to share the life of God. Consider this.

WHAT THE LESSON MEANS FOR TODAY

Basic to all true discipleship is to know God and to love and serve him. Such discipleship draws on all that any person is. It involves heart, might, mind, and strength. It is nourished in worship. It is patterned after the life of the Lord Jesus.

Chapter 45

"I WILL COME AGAIN"

After the ascension of the Lord Jesus, the disciples thought over many of his sayings and so interpreted them as to look for their fulfillment in his early and visible return. Although the time of this return was hidden[1] it was quite clear that Jesus had promised he would come. To the high priests Jesus had said: "Ye shall see the Son of man sitting on the right hand of power, and coming in the clouds of heaven."[2] He had warned his disciples that he himself did not know the time of his coming,[3] but immediately thereafter he had said:

> The Son of man is as a man taking a far journey, who left his house, and gave authority to his servants, and to every man his work, and commanded the porter to watch. Watch ye therefore; for ye know not when the master of the house cometh, at even, or at midnight, or at the cock-crowing, or in the morning; lest coming suddenly, he find you sleeping. And what I say unto you, I say unto all, Watch.[4]

Similarly, in the parable of the nobleman and his servant, he said: "Occupy till I come."[5] In his last conversation with his disciples prior to his crucifixion he had said: "I go to prepare a place for you. And when I go, I will prepare a place for you, and come again, and receive you unto myself."[6]

Despite these promises of his return there are many New Testament passages which indicate that Jesus anticipated delay in his coming. He took careful pains to correct the thought "that the kingdom of God should immediately appear."[7] The gospel must be preached to all nations before the end comes.[8] The "times of the Gentiles" must be fulfilled.[9] He warned against false prophets,[10] and spoke frequently of the strain upon faith due to delay in his appearance.[11]

For the time being, they would be denied the visible

presence of the Master, but they would not be alone. Jesus had promised them another Comforter who would be to them all that he himself had been. Under the guidance of this Comforter, they were to carry on the work and the burdens of world evangelization, in active partnership with Jesus, and so become more like him. They remembered that "Enoch walked with God,"[12] that "Noah was a just man. . . .and walked with God,"[13] and that others of the ancient worthies had lived in the presence of Divinity on terms of righteousness. It is small wonder that the desire to grow like the Master so as to be ready to welcome him at his return became one of the cardinal motivations of the early Christians.

In a short letter to the Thessalonian saints, Paul used the word *parousia* four times. This word was used to indicate the visit of a king. The saints were waiting for their king to come from heaven and take his throne. They had "turned. . .to serve the living and true God; and to wait for his Son from heaven, whom he raised from the dead, even Jesus."[14] This note of expectation pervaded the entire life of the early Christians. The actual phrase "second coming" is to be found only once: "Unto them that look for him shall he appear the second time, without sin, unto salvation."[15] The basic idea, however, is constantly recurring. In the same letter we read, "Yet a little while, and he that shall come will come, and will not tarry."[16] Peter reminded the saints, "The end of all things is at hand; be ye therefore sober, and watch unto prayer."[17] In his general epistle, James said, "Be ye also patient; stablish your hearts; for the coming of the Lord draweth nigh."[18]

Paul repeatedly cited the imminence of the second coming as a reason for right living. He charged Timothy to be faithful in his ministry for this reason,[19] and wrote to Titus that this was a major reason for repentance.

Peter, similarly, pointed out that their hope of the second coming was a reason for the saints to be steadfast in the faith.[20] Later the same apostle used the same reason when pleading with the saints to be diligent that they might be "found of him in peace, without spot and blameless."[21] John, too, admonished the saints: "Abide in him; that, when he shall appear, we may have confidence, and not be ashamed before him at his coming."[22]

This expectation of the immediate return of their Lord had some unwholesome effects in the church. It naturally tended to emphasize otherworldliness, distracting attention from the immediacy of some of the more practical problems and encouraging a mysticism which was superstitious rather than spiritual. Among those who had caught the real spirit of the new evangel, however, the undesirable results of their expectancy were reduced to a minimum. Instead, the clouds of lesser interests were rolled away; ultimate values and eternal issues stood out before them stark and clear, as never before or since in the history of our race.

For the saints the anticipation of the Lord's return was an expectation of victory. But this was not all. The Lord will also return in judgment. Although the gospel is preached in all the world, there is no promise that it will be accepted and obeyed by all people.

The return of the Lord Jesus does not mean that in the intervening years the world is to become something of a paradise on earth. The opposite is true. Wicked people pursue their godless ways. But while they do this with an illusion of safety, "in history's other rooms, the table is already being set for the royal wedding feast, and the trumpets of the final judgment are slowly being raised."[23]

The more carefully we think about the second coming of Jesus, the more reasonable it appears to be. Indeed, belief in the visible personal appearance of our Lord, to reign over his people on the earth, seems to follow from the convictions already held by most of us in the light of our fundamental Christian experience. We believe that Jesus rose from the dead and is actually alive today and that he is working patiently and persistently to win us to his own way of life. For the present it is well that he shall continue to work behind the veil which hides him from us. In this way, he can guide us into all truth by the benign influence of his Spirit.[24] But when a generation of his followers shall grow so like him as to be happily responsive to every indication of his will, then surely he will come from behind the veil and visit the earth which he once trod with such joy and which was created by him in love as our home.

Jesus said he would come again. The apostles felt an assurance within their very souls that this was true. But not even Jesus knew the day of his coming during his earthly ministry. Time was not important. What was important was the absolute certainty of the coming crisis when he would return to the earth in power and great glory to meet a people worthy to meet him—mature, righteous, responsive. Such a consummation does not come because a certain date has arrived but because a certain people have grown up.

This is not to say that we must work out our salvation alone and that Jesus is awaiting our success before he will return. The Lord Jesus is working with us and for us. We work within a certain larger framework of events. These events are not predetermined by a celestial calendar which forces us into a pattern and takes away our freedom. They are determined, rather, by the fact that God has his agency as well as we, and he does intervene in the life of his world to bring to pass his eternal purpose.

Our heavenly Father, by his Spirit, is constantly

tempting us upward, educating the conscience of nations as well as the insight of individuals, so that we may someday be ready for uninterrupted communion with him. We can cooperate to mold history to a degree, but God is also molding history. The second coming will occur when enough of us shall have achieved a certain spiritual standard; God is at work seeing to it that we shall have every opportunity to achieve that standard. He will win, and we shall win.

NOTES

1. John 16:1-12.
2. Matthew 26:65.
3. Matthew 24:36, KJ.
4. Mark 13:34-37, KJ.
5. Luke 19:13.
6. John 14:23.
7. Luke 19:11.
8. Mark 13:10, KJ; 14:9.
9. Luke 21:24, KJ; 23, IV.
10. Matthew 24:3-6.
11. Luke 12:37, 38, KJ; 40, 41, IV; 18:8.
12. Genesis 5:24, KJ; 6:41, IV.
13. Genesis 6:9, KJ; 8:16, IV.
14. I Thessalonians 1:9, 10.
15. Hebrews 9:28, KJ.
16. Hebrews 10:37.
17. I Peter 4:7.
18. James 5:8.
19. II Timothy 4:1, 2.
20. I Peter 1:13.
21. II Peter 3:14.
22. I John 2:28.

23. See *I Believe in the Christian's Creed,* from Count Lahndorff's East Prussian Diary, p. 207.

24. John 16:13.

Study Helps for

Chapter 45

LESSON PURPOSE

To call attention to the scriptural teachings concerning the return of the Lord Jesus Christ. To encourage believers to consider the promise of the second coming as a means of becoming "partakers of the divine nature" (II Peter 1:3-4).

SCRIPTURE REFERENCES

Acts 1:1-11; I Thessalonians 1:9-10; 3:12-13; 5:1-9.

HIGH POINTS OF THE LESSON

- The hope and expectation of personal communion with the Lord Jesus has strengthened the saints in generation after generation.
- The promises of the second coming should be studied with wisdom and in the spirit of worship.
- Jesus said to his disciples that he had many things to say to them, but that they could not yet bear them. There is a time element in understanding. But where the promises are sure understanding should be pursued.

QUESTIONS AND DISCUSSION TOPICS

1. There have been several anticipations of the return of the Lord Jesus. Consider in this connection what the visible presence of Jesus did for the disciples of the first generation; what their experience of the spirit of Jesus has done for many of the faithful.

2. Comment on the meaning of "parousia" and its pertinence in reference to the return of the Lord.

3. What unwholesome effects did their expectation of the early return of Jesus have in the lives of some of the saints of the apostolic age? How did the apostles meet this?

4. What values accrued to the early saints who waited in wisdom and patience but also in faith for the return of the Lord?

5. What values might we conserve among the predominantly secular emphases of our times by consideration in the spirit of worship of the promised return of our Lord?

6. Comment on the many references to the return of the Lord which occur in the early revelations to the Restored Church: The Lord will come quickly: D. and C. 34:66d; 49:5d; 85:38c; 105:13a. We should prepare for this: D. and C. 32:3e; 65:1e. He will come in glory: D. and C. 45:10b, etc. . . .to his temple, suddenly: D. and C. 35:3b, 42:10c. . .to a gathered people among whom he will reign in righteousness: D. and C. 36:13-14.

WHAT THE LESSON MEANS FOR TODAY

Many of us are engrossed in the affairs of our times suffering, it has been said, from the "disease of contemporaneity." We need to judge our times, as well as others, against the background of the purpose and intention of God, to remember his promises as well as what he has done for us.

Chapter 46

THE NEW AGE

In the weeks of study and prayer following immediately after the resurrection, the apostles and other disciples entered into life of larger dimensions than they had ever known before—the life of the Messianic Age. This had not been possible until this time. Jesus himself had said to them, "I have yet many things to say unto you, but ye cannot bear them now."[1] Their full understanding had to wait until the pertinent facts were available. Now the facts were known and were being savored.

Jesus had referred to this new age when he had taught concerning the preparatory ministry of John the Baptist. At that time he had said:

> What went ye out for to see? A prophet? Yea, I say unto you, and more than a prophet. For this is the one of whom it is written, Behold, I send my messenger before thy face, which shall prepare thy way before thee. Verily, I say unto you, Among them that are born of women, there hath not risen a greater than John the Baptist; notwithstanding, he that is least in the kingdom of heaven, is greater than he.[2]

Again, in the same connection, Jesus had said:

> Verily I say unto you, many righteous prophets have desired to see these days which ye see, and have not seen them; and to hear that which ye hear, and have not heard.[3]

Remembrance of these sayings, together with the enlightenment of the Spirit which came to them as they thought of the deeper meanings of the resurrection, brought and confirmed in the apostles such recognition of the new age that Peter, "standing up with the eleven,"[4] could say: "Jesus of Nazareth . . . God hath raised up, having loosed the pains of death; because it was not possible that he should be holden of it."[5] Later in that same sermon he affirmed that Jesus, "being by the right hand of God exalted, and having received of the Father the promise of the Holy Ghost, he hath shed forth this, which ye now see and hear."[6]

When thinking of Pentecost we tend to dwell on the marvelous outpouring of the Spirit experienced at that time—the tongues, the proclamation, the conversions. Great as were the events of that day we must not forget that, as far as one day could do so, Pentecost marked the inauguration of the great age of culmination. The people of God were now pressing forward into the opening days of the "dispensation of the fullness of times" when it was the purpose of God to "gather together in one all things in Christ."[7]

At Pentecost the Apostle Peter elaborated on this theme, explaining that the outpouring of the Holy Spirit which they had witnessed was indicative of the coming of the new era. It was that outpouring of the Spirit of God which the prophet Joel had said should come to pass "in the last days."[8]

There are places in the New Testament where Peter's phrase, "the last days," appears to have primary reference to time, and we frequently think of it in this connection. At Pentecost, however, Peter gave it a much deeper significance. Here he presented "the last days" as the time of culmination. What God had been seeking to bring to pass, and what Joel and the other great prophets had seen in prospect, had now become a reality. They were living in a new age.

The Apostle John shared the joy of the other believers. When he wrote the gospel which bears his name, his story ran parallel to the story of the creation in Genesis, but central to it was his testimony that the Lord reigns over both creation and redemption:

> All things were made by him; and without him was not anything made that was made. In him was the gospel, and the gospel was the life, and the life was the light of men. . . . As many as received him, to them gave he power to become the sons of God; only to them who believe on his name. He was born, not of blood, nor of the will of the flesh, nor of the will of man, but of God.[9]

The resurrection was an act of revelation. As does all revelation, it provoked reflection. This reflection was on the wonder of what God had done and on what newly perceived word of truth God sought to convey by it. The disciples were required to remember from their new vantage point all that had gone before and to regard current happenings in a new light. As they did this they were filled with confident expectations of even greater things to come.[10]

The idea of newness is an essential feature of the New Testament. After Pentecost the disciples spread in every direction, testifying that God had inaugurated a new order based on a new covenant which fulfilled or went beyond the old covenant which he had made with Israel. by the grace of God the disciples now walked "in newness of life."[11] They were empowered by a lively hope. Peter wrote:

> Blessed be the God and Father of our Lord Jesus Christ, which according to his abundant mercy hath begotten us again unto a lively hope by the resurrection of Jesus Christ from the dead, to an inheritance incorruptible, and undefiled, and that fadeth not away, reserved in heaven for you, who are kept by the power of God through faith unto salvation ready to be revealed in the last time.[12]

The completion of the earthly ministry of the Lord Jesus had laid the foundation for the more comprehensive ministry of the Holy Spirit. Paul contrasts the characteristics of life under the old covenant with life guided by the Spirit which is now possible under the new covenant. He wrote: "Our sufficiency is of God; who also hath made us able ministers of the new testament; not of the letter, but of the Spirit; for the letter killeth, but the Spirit giveth life."[13]

The ancient scriptures also took on new life. For the first time the disciples saw them as the inspired record of God's dealings with people. These dealings had now come to a climax in the life, ministry, death, and resurrection of the Lord Jesus, and in so doing had given meaning to all that had gone before. This new awareness was to be expected, since Jesus had opened up the scriptures to them.[14] Now, as the disciples studied the prophets and the psalmists, they saw everything grounded in Christ.

The early saints knew that they were called to grow in understanding of the Lord. They also knew that no revelation which the tomorrows might bring would be a greater disclosure of the truth than was already available to them. They proclaimed with confidence, "Jesus Christ the same yesterday, and today, and forever,"[15] and:

> Grace and peace be multiplied unto you through the knowledge of God, and of Jesus our Lord, according as his divine power hath given unto us all things that pertain unto life and godliness, through the knowledge of him that hath called us to glory and virtue; whereby are given unto us exceeding great and precious promises; that by these ye might be partakers of the divine nature, having escaped the corruption that is in the world through lust.[16]

NOTES

1. John 16:12.
2. Matthew 11:9-11.
3. Matthew 13:16.
4. Acts 2:14.
5. Acts 2:22, 24.
6. Acts 2:33.
7. Ephesians 1:10.
8. Acts 2:16-18.
9. John 1:3, 4, 12, 13.
10. John 1:50.
11. Romans 6:4.
12. I Peter 1:3-5.
13. II Corinthians 3:5-6.
14. Luke 24:32, 45, KJ; 31, 44, IV.
15. Hebrews 13:8.
16. II Peter 1:2-4.

Study Helps for

Chapter 46

LESSON PURPOSE

To show that after the ascension the disciples entered into life of larger dimensions than they had ever known before, and that this larger life is available to us on the same terms as it was to them.

SCRIPTURE REFERENCES

John 15:1-10; 16:12-13

HIGH POINTS OF THE LESSON

- After the ascension and Pentecost it was demonstrably true that the disciples "walked in newness of life."
- Pentecost marked the beginning of a new age, the age of "the spirit of life in Christ Jesus" (Romans 8:2).

QUESTIONS AND DISCUSSION TOPICS

1. For the intimate disciples of Jesus, the days had passed when they could not bear what he had to say to them. Describe the change in them.

2. At Pentecost Peter referred to the last days as days when the Lord would pour out his Spirit upon all flesh. Nothing like this had ever happened before. The fullness of revelation through Christ was attested by the power of the testimony of the Spirit. It indeed marked a new age.

3. John the Baptist and the other prophets to whom Jesus referred (Matthew 11:9-11) were called of God and played an important part in the Lord's program of redemption. But they served before the climax was reached at Calvary and Easter. Note how all that they taught lacked fullness because of this.

4. Comment on the meaning of the phrase "the fullness of times" noting the statement of Paul in Ephesians 1:8-10.

5. Note John's correlation of creation and redemption with that of Paul: "if a man be in Christ he is a new creature" (II Cor. 5:17). It is the power of God which makes new creatures, and creatures made new after his likeness build the new age.

6. Comment on the "lively hope" which characterized the early saints.

7. Note the sounder understanding of the scriptures which the early disciples received when they read them in light of the life and ministry of Jesus.

8. Many stirring phrases have come to us from this period. Note, for example, "grace and peace be multiplied unto you." Can you think of others?

WHAT THE LESSON MEANS FOR TODAY

Life in the new age in Christ calls for deep and stable faith, integrity, courage, patience, endurance, high endeavor, and similar qualities. But it should also be characterized by what Peter called "joy unspeakable and full of glory" (I Peter 1:8). While this is given us in many ways one of the chief of these is the study of the word of God in the spirit of worship.

Chapter 47

JESUS CHRIST IN THE BOOK OF MORMON

Latter Day Saint students of the life and ministry of the Lord Jesus Christ necessarily give some attention to what the Book of Mormon says in this connection. There is one clear and wise approach. It is to study what the book itself says about our Savior.

Many of us have been distracted from this approach to another approach which is important and, indeed, inescapable, and have concerned ourselves with the credentials of the Book of Mormon. We have concerned ourselves with the manner of the book's emergence, the details of its translation, the testimonies of the witnesses, the collateral events noted in the book, etc. This kind of investigation goes on all the time in connection with the Bible. And the more the Book of Mormon attracts the attention of students—believers and nonbelievers—the more it is likely to be the subject of similar scrutiny. We should not decry this approach. But in the nature of the situation it is secondary.

In the long run the Book of Mormon will be accepted or rejected on the basis of the quality of its teachings. Dr. Roy A. Cheville affirmed this in his able book *The Book of Mormon Speaks for Itself*[1] (Herald House 1971). It has been affirmed by a number of Mormon writers.

What, then, does the Book of Mormon say of the life and ministry of the Lord Jesus? Obviously we cannot treat this in minute detail. Nor can we expect it to differ in principle from the record in the Bible for it is an additional witness, not an independent witness. The Book of Mormon itself reads:

> I, the Lord your God, have created all men, and . . . I remember those who are upon the isles of the sea; and . . . I rule in the heavens above, and in the earth beneath; and I bring forth my word to the children of men, even

upon all the nations of the earth. . . . Know ye not that the testimony of two nations is a witness to you that I am God, that I remember one nation like another?. . . I do this that I may prove to many that I am the same yesterday, today, and forever; and that I speak forth my words according to mine own pleasure.[2]

The Universality of the Divine Concern

Jesus likened himself to the Good Shepherd. The disciples who were with him in Galilee and in Judea and had heard his teaching and particularly his parables, did not find this hard to understand. But Jesus broadened their outlook, saying to them, "Other sheep I have, which are not of this fold, them also I must bring" (John 10:16).

Latter Day Saints have generally held this to be a reference to the ministry of the Lord Jesus in the western hemisphere, and this has some support in the Book of Mormon itself. But the Book of Mormon goes further. Here Jesus is reported as saying to his Nephite disciples,

> [Y]e are they of whom I said, "Other sheep I have which are not of this fold; them also must I bring, and they shall, hear my voice, and there shall be one fold, and one shepherd. . . . And verily, verily, I say unto you that I have other sheep which are not of this land; neither of the land of Jerusalem; neither in any parts of that land round about, whither I have been to minister. For they of whom I speak, are they who have not as yet heard my voice; neither have I at any time manifested myself to them.[3]

This broader statement is in harmony with the words of Mormon which are used as an introduction to the Book of Mormon and state that a major purpose of the book is "the convincing of the Jew and Gentile that Jesus is the Christ, the Eternal God, *manifesting himself to all nations"* (p. iii).

There was prophetic preparation for the coming of Jesus.

The prophet Amos declared that "surely the Lord God will do nothing, until he revealeth the secret to his servants the prophets" (Amos 3:7). This insight has been verified again and again down through the centuries. God prepares his way before him. He did this in relation to the life and ministry of his Son in Palestine. He also did it in relation to the ministry of his Son among the Nephites and their people (Genesis 49:22-26; Isaiah 29:11-12; Ezekiel 37:15-23, 28).

According to the Book of Mormon about six hundred years before the birth of Christ immediately prior to the Babylonian captivity, a small group of men and women left Jerusalem under the guidance of Lehi, a godly man of the tribe of Manasseh.[4] This colony migrated to America and grew in numbers until they became a mighty people. Although many of them forsook the religion of their fathers, others were faithful to the law of Moses and enjoyed the ministry of a long line of prophets. The favorite theme of these prophetic leaders was the coming of the Messiah, Many of their prophecies were parallel to those in the Old Testament. Some were more detailed. Thus Lehi, while yet a short distance from Jerusalem on the journey west, predicted the time and place and manner of the coming of the Messiah, the work of John the Baptist, something of the ministry of Jesus and his death and resurrection.[5] This prophecy was reaffirmed and elaborated as to detail by Nephi (I Nephi 5:236-257; II Nephi 11:21-28), Abinadi (Mosiah 8:28-38), Alma (Alma 16:196-197), Amulek, (Alma 16:201-207), and others. Five years before the birth of Jesus the most specific of these prophecies was given through Samuel, the Lamanite prophet.[6]

This high expectation conditioned the lives of those who believed.

Jesus is the author and guarantor of our salvation.

This is the theme of the Book of Mormon. It is stated directly and lies behind many less direct teachings and affirmations. Nephi taught it constantly. Here are some excerpts from his writings:

> [T]here is but one Messiah spoken of by the prophets, and that Messiah is he who should be rejected of the Jews. . . . As the Lord God lives, there is no other name given under heaven, save it be this Jesus Christ of which I have spoken, whereby man can be saved.[7]
>
> For we labor diligently to write, to persuade our children, and also our brethren, to believe in Christ, and to be reconciled to God; for we know that it is by grace that we are saved, after all we can do.[8]
>
> And we talk of Christ, we rejoice in Christ, we preach of Christ, we prophecy of Christ, and we write according to our prophecies, that our children may know to what source they may look for a remission of their sins.[9]
>
> [T]he right way is to believe in Christ, and deny him not; and Christ is the Holy One of Israel. Wherefore you must bow down before him and worship him with all your might, mind, and strength, and your whole soul, and if you do this, you shall in no wise be cast out.[10]

Jesus ministered in person in the West.

In III Nephi chapters five, six, seven, and eight is the record of the ministry of the Lord Jesus in the West. It is needed to fulfill what had been prophesied. It is also the most reassuring section of the book for many who have read it in faith. But it is possibly the most difficult for those who do not make this approach. It may be helpful to recall what had happened when Jesus joined Cleopas and his friend as they walked to Emmaus immediately after his resurrection. It will be remembered that Jesus opened the scriptures and explained them in terms of what had now happened, and that after they had recognized him and he had left them they said to one another, "Did not our heart burn within us, while he talked with us by the way, and while he opened to us the scriptures?" (Luke 24:31).

What Jesus said and did in Bountiful sounds familiar to those who have studied the New Testament record of the teachings of Jesus. But if the gospel was to be planted in the West it had to be set forth there also. It must not be another gospel. The gospel of Jesus Christ is the way of salvation, and the only way. So, Nephi says, the ministry was called and commissioned, the principles were taught, the sacraments were administered, the power of the Spirit was made evident, and the Saints rejoiced.

God wills our salvation, but respects our agency.

The Book of Mormon teaches, as does the Bible, that although God loves us, and through all history has reached out after us, he will not force us to obey him. We must decide freely what is to be our way of life, and are responsible for the choices which we make. Samuel, the Lamanite, put it this way: "You are free; you are permitted to act for yourselves; for behold, God hath given to you a knowledge, and he has made you free" (Helaman 5:85-86). See, also, II Nephi 1:99, 7:40.

Though we are free, we are not left alone as we face the choices between good and evil. We are constantly "tempted upward." In his last admonitions to his sons Lehi warned them of the enticements of evil but also said, "Look to the great Mediator, and hearken to his great commandments, and be faithful to his words, and choose eternal life, according to the will of the Holy Spirit" (II Nephi 1:122-23). It is within our power to do this. Nephi told his father, "I will go and do the things which the Lord has commanded, for I know that the Lord gives no commandments to the children of men save he shall prepare a way for them that they may accomplish the thing which he commands them" (I Nephi 1:65).

NOTES

1. Roy A. Cheville, *The Book of Mormon Speaks for Itself,* Herald House, 1971, p. 152 ff.
2. II Nephi 12:56-57, 59, 62.

3. III Nephi 7:20, 24-25.
4. Alma 8:3.
5. I Nephi 3:4-15.
6. Helaman 5:55-61; 75-82.
7. II Nephi 11: 34, 39.
8. II Nephi 11:43-44.
9. II Nephi 11:48.
10. II Nephi 11:55-56. See also II Nephi 1:71, 72-73, 116; Mosiah 1:109; 8:90-91.

Study Helps for

Chapter 47

LESSON PURPOSE

To examine, briefly, the teachings of the Book of Mormon in relation to the life and ministry of the Lord Jesus

SCRIPTURE REFERENCES

Acts 10:34-35; 46-48; John 10:11-16

HIGH POINTS OF THE LESSON

- Let the Book of Mormon speak for itself.
- Its message is akin to that of the Bible.
- It quickens concern for the Christian outreach into other nations.

QUESTIONS AND DISCUSSION TOPICS

1. Why was Lehi commanded to leave Jerusalem? Compare this with the departure of Abraham from Ur (Genesis 12:1-2). What lesson has it for us about the primacy of spiritual values over material possessions?

2. Comment on the statement of Jesus about his "other sheep." Why deal with them separately, and not all together?

3. Who are the prophets to whom God reveals his secrets? Some have left the record of their prophecies in the scriptures. Are there others? Poets, for example?

4. If some modern Cleopas studied the Book of Mormon as it was opened to him by a godly man, a believer, what result would accrue? (Note Moroni 10:5 in this connection.) Is there any time limit to the understanding promised?

5. III Nephi, chapters five to nine, reports the ministry of Jesus in the West. Can you suggest anything which was omitted? Was anything added which was inconsistent with the total message?

6. The doctrine of agency which is noted here, and which is basic to the Sermon on the Mount and other teachings of Jesus, is related to the doctrine of stewardship and such other matters as the rights and responsibilities of

Christians at every level. Having noted this, comment on what the observance of this principle might have done to prevent the decay of the Christian social order which followed the period of Nephite unity after the ministry of Jesus.

7. What provisions did Jesus make for the continuance of his ministry in the West? The twelve disciples especially commissioned by Jesus were not called "apostles." Did this mean that no such apostolic function as was entrusted to their counterparts in Palestine were also entrusted to them? Is this important?

8. What did Jesus teach about the promises of God to Israel? Why was this important?

WHAT THE LESSON MEANS FOR TODAY

God has invited our consideration of the whole world for all the time that is yet to come as giving us spiritual opportunities and laying on us major spiritual responsibilities. We are now strengthening or laying foundations for far richer tomorrows than our forebears ever dreamed. This is not because we are especially able, but because of the love and power of God and the fact that, as Paul wrote, "[We] can do all things through Christ which strengtheneth [us]" (Philippians 4:13). (Note that this has been put into the plural.)

Chapter 48

THE DOCTRINE OF JESUS

Jesus was a great doctrinal preacher and teacher. In our day this is not generally recognized because there has been widespread reaction against doctrine. It is nevertheless quite true.

An informed person using the word *doctrine,* is not referring to antiquated ideas about God and people—ideas hoary with age and long since left behind by the thinkers and leaders of our time. The searcher is concerned, rather, with sound and fundamental statements of what is held to be true. The word *doctrine* is closely related to the word *doctor,* and a doctor—in the original sense of the word—is a teacher, a competent dispenser of truth. A doctrine, then, is a considered and fundamental pronouncement. It is in this sense that physicists talk of the doctrine of entropy; statesmen, of the Monroe Doctrine; and Marxians of the doctrine of economic determinism. When informed disciples talk of the doctrine of Christ, they have in mind the fundamental affirmations of Jesus concerning God and man.

Some who have not understood the nature of the doctrine of Christ have regarded it as a system of arbitrary edicts having little to do with the realities of daily life. Nothing could be further from the truth. The doctrine of Christ deals with necessities rising out of the nature of God and persons—principles rooted in the nature of things as they truly are. There is nothing arbitrary about such basic admonitions as the following:

> Have faith in God.[1]
>
> Repent ye, and believe the gospel.[2]
>
> He that believeth and is baptized, shall be saved; but he that believeth not, shall be damned.[3]

These principles of the doctrine of Christ have to do with the business of living effectively, and they are true in every land and in every age. They were enunciated by Jesus Christ, who said of himself: "I am . . . the truth."[4] Those who respect the credentials presented by the Lord Jesus will submit themselves to the disciplines indicated in these doctrines and expect them to be justified in their own experience. Jesus has advised just such a course: "My doctrine is not mine, but his that sent me. If any man will do his will, he shall know of the doctrine, whether it be of God."[5]

It is the strength and glory of the doctrine of Jesus that this doctrine and its adequacy were so marvelously illustrated in his own life. Jesus is "the way, the truth, and the life." When we talk of faith in God we mean such faith in God as Jesus demonstrated. When we consider repentance from sin we are concerned with such adjustment to the divine purpose as Jesus constantly manifested. When we talk of baptism of water and of the Spirit we have in mind the enlistment with others under God which Jesus himself practiced. Any who seek to understand the secrets of Jesus' wisdom and power but fail to consider the fundamental convictions by which he lived are impractical and unscientific and are foredoomed to disappointment. Out of his own assurance of this fact, John wrote:

> Whosoever transgresseth, and abideth not in the doctrine of Christ, hath not God. He that abideth in the doctrine of Christ, he hath both the Father and the Son.[6]

Unfortunately, in some circles doctrine has been related at times to beliefs rather than to practice; to acceptance and not necessarily to action. Jesus had no such passive attitude. He said:

> It is not everyone that saith unto me, Lord, Lord, that shall enter into the kingdom of heaven; but he that doeth the will of my Father who is in heaven. . . .
>
> Therefore, whosoever heareth these sayings of mine and doeth them, I will liken him unto a wise man, who built his house upon a rock. . . .
>
> And everyone that heareth these sayings of mine, and doeth them not, shall be likened unto a foolish man, who built his house upon the sand.[7]

It may be that this tendency to regard belief as passive acceptance is due to greater emphasis on the intellectual aspect of belief than the scriptures warrant. Careful reading of the scriptures will show that belief has to do with the whole person and includes an attitude of both mind and heart. The real meaning of belief is to be faithful, to carry one's belief into appropriate action. A helpful modern translation of the apostolic commission reads thus:

> Go ye into all the world, and preach the gospel to every creature. He that is faithful and is baptized shall be saved; but he that is unfaithful shall be condemned.[8]

In line with this thought, we note that in his arresting portrayal of the final judgment Jesus showed clearly that reward or punishment in the hereafter will be according to our actions. Sound and deep convictions are important because they lead to sound and effective actions.

The more squarely we face the opportunities and demands of life, the more highly we shall value the great principles of action by which Jesus lived and died. Foremost among these principles is confident faith in God. Indeed, as we have seen, Jesus made it clear that people of faith live on one level of life and people lacking faith live on a much lower level. The essential difference between life on these two levels is not a matter of money or of social position or any other secondary thing; it is essentially a matter of faith in God.

Another doctrine of major importance in the life of Jesus is the principle of the supreme value of the human soul. By the light of this principle, Jesus lived for people and died for people—not for rich or poor, black or white but for all. In his sight people are so important as individuals that such incidentals as color and station are far too trivial to add to or to detract from their intrinsic worth. The sublime indifference of the Master to the blandishments of wealth and power can be explained only when we give its rightful weight to the deep conviction he held concerning the worth of persons. The life of Jesus confirms his conviction that there is no true wealth other than character, no lasting power apart from righteousness, no real glory except the light of truth.

The convictions Jesus held concerning God and persons gave rise to the great Christian doctrines concerning sin and forgiveness. He thought of people as the prodigal children of a good and wise and generous father, children who go to far countries and there live on husks while the heart of their father yearns over them. In the eyes of Jesus this is sin, and sin is a crime against the love of the Father. To shut one's eyes to the fact of sin does not destroy that fact nor heal the broken heart of the Father. The only solution to the problem of sin lies in the continuing love of God and the creative power of the forgiveness he extends to all who can be persuaded to repent. The Master knew in his soul that sinners can be reclaimed whenever the grace of forgiveness is given a chance to operate.

Jesus has great respect for the importance of this present life, but he knows that wise persons live today in the light of eternity. To him the destruction of the body is an incident, but the destruction of the soul is the ultimate tragedy. In his eyes this present life is the time when the ultimate purposes of life are envisioned and registered. Survival after death is important because it guarantees opportunity for achieving the values we envision in this present life but which so often elude our grasp. Because he had such confident and living faith in God, Jesus was sure of the immortality of the soul.

The convictions by which Jesus lived became the basis of the doctrines of the church. They carried the certitude given them by his authority. He knew they could not be changed by time or circumstance; that there never can be any situation in which faith in God will be outmoded; that people are of infinite worth to God; that those who acknowledge themselves to be sinners and who repent and accept the forgiveness so graciously extended out of the love of God will in this way find salvation; that all persons must bear responsibility for their own eternal destiny; that to build the kingdom of God is to serve God and to live selfishly—with no sense of stewardship—is to fail God; that, beyond all debate, life here which ignores the hereafter is neither safe nor adequate.

The doctrine of Christ, illustrated in the life of Christ, is so important that Jesus said to his apostles, "He that believeth not, shall be damned."[9] To refuse to believe truths as fundamental as these is itself damnation, for to disregard principles so vital to eternal life is to miss the purpose of life itself. It was for this reason that Jesus told his disciples:

> Go ye therefore, and teach all nations, baptizing them in the name of the Father, and of the Son, and of the Holy Ghost; teaching them to observe all things whatsoever I have commanded you; and, lo, I am with you always, unto the end of the world.[10]

It was for this reason also that the apostles, carrying on his tradition, laid such emphatic stress on the importance of the right understanding of God's will and his purposes for us. It was for this reason that the leaders of the early church classed heresy and unbelief with drunkenness, fornication, and murder.[11]

Despite the limitations of his earthly life, Jesus exercised a freedom and power which no other person had ever known. These qualities were rooted in his deep convictions, and these beliefs in turn were won and held in communion with his Father. Jesus called his followers to this same freedom and this same power, rooted in similar convictions and in similar communion. He did not call people from the half-truths they had believed heretofore to a freedom which was divorced from belief. He called them from small convictions which would not stand the test of enlarged experience to great convictions that would stand the scrutiny of time and eternity. He called them from their vain speculations regarding God and persons to the eternal truth revealed in him and loved by those who share his mind and his Spirit. He called them from petty living to high and noble adventures in the great crusades of faith, from contented grubbing in the old world to new exploration and new life with God in the new world; and the watchword in all this adventuring has always been, "Ye shall know the truth, and the truth shall make you free."[12]

From the time that Jesus chose his disciples, Christianity has always meant following Jesus. The Christians were so named at Antioch because they were followers of Christ. But following Jesus includes much more than physical or intellectual "going after." It also includes a sincere effort to secure the point of view of Jesus, to abide by this point of view, and to live on the basis of this point of view. It includes sharing the assurance of Jesus about God, about the quality and purpose of life, about the value of the human soul, about the necessity for rebirth, about the supremacy of the kingdom of God, about immortality and eternal life. We can choose whether or not we will be Christians; but if we *are* to be Christians, then we must subscribe to the same certitudes by which Jesus governed his life. The emphasis on truth which we must accept and live if we are to gain abundant life must become more and more like the emphasis Jesus taught.

NOTES

1. Mark 11:24.
2. Mark 1:13.

3. Mark 16:15.
4. John 14:6.
5. John 7:16, 17.
6. II John 9.
7. Matthew 7:30, 34, 35.
8. See *The Case for Christianity,* by Clement F. Rogers, pages 112, 113; Harper & Brothers, Ltd., N.Y.
9. Mark 16:15.
10. Matthew 28:18, 19.
11. Galatians 5:19-21. See also I Corinthians 1:10; 10:17; Galatians 1:9, KJ; 8, IV; Romans 16:17; Ephesians 4:5.
12. John 8:32.

Study Helps for

Chapter 48

LESSON PURPOSE

To indicate the importance of sound doctrine as a means to effective life

SCRIPTURE REFERENCES

Matthew 28:18, 19; Galatians 1:8-12.

HIGH POINTS OF THE LESSON

- The vital importance of sound doctrine.
- The relation between belief and practice.
- The unchangeability of basic doctrines.

QUESTIONS AND DISCUSSION TOPICS

1. What do we mean by *doctrine?* Why is doctrine important for life?

2. It has been said that "the golden rule is only gilt unless it is practiced by people who love God." Under what circumstances is this true?

3. Analyze and explore the meaning of: "He that abideth in the doctrine of Christ, he hath both the Father and the Son" (II John 9).

4. Explore the relation between belief and faithfulness. (Read I Kings 8:18.) Explain how you believe good intentions will be weighed in the day of judgment.

5. Enumerate some of the great principles by which Jesus lived. Phrase them in your own words. Discuss their importance for us to live by.

6. Although basic doctrines do not change, it sometimes happens that sound doctrinal teaching demands changing modes of expression. Comment on the importance of habitual scripture study as a safeguard here.

7. Discuss the meaning of the Master's statement: "Ye shall know the truth, and the truth shall make you free."

8. Consider briefly the cost of learning the truth in such fields as chemistry, aeronautics, human relationships. Can people ever acquire knowledge of the truth cheaply? What is the difference between knowing the truth and giving it intellectual assent?

WHAT THE LESSON MEANS FOR TODAY

In the modern world the planned life is the effective life, and successful planning is possible among those of us who know the principles of effective living. In planning our lives it is of vital importance that we shall be clear as to the principles of life in its larger reaches. These principles cannot be discovered by us, for we do not have access to some of the aspects of the large life. The principles must be revealed by One who knows life in its entirety. Wise people seek to follow and to understand his teachings.

Chapter 49

THE HOLY SPIRIT

Throughout the New Testament we are impressed by the important part played by the Holy Spirit. Nowhere is this more clearly demonstrated than in the ministry of the Lord Jesus Christ, whose birth and earthly labors and resurrection were all attended by the power of the Holy Spirit, as is his ministry among people to this present hour.

Long before Jesus was born, the way was prepared for his coming by the testimony of the prophets,[1] who "spake as they were moved by the Holy Ghost."[2] Then, in the meridian of time, the Incarnation was brought about by the operation of the Holy Ghost, which is the spirit of divine love.[3]

> The birth of Jesus Christ was on this wise. After his mother, Mary, was espoused to Joseph, before they came together, she was found with child of the Holy Ghost. Then Joseph, her husband, being a just man, and not willing to make her a public example, was minded to put her away privily. But while he thought on these things, behold, the angel of the Lord appeared unto him in a vision, saying, Joseph, thou son of David, fear not to take unto thee Mary thy wife; for that which is conceived in her, is of the Holy Ghost.[4]

Under the guidance of the Holy Spirit the boy Jesus "increased in wisdom and stature, and in favor with God and man"[5] and in time came to John to be baptized. Immediately after this, "The Holy Ghost descended, in bodily shape like a dove, upon him; and a voice came from heaven, which said, Thou art my beloved Son, in thee I am well pleased."[6]

As the Master prepared for his public ministry, he was attended by the Holy Spirit[7] which continued with him as he began his work in Galilee[8] and was clearly present in the synagogue of Nazareth when the Lord applied to himself the prophetic words of Isaiah:

> The Spirit of the Lord is upon me, because he hath anointed me to preach the gospel to the poor; he hath sent me to heal the brokenhearted, to preach

deliverance to the captives, and recovering of sight to the blind, to set at liberty them that are bruised, to preach the acceptable year of the Lord.[9]

Throughout his life the influence of the Spirit continued as Jesus yielded himself naturally and without reservation to the will of his heavenly Father. As Peter testified in the home of Cornelius:

God anointed Jesus of Nazareth with the Holy Ghost and with power; who went about doing good, and healing all that were oppressed of the devil; for God was with him.[10]

Since the Holy Spirit was such a vital force in the life of the Master, he was fully aware that if his work among people was to continue the Spirit must work with and in them, too. As he approached the end of his earthly ministry, he therefore promised his disciples:

I will pray the Father, and he shall give you another Comforter, that he may abide with you forever; even the Spirit of truth; whom the world cannot receive, because it seeth him not, neither knoweth him; but ye know him; for he dwelleth with you, and shall be in you.[11]

To the surprise of the disciples, Jesus then went on to assure them that the coming of the Comforter, the Holy Spirit, was not a mere compensation to be regarded as a desirable but secondary adjustment made necessary by the wickedness of the Jews. It would actually be better for them if he himself should leave them in order that the Comforter might come:

I tell you the truth; It is expedient for you that I go away: for if I go not away, the Comforter will not come unto you; but if I depart, I will send him unto you.[12]

This was very difficult indeed for the sorrowing disciples to understand, even as it is for us today. But, as Jesus carefully pointed out, what he said was both true and important. If he should remain visibly present among his disciples after they knew the fullness of his greatness, his presence would overawe them. If they were to be truly free, God must continue to guide them as he had done in the life of Jesus; but this guidance must not be too apparent. It must leave room for their free response. The continuance of Jesus in their lives, through the Holy Spirit, would require of them a much more profound faith than could be achieved by his continuance in their midst as a visible and immediately accessible example whose evident greatness would overpower them.

This retirement of the Lord Jesus at the point where his presence might so easily prove a deterrent to the growing maturity of his followers was consistent with the practice of Divinity from the beginning. At any time, by permitting some great physical catastrophe or some stupendous display of power, God could have brought every child of Adam to his knees. If he had done so, however, their obeisance would have had no genuine spiritual significance. The purpose of God is to convince persons, not to coerce them. This demands persuasion, not display. It was in light of this truth that Jesus prayed his Father that he would now send the Comforter. The battle for souls had been carried on among them. Now it was to go forward within them.

In this connection it is helpful to remember that the basic meaning of the word *comfort* is strengthen. The Holy Ghost is the Comforter because it strengthens the believing followers of the Lord Jesus Christ in the inner person quickening in them a living testimony, reminding them of the great things God has done for them, giving them assurance for all the tomorrows, and making them valiant in testimony of all these things.[13]

When the time came the prayer of Jesus was answered and the Comforter, which is the Holy Spirit, ministered to the disciples in great power, continuing what the Lord Jesus had begun. The New Testament writers speak of being "sent forth by the Spirit," "led of the Spirit," and "pressed by the Spirit." But this pressure, as is shown by the context, was always congenial. What the disciples experienced was a divine companionship in which their outlook was so changed that their wills began to move in harmony with the purpose of God. The guidance of the Holy Spirit was expressed in sense of personal relationship, akin to what they had had with Jesus, creating within them exactly what Jesus had sought to create.

It was the conviction of the early saints that as God had sent forth his Son into the world, so, when the Son's work here was finished, God had sent forth his Spirit to continue the work under different conditions. When they found themselves possessed of new aims and new motives, new disposition and character, new joy and new hope in living, they recognized the new spirit working with them as the living energy of Divinity. It was not the hand of God from without, remolding the vessel he had made, but his own life, dwelling and working within:

> Know ye not that ye are the temple of God, and the Spirit of God dwelleth in you?[14]
>
> As many as received him, to them gave he power to become the sons of God.[15]

The Apostle Paul told what was happening when he wrote to the Corinthian saints:

> If any man live in Christ, he is a new creature; old things are passed away; behold, all things are become new.[16]
>
> We. . .are changed into the same image from glory to glory, even as by the Spirit of the Lord.[17]

What Paul was seeking to express here was not the thrusting into the human soul, by an outside power, of something wholly alien to its true nature. Rather, he was convinced that people had been made in the image of God and that now, by the grace of God, faithful believers were being won back to their true selves. The "I" which Paul said had been "crucified with Christ" was a usurper, occupying the place of Paul's true self; his true self was the "I" which now lived because Christ lived in him.[18]

Practically all that Paul says about the Spirit working in us can be duplicated in what he says about Christ working in us. The work of the Spirit is the work of Christ, and the work of either or both is the work of God. The Spirit of Truth is the power by which we see and understand the things of Christ. He (the Spirit) has not come as an independent divine agent to teach us the truth; he comes to make Christ, who is the embodiment of truth, real to us and in us:

> No man can say that Jesus is the Lord, but by the Holy Ghost.[19]
>
> It is the Spirit that quickeneth; the flesh profiteth nothing; the words that I speak unto you, they are spirit, and they are life.[20]
>
> As many as are led by the Spirit of God, they are the sons of God.[21]
>
> Where the Spirit of the Lord is, there is liberty.[22]

Early Christinaity was, above everything else, the religion of the Spirit. To the first Christians the Spirit meant Jesus' spiritual presence, triumphant over death and now present as Comforter, Guide, and Energizer. This Spirit filled them with wisdom and power, raising their whole beings to a new level of insight and effectiveness.

The Spirit kept the life of the disciples and of the church fresh and current. Had the Spirit not been with them, the disciples would have looked back to the earthly ministry of the Master instead of facing forward with him. As long as they lived for and under the Holy Spirit, they knew Jesus as their Lord and faced the events of time and eternity with hope and courage.

NOTES

1. Genesis 49:10; Isaiah 9:6; 42:1-4; Jeremiah 23:5, 6.
2. II Peter 1:21.
3. John 3:16.
4. Matthew 2:1-3, IV.
5. Luke 2:52.
6. Luke 3:29.
7. Matthew 4:1, IV.

8. Luke 4:14.
9. Luke 4:18, 19, KJ.
10. Acts 10:38, IV.
11. John 14:16, 17.
12. John 16:7.
13. John 14:26.
14. I Corinthians 3:16.
15. John 1:12.
16. II Corinthians 5:17.
17. II Corinthians 3:18.
18. Galatians 2:20.
19. I Corinthians 12:3, KJ.
20. John 6:63.
21. Romans 8:14.
22. II Corinthians 3:17.

Study Helps for

Chapter 49

LESSON PURPOSE

To explain the relation between Jesus and the Holy Spirit and to emphasize the importance of the Holy Spirit in the life of the church today.

SCRIPTURE REFERENCES

John 14:13-26; 16:6-15.

HIGH POINTS OF THE LESSON

- The work of the Holy Spirit in relation to Jesus Christ.
- The necessity that Jesus go away in order that the Comforter might come.
- The work of the Holy Spirit in the life of the disciples of the Lord.

QUESTIONS AND DISCUSSION TOPICS

1. Name several ways in which we believe that people were prepared for the earthly ministry of Jesus Christ.

2. Recount evidences of the ministry of the Holy Spirit in connection with the earthly ministry of Christ.

3. Why was it necessary for Jesus to leave his disciples in order that they might receive the ministry of the Comforter? What is the basic principle involved here?

4. What is the meaning of the title "the Comforter"? What is the most enduring comfort that can come to anyone?

5. What was the central ministry of the Holy Spirit among the disciples after the ascension of Jesus Christ? What other important ministries were promised by Jesus through the Comforter? Give examples of the fulfillment of this promise among the early disciples.

6. What is the relation of the ministry of the Holy Spirit to the agency of believers? Explain how it happens that disciples are more truly themselves when they are obedient to the guidance of the Spirit than when they assert their own will against such guidance.

7. Enumerate some of the gifts of the Holy Spirit enjoyed in the early church. What are some of the fruits of the Spirit enjoyed among the early saints? By us?

8. What are the evidences that the Spirit of God is at work in the church today? Under what conditions can we expect a richer ministry of the Holy Spirit?

WHAT THE LESSON MEANS FOR TODAY

It is becoming increasingly apparent that the world will not be saved through the increase of knowledge. Our need is for spiritual growth, not just intellectual advance or the improvement of our technical skills. Such spiritual growth is achieved by those who make a worthy surrender to the rightful leadership of Divinity.

Chapter 50

JESUS AND HIS FATHER

As we have seen, Jesus had difficulty first of all in teaching the Jews that he was truly the Messiah and then in persuading them of the nature of his messiahship. Much which his disciples had but dimly perceived at first became clear to them after the Resurrection and during the ensuing forty days. Even so, these early saints still did not know just where to place Jesus in relation to God the Father. Their Jewish upbringing was both a help and a hindrance at this point. Their idea of the Messiah did take them a long way toward the truth, but their deep conviction that God is One and Supreme made it difficult for them to see that Jesus was in truth much more than their Messiah. It was hard to recognize him as the Son of God.

Christianity is first of all an experience, not an argument about theology. The theololgy comes later. The early disciples shared the new life which came to them from God through Jesus Christ and through the Holy Spirit. This was fundamental. But it was also important that they should think about the implications of their new experience. Otherwise they could not explain it adequately to thoughtful inquirers. As they applied their minds to an exploration of their faith they became aware that the Holy Spirit was reminding them of things the Master had said to them which they had only dimly understood at the time; they also realized that this same Spirit of Truth was leading them toward heights of understanding they could not have scaled while the Master was wtih them.[1]

Among the things which Jesus had said concerning his relation with his Father, one of the most important which the disciples must have pondered many times, is recorded by Matthew:

> No man knoweth the Son, but the Father; neither knoweth any man the Father, save the Son, and they to whom the Son will reveal himself; they shall see the Father also.[2]

Here, they realized, the Master claimed for himself the closest possible intimacy with his Father—intimacy much closer than anything to which persons might attain.

This awareness of Jesus of his unique relation with his Father is reflected in some of the parables. In the story of the Lord of the vineyard and the wicked husbandman, for example, it is clear that there is great difference between the messengers for whom the husbandman should have shown respect and the Lord's own son for whom they should have shown reverence.[3]

Looking back again, with eyes no longer clouded, the disciples reflected that the Master had actually encouraged them to expect the work of God at his hands. He had taught them to look to him for relief from all manner of distress—physical, mental, and spiritual. He promised rest to the weary and overburdened, forgiveness for repentant sinners, and light to those searching for truth. He set himself forth as the final and infallible judge of all humankind. He told his disciples to pray "our Father" and talked to them of "your Father," but when he himself was involved he always spoke of "my Father."[4]

As has already been indicated, it is probable that during the early days of the apostolic age the twelve and their associates were so deeply impressed by the fact of the Resurrection and their current experience with the endowment of the Holy Spirit that they thought of Jesus as "both Lord and Christ" (i.e., the Messiah and even more than the Messiah) without working out any more careful statement of their theology.[5] As they looked backward under the enlightening influence of the Spirit, the sayings of the Lord Jesus bore their own testimony and demanded that the believers face the full truth about their Lord. It was not long until Peter was to be found telling the rulers of the Jews:

> This [Jesus] is the stone which was set at naught of you builders, which is become the head of the corner. Neither is there salvation in any other; for there is none other name under heaven given among men, whereby we must be saved.[6]

Shortly after this Peter was associated with John in a mission to Samaria concerning which Luke says:

> Who, when they were come down, prayed for them, that they might receive the Holy Ghost. (For as yet he was fallen upon none of them; only they were baptized in the name of the Lord Jesus.) Then laid they their hands on them, and they received the Holy Ghost.[7]

Again, the same Peter preached in the house of Cornelius:

> It is he [Jesus] which was ordained of God to be the Judge of quick and dead. To him give all the prophets witness, that through his name whosoever believeth in him shall receive remission of sins.[8]

In the earliest record we have of the New Testament saints, it is therefore apparent that they already thought so highly of the Lord Jesus Christ that it was only a question of time until the logic of their own experience pushed them still further and helped them to see that Jesus Christ is in fact the Son of God, sharing in full glory the character and the purpose of his Father.

The Apostle Paul is the first of the disciples who is on record with a reasoned statement that Jesus is God.[9] In his later ministry, Paul emphasized this central truth again and again:

> That the name of our Lord Jesus Christ may be glorified in you, and ye in him, according to the grace of our God and the Lord Jesus Christ.[10]
>
> Looking for that blessed hope, and the glorious appearing of the great God and our Savior Jesus Christ.[11]
>
> For in him dwelleth all the fullness of the Godhead bodily.[12]

Furthermore, the Apostle Paul was so fully convinced that the Father and the Son are each divine that his writings indicate that we may sin against Christ as we sin against God;[13] we may tempt Christ as we tempt God;[14] the judgment seat of God is the judgment seat of Christ;[15] the kingdom of God is the kingdom of Christ;[16] the church of God is the church of Christ;[17] and the Spirit of God is the Spirit of Christ.[18] In his writings, the Lord is continually associated with the Father as the source of grace and peace.[19] Jesus is represented as the supreme lawgiver,[20] the giver of light,[21] the bestower of authority,[22] the transformer of character.[23]

in the letter to the Hebrews, the divinity of Jesus Christ, the Son of God, is fully and clearly portrayed. Indeed, this is one of the dominant notes of the epistle, presenting Jesus as the

> Son, whom he [God] hath appointed heir of all things, by whom also he made the worlds; who being the brightness of his glory, and the express image of his person, and upholding all things by the word of his power, when he had by himself purged our sins, sat down at the right hand of the Majesty on high.[24]

In the Gospel of John, which was the last of the Gospels to be written, the divinity of the Lord Jesus Christ is proclaimed from the first verse:

> In the beginning. . .the Son was with God, and the Son was of God.[25]
>
> The gospel was after the power of an endless life, through Jesus Christ, the Only Begotten Son, who is in the bosom of the Father.[26]
>
> We beheld his glory, the glory as of the Only Begotten of the Father, full of grace and truth.[27]

Chrysostom, one of the early fathers of the church, rendered this last sentence: "We have seen his glory, such glory as it was becoming and right that the Only Begotten and true Son of God should have."

As the thoughts of the disciples matured under the guidance of the Holy Spirit and in reawakened appreciation of what Jesus himself had taught them, they thus came to see that the Lord Jesus Christ is indeed the Son of God and so intimately associated with his Father in the work of creation and of redemption that much which is said of one may be said with equal truth of the other. Moreover, the best revelation we can have of the nature of God is summed up in a phrase which the Apostle Paul used in four of his letters: God is "the Father of our Lord Jesus Christ."[28] Nevertheless, the distinction between the Father and the Son was always clear. It is the Father who has sent forth both the Son and the Spirit:

> When the fullness of the time was come, God sent forth his Son, made of a woman, made under the law, to redeem them that were under the law, that we might receive the adoption of sons. And because ye are sons, God hath sent forth the Spirit of his Son into your hearts, crying, Abba, Father.[29]
>
> Jesus said unto them, If God were your Father, ye would love me; for I proceeded forth and came from God; neither came I of myself, but he sent me.[30]

Although the work of the Son is the work of the Father also, so that each is fully involved in all the other does, the Father and the Son are two persons. The verbiage used in the scripture to express this unity and separateness is at times difficult to understand, since there is nowhere in the universe any parallel to which we can liken it; yet—as modern revelation emphasizes—the unity and the separateness of the Father and the Son are part of our Christian testimony.[31]

The divinely guided meditation and understanding of the early saints in this field is of immense importance to us today. Far more than many of us realize, we need the deep and sound assurance that there is no place in the universe, in time or in eternity, where we cannot find "the God and Father of our Lord Jesus Christ" in whom is our hope of eternal salvation. God, the Father, is available. God, the Son, is available. Every attempt made by misguided thinkers to separate the Father and the Son leads to the conclusion that God is too remote to be available or that the Son is not quite adequate to the universal demands laid on him by our deepest necessities. We must think of the Father and the Son, as the scripture teaches, as inseparably associated. "He that hath seen me," said the Master himself, "hath seen the Father."[32] There is no exact parallel to this in our experience, but we get a hint from the statement of how the Master regarded truly married persons: "They are no more twain, but one flesh. What, therefore, God hath joined together, let no man put asunder."[33]

Nevertheless, such sincere but misguided persons as would have us completely identify the Father and the Son are also in error. The Father and the Son are "twain" despite the fact that they are one. And this, also, is important; for our highest thought of personality is social. We must not think that God the Father ever was isolated by the solitary splendor of his unapproachable divinity. The Son was in the beginning with God,[34] for God is love, and love demands an object through which to express itself. The Son was related to the Father in love before the world was.

Any persistent thought concerning the relation of the Father and the Son soon takes us beyond our depth. We can see clearly enough, however, to know that Christ is necessary not only to our understanding of ourselves but to our understanding of the Father.

NOTES

1. John 14:26; 16:21-25.
2. Matthew 11:28, IV. The parallel passage in Luke 10:22, IV, is best understood in light of the Matthean statement.
3. Mark 12:1-9. See also Mark 8:31-38, KJ; 33-41, IV.
4. Epitomized from *A New Commentary on Holy Scripture,* Gore, etc., Macmillan Company, New York.
5. John 20:28 is the strongest statement in this connection prior to this time, but there is some question as to the exact meaning of Thomas.
6. Acts 4:11, 12.
7. Acts 8:15-17.
8. Acts 10:42, 43.
9. Acts 9:20. See *A New Commentary on Holy Scripture,* by Gore, "New Testament," p. 413 ff.; *Belief in Christ,* by Gore, pp. /5, 87 ff.

10. II Thessalonians 1:12.
11. Titus 2:13.
12. Colossians 2:9.
13. I Corinthians 8:12.
14. I Corinthians 10:9.
15. Romans 14:10; II Corinthians 5:10.
16. Romans 14:17, 18; Ephesians 5:5.
17. I Corinthians 10:32; Romans 16:16.
18. I Corinthians 2:11; Romans 8:9.
19. Galatians 1:3; I Timothy 1:2.
20. I Corinthians 7:10; 9:14-21.
21. Ephesians 5:14.
22. Romans 1:5.
23. I Thessalonians 3:12.
24. Hebrews 1:2, 3. Note the distinction in the scriptures between God and Christ. The Son "sat down at the right hand of the Majesty on high."
25. John 1:1, IV.
26. John 1:18, IV.
27. John 1:14.
28. Romans 15:6; II Corinthians 1:3; 11:31; Ephesians 1:3; Colossians 1:3.
29. Galatians 4:4-6, IV.
30. John 8:42, IV.
31. Doctrine and Covenants 17:5; 90:2.
32. John 14:9.
33. Matthew 19:6.
34. John 1:2, IV.

Study Helps for

Chapter 50

LESSON PURPOSE

To consider the completeness of the revelation of God in the Son Jesus Christ.

SCRIPTURE REFERENCES

John 1:1-5, IV; Acts 2:29-36; I Corinthians 1:30, 31.

HIGH POINTS OF THE LESSON

- Jesus Christ is the Son of God.
- Jesus is the author and finisher of our faith (Hebrews 12:2).
- "In him [Christ] dwelleth all the fullness of the Godhead bodily" (Colossians 2:9).

QUESTIONS AND DISCUSSION TOPICS

1. How did their Jewish background help the early disciples to understand the true nature of the Lord Jesus Christ? In what respects did it make understanding more difficult? What was the heart of their problem?

2. What is the relationship between religious experience and doctrinal teachings? How are these factors related in our becoming effective disciples?

3. Why was the true nature of Jesus not made fully clear by the Holy Spirit at the very beginning of the apostolic experience? Why were the early disciples so long in realizing that the gospel was intended for the Gentiles as well as for the Jews? What light does this throw on the place of experience in the achievement of spiritual understanding? Note in this connection the instruction that the Holy Spirit is to "guide" us into all truth.

4. Read Matthew 11:28. William Barclay, in commenting on this concept, says: "The greatest claim that Jesus ever made, the claim which is the center of the Christian faith, is that he alone can reveal God to humankind. Other men may be sons of God; he is *The Son.* John put this in a different way, when he tells us that Jesus said, 'He who has seen me has seen the Father' (John 14:9).

5. Enumerate some of the evidences that Jesus knew himself to be the Son of God, closer to his Father than any other person could be.

6. Explore the meaning of these scriptural statements: "They were baptized *in the name of the Lord Jesus*"; "There is none other name under heaven given among men whereby we must be saved." Was the Father involved?

7. Jesus said of a man and his wife that "they twain shall be one flesh" (Matthew 19:5). Comment on this as an illustration of the identity and separateness of the Father and the Son.

8. What has been the result of attempts to divide the Father and the Son, as though the Son in some way lacked the fullness of Divinity? What has been the result of attempts to identify the Father and Son so completely that there is no distinction whatever between them?

WHAT THE LESSON MEANS FOR TODAY

Our Lord and Savior Jesus Christ is the source and center of our redemption. Any true thought of God comes to us through him. Our best thought of God is as the "God and Father of our Lord Jesus Christ" (I Corinthians 8:6, etc). There is no salvation apart from him.

Chapter 51

JESUS AND THE RESTORATION

Throughout the apostolic age vivid memories of the ministry of Jesus, the expectation of his early return, the enlightening influence of the Holy Spirit, and the high cost of discipleship combined to keep the church comparatively free of subversive elements and reasonably faithful to the purpose of God for his people. As the years passed, and the expectation of the immediate return of Jesus was tempered by experience, the spiritual vitality of the church perceptibly declined. There were situations where this decline was hastened, curiously enough, by the very values to which Christianity ministered. People who were thrifty and industrious and honest tended to become persons of substance and were tempted by pride and vainglory. Earnest and sober-minded persons who were attracted to Christianity by the lives of the Christians tended to put too high a value on the social results of Christianity and failed to relate these to the spiritual passion which is a vital part of true discipleship.[1] Respectability and decency, which were eminently desirable as evidences and results of Christianity, became substitutes for it.

Then, too, the growth of the church made organization necessary, and organization put a premium on administrative ability. With the passing of the years, the old conflict between the prophet and the priest was renewed. Men of prophetic temper of mind sought to keep in close touch with God and to attune their lives in a constantly finer harmony with the divine purpose. The need for unity and stability was obvious, however, and called for the services of men of priestly temper of mind. These came to the fore and spiritual vitality was sacrificed to order. So, gradually, the church was institutionalized. The questing spirit, the human contribution to the experience of revelation, was lost. Tradition, law, and precedent took its place.

The state, which had at first opposed the church, turned from persecution to toleration, from toleration to acceptance, and—in time—to domination. The emperor came to regard the church as an instrument of government and when it suited his purpose called or authorized councils which passed on matters of faith: the creedal statements of Nicea (325), Chalcedon (431), and others. Bishops and other influential church leaders were appointed or removed for political reasons. By the time the Roman Empire collapsed the papacy was ready to take over and thereafter ruled with sovereign authority.

In the course of its long history, Christianity has entered into all sorts of peculiar compromises and undesirable alliances with corrupt political and economic systems. Yet the world owes Christianity more than it can ever repay, for when all that can be said against historic Christianity has been said, we must still recognize that it has always cultivated some sort of relationship with Jesus.

Although the church as a whole drifted far from what the Lord had taught, there arose with the church many small groups or individuals who glimpsed anew the fresh and vitalizing significance of Jesus. Though the light shining from the lives of these men and women was not such as could banish the gloom of the Dark Ages it was revealing enough to quicken the spiritual desires of many common people and to create in their hearts the readiness to receive greater light when it should become available. Robert A. Baker wrote in this connection:

> The difference between the New Testament pattern and that of the Roman Catholic Church in the thirteenth century was great. The Roman Bishop had become dominant. His authority was recognized in spiritual and secular areas. His organization was strong and well disciplined. The doctrinal

definition of Rome's principal tenets was almost complete. New monkish orders provided recruits for every kind of special service. The future seemed bright. But there were elements which would have disturbed an observant onlooker. Dissent was widespread. . . . The foregleams of the dawn were casting light against which the Roman system could not continue to dominate the minds and hearts of men.[2]

It is impossible to believe that the God and Father of our Lord Jesus Christ turned a deaf ear to those who hungered and thirsted after righteousness throughout the dark night of apostasy. It was in the nature of the situation that recovery from that which had developed so gradually and imperceptibly should itself go forward little by little. When the elements of this recovery began to appear they seemed to be of little consequence, but soon they were augmented from every quarter. The translation of the Bible and the almost simultaneous invention of movable type made it possible for the first time for the common people to study the word of God for themselves. Less obviously, the Renaissance, the discovery of the New World, the rise of nationalism, the introduction of new economic systems, and a thousand other developments made for freedom of thought and action and worship. In the monasteries, the abbeys, and the universities earnest men and women found time and opportunity for study, prayer, and worship. The cost was tremendous but, once again, the blood of the martyrs became the seed of the church.

The roll of the pioneers of the coming Reformation is too long to be recapitulated here. Some are known to even the most casual students of history—John Huss of Bohemia (1369-1415), Martin Luther of Germany (1483-1546), John Calvin of France and Switzerland (1509-1564), John Wycliffe of England (1520-1584), George Fox of England (1624-1691), John and Charles Wesley of England (1703-1791; 1707-1788). The denominations which grew out of the labors of these men keep fresh the memory of their teachings. What we rarely remember is the devotional guidance given believers by such men as Thomas a Kempis (*The Imitation of Christ*) and John Bunyan (*Pilgrim's Progress*).

In the newly published *Hymns of the Saints* there is interesting evidence of the indebtedness of today's worshipers to lovers of the Lord Jesus who lived before the Reformation. Note, for example,

"All Glory, Laud, and Honor" (23) by Theodulph of Orleans (c. 760-821).

"Come, O Creator Spirit, Come" (283) attributed to Hrabanus Maurus (776-856).

"Jesus, the Very Thought of Thee" (167), Bernard of Clairvaux (1091-1153).

"Jesus Christ Is Risen Today" (278), a fourteenth century Latin carol.

And from the early Reformation period come

"A Might Fortress" (142), Martin Luther (1483-1546).

"Now Thank We All Our God" (60), Martin Rinkart (1586-1649).

"Teach Me, My God and King" (439), George Herbert (1593-1633).[3]

In this connection it is also well to note the call of Emma Smith to "make a selection of sacred hymns" for use among the Saints.[4] The hymns chosen were well known before the Restoration came into being.

The Restoration was primarily a new awakening of people to Christ. It centered in the ever loving, ever revealing presence of Jesus Christ. It began, as far as such an event can be dated, on a day in the early spring of 1820 when Joseph Smith retired to a grove near his home and there pleaded with God to help him choose the right church from among the various churches of the vicinity. The answer to his prayer is recorded in his own words:

> I saw a pillar of light exactly over my head, above the brightness of the sun; which descended gradually until it fell upon me. . . .When the light

rested upon me I saw two personages (whose brightness and glory defy all description) standing above me in the air. One of them spake unto me, calling me by name, and said (pointing to the other), "This is my beloved Son, hear him."[5]

After this experience, and in harmony with the further instructions of a heavenly visitant, Joseph became an even more careful student of the scriptures but he did not join any of the churches of the vicinity.

Three years later Joseph again received a visit from a heavenly messenger; as a result of the instructions received at that time, the plates of the Book of Mormon were unearthed from their hiding place in western New York. They were subsequently translated by Joseph and thus given to the world. The Book of Mormon was first published in 1830. Its title page states that the purpose of the record is "the convincing of the Jew and Gentile that Jesus is the Christ, the Eternal God, manifesting himself unto all nations."

While these events were transpiring, and before the Book of Mormon was published, authority to baptize was recommitted to the earth under the hands of John the Baptist, the "forerunner" of Jesus. In transmitting his authority to Joseph Smith and his associate, Oliver Cowdery, John said:

> Upon you, my fellow servants, in the name of the Messiah, I confer the priesthood of Aaron, which holds the keys of the ministering of angels, and of the gospel of repentance, and of baptism by immersion, for the remission of sins; and this shall never be taken again from the earth, until the sons of Levi do offer again an offering unto the Lord in righteousness.[6]

Thus the work of preparation was again initiated. Just as John had prepared the way before the Master prior to the earthly ministry of Jesus, so now the men of the priesthood and the church as a whole were commissioned to prepare the way for the second coming of the Master.

The outstanding message of the newly commissioned ministry was that Jesus Christ still lives and is eager to manifest himself to those who will receive him. This principle of divine revelation was made clear in the experience of the boy Joseph in the spring of 1820, and it was repeatedly reaffirmed in the further divine guidance which he received and which culminated in the organization of the church on April 6, 1830. In February 1832, Joseph Smith and Sidney Rigdon, one of his immediate associates, inquired of the Lord regarding the meaning of a passage of scripture they were studying together. In answer to their seeking they were granted a vision of the Master, of which they bore this most wonderful testimony:

> And, now, after the many testimonies which have been given of him, this is the testimony, last of all, which we give of him, that he lives; for we saw him, even on the right hand of God; and we heard the voice bearing record that he is the Only Begotten of the Father; that by him, and through him, and of him, the worlds are and were created; and the inhabitants thereof are begotten sons and daughters unto God.[7]

A few years later, soon after the wonderful endowment received at the dedication of Kirtland Temple, Joseph Smith and Oliver Cowdery retired behind the temple veil and during the ensuing prayer received the personal ministry of Jesus the Lord. These and similar experiences have become forever part of the heritage of Latter Day Saints; they find their echo in the continuance of the apostolic witness that Jesus is the Christ.[8]

Notwithstanding the experiences of the past, the Saints of today at times tend to exalt the principles of the gospel as ends in themselves instead of as means to the great end that Christ shall live in the lives and hearts of all people. Against such a tendency we must be constantly on our guard. Twenty centuries ago John the Beloved declared that "He that abideth in the doctrine of Christ, he hath both the Father and the Son."[9] This is still true. All the teachings of the church center in the fact of Jesus Christ and in his message of the love of God. No attempt to express in permanent institutions the spirit of that message must be permitted to destroy the liberty and freedom of personal experience with the Master. It is essential that our expanding understanding of the ways of Divinity shall become the prized possession of the whole body of the church, and shall be incorporated into our church institutions so as to mold the thinking and the understanding of those who come after. But these institutions must reflect the mind of Christ. They must be guided by his Spirit and find their justification in the extent to which they register and fulfill his purpose.

Our Latter Day Saint experience has been that Jesus is our final source of inspiration and power. When we have made mistakes—and we have made them often—it has been because we have failed to understand him or have been untrue to him through blindness or unwillingness to pay the price of discipleship. In our brief experience as a people, we have been called back again and again to the Man of Galilee and to his way of life. Whenever we heed his call, we expect him to lead us on to new continents of spiritual understanding. He is even now preparing us for still richer endowments of spiritual power and insight. We expect that our love for each other will become more wise and more willingly sacrificial, and therefore more effective, as we journey in the way with him. We find ourselves troubled, as his early disciples were troubled, by the temptation to judge the process of his kingdom by the standards of an ungodly world. In so doing we think too much of the "forms of godliness" and too little of the power given to persons of spiritual integrity.

Sometimes we find ourselves thinking of his kingdom in material terms, very much as the disciples of an earlier age tended to do. Although we can repeate the words of the promise of Christ, we do not yet understand with our hearts that all things we need shall be added if we seek first to build up the kingdom of God and to establish his righteousness.[10] We are sure, however, that Jesus our Lord has the words of Eternal Life for our age and for every other age. We know that every quickening of the forces which make for more abundant life comes from God and is made available to us through the Spirit of the Lord Jesus. The way of the future is the way of growing intimacy with him and growing devotion to his person and his purpose.

NOTES

1. Note the Book of Mormon parallel in IV Nephi 1:26-28.
2. *A Summary of the Christian History,* Broadman Press, Nashville, TN, 1959, page 143.
3. See also hymns 30, 40, 211, 238, 260, 262, 276, 289.
4. Doctrine and Covenants 24:3b.
5. *The History of the Reorganized Church of Jesus Christ of Latter Day Saints,* Vol. 1, p. 9.
6. Ibid., pp. 34-36.
7. Doctrine and Covenants 76:3g, h.
8. Doctrine and Covenants 26:3; 104:12, 13.
9. II John 9.
10. Matthew 6:38, IV.

Study Helps for

Chapter 51

LESSON PURPOSE

To emphasize the central place of Christ in the Restoration movement.

SCRIPTURE REFERENCES

I Corinthians 2:5-16; 3:6-11; Revelation 14:6-7.

HIGH POINTS OF THE LESSON

- The gradual drift of the New Testament church into periods of apostasy.
- The gradual change of persecution to domination by the government.
- The gradual turning from sinfulness to awareness by people blessed of God.
- The new awakening of people to Christ through the Restoration.

QUESTIONS AND DISCUSSION TOPICS

1. What changes in the New Testament church made it possible for tradition and precedent to take the place of spiritual vitality?
2. What changes made it possible for the government to dominate the church?
3. How was the Reformation a necessary part of history? How is the Restoration a part of this flow of history?
4. Why is it impossible to believe that God "turned a deaf ear to those who hungered and thirsted after righteousness throughout the dark night of apostasy"?
5. Name some of the great leaders of Christian history and their contributions.
6. What is the central theme of the Restoration message? What is the purpose of the Book of Mormon?
7. What was the nature of the endowment that Joseph Smith and Oliver Cowdery received in Kirtland Temple? Under what circumstances can we participate in such an experience?
8. What is the danger of exalting the principles of the gospel as ends in themselves and emphasizing some methods opposed to others in our teaching experience? What are the outstanding characteristics of a true disciple of Jesus in our day?

WHAT THE LESSON MEANS FOR TODAY

The task of our day is to achieve personal loyalty to Jesus our Lord, and to express this loyalty in terms which he has already indicated and which will be clarified in expanding experience. The threat of apostasy exists throughout our history. In earlier days this robbed religion of its effectiveness. There is a danger that we shall substitute good ideas and even good works for the distinctive work which our Master wants us to do under his personal guidance. The slogan is still, "Hear ye Him."

Chapter 52

OUR LORD AND SAVIOR, JESUS CHRIST

The early disciples followed Jesus because they already had deep spiritual concern. Several of them had been close followers of John the Baptist and followed the Lord on John's recommendation. Later, all of them followed him on the specific invitation of the Lord himself. Matthew tells us that Jesus,

> walking by the Sea of Galilee, saw two brethren, Simon, called Peter, and Andrew, his brother, casting a net into the sea; for they were fishers. And he said unto them, I am he of whom it is written by the prophets; follow me, and I will make you fishers of men. And they, believing on his words, left their nets, and straightway followed him.[1]

In like fashion, James and John also followed him.[2]

The record says that the disciples left their nets and followed "straightway" and "immediately." Quite evidently the prospect of becoming "fishers of men" was attractive to them, but this calling was not to be undertaken singly. The invitation was phrased in the plural. In accepting the invitation the disciples (who in time would become apostles) became members of a fellowship of commissioned witnesses.

These men came to share transforming convictions about God and people and the divine purpose in creation. Their Christianity, however, was more than a matter of belief. It was, essentially, a mode of existence patterned on the life and teachings of the Lord who had said, "I am the way."[3] Those who believed in Christ were said to be "of the way."[4]

The titles and designations which the saints applied to Jesus give some indication of what the Lord came to mean to them. Some of the names were taken from the Old Testament, for in their newly alert study of the scriptures in light of the Resurrection the saints felt that these were clearly appropriate to him.[5] Thus he was referred to as "a prophet like unto Moses,"[6] the "Holy One,"[7] the "Redeemer,"[8] and the "King."[9] Again, he was known as Emmanuel (God with us).[10] Isaiah's prophecies concerning the coming "Wonderful, Counselor, The mighty God, the "Everlasting Father" (literally the Father of eternity), the "Prince of Peace," were applied to him.[11]

In the early days of his ministry Jesus was generally known by that name, but "Christ" (the Greek equivalent of the Hebrew "Messiah" or "the Anointed") soon replaced it. The name "Christ" is weighted with the entire content of his claim.[12]

We may note in passing that in the New Testament the word *Lord* was commonly used simply as a polite form of address which we properly translate by *Sir.* It is used in this sense in Matthew and Mark in particular. But we must go deeper than this if we are to know its loftier meaning.

Jesus was called Lord by the angel who announced his birth[13] and by John the Baptist, who was his forerunner.[14] Jesus himself also used this term during his last days.[15] Its more frequent use after the Resurrection indicated growing awareness of the Lord's right to reign. To call him Lord was both a confession of faith and loyalty and a claim to be his disciple.[16]

In the apostolic church *Lord* tended to replace *Jesus,* which was now felt to be too familiar. It often replaced *Christ* also, for this was sometimes thought to be too formal. Sometimes the two designations were joined and became *Lord Jesus.*[17]

As the early saints were awakened to the signficance of the Resurrection, the lordship of Jesus Christ came to mean absolutely unique lordship. Affirmation of this sovereignty was equivalent to an affirmation that other lords are false. He is Lord; there are no other lords. He is far above all principality and power and might and dominion and every name that is named, not only in this world but also in the world which is to come.[18]

There were times when the Lord Jesus referred to himself as "the Son of Man." This expression was used by Gabriel when he came to Mary to announce the birth of Jesus and said, "He shall be called the Son of the Highest...the Son of God."[19] After his baptism the Father testified, "This is my beloved Son, in whom I am well pleased."[20] John said that his gospel was written "that ye might believe that Jesus is the Christ, the Son of God; and that believing ye might have life through his name."[21]

The use of this designation by Jesus constituted a specific claim to a deep intimacy with the Father whom he came to make known.[22] This was not immediately apparent to all of the saints, but they recognized the expression as a quotation from the prophecies of Daniel.[23] It became one of the many factors helping them to realize that the earthly ministry of the Lord was the high point of the revelation of God through his prophets down the ages.

The title most beloved by the saints down the generations, however, is *Savior.* Although the specific term—like *Redeemer*—is used infrequently, it has abundant New Testament justification. Joseph was told by the angel "Thou shalt call his name Jesus; for he shall save his people from their sins."[24] And to the astonished shepherds the angel said,

> ...for behold, I bring you good tidings of great joy, which shall be to all people. For unto you is born this day, in the city of David, a Savior, who is Christ the Lord.[25]

Peter declared to the Council that "The God of our Fathers raised up Jesus....Him hath God exalted with his right hand to be a Prince and a Savior."[26] And at Antioch Paul declared that God, "according to his promise, raised unto Israel a Savior, Jesus."[27]

Basic to the whole message of Jesus was his passion and concern for the salvation of humankind—for all who do not know God as he truly is and so neither love him nor serve him truly.

Jesus himself said that the Son of Man is come to save that which is lost.[28] Notable among his parables was the one telling of a man who had a hundred sheep but left the ninety and nine and went into the mountains to seek one who had "gone astray" and continued his search "until he found it." When he found it, he called together his friends and neighbors, saying, "Rejoice with me; for I have found my sheep which was lost."[29]

In the ordinary traffic of daily life to say that something is lost means that it is missing from where it belongs, as a lost book, a lost child, a lost coat, lost luggage. Sometimes an article reported as "lost" would be better described as "misplaced"; it can usually be recovered without undue inconvenience. But if a girl has wandered away from her parents with whom she was on a vacation in a strange country, whose language she does not speak, what then? Someone who knows the country and the language must volunteer or be drafted to help or there is tragedy in the making.

While people today tend to find obnoxious the very idea that they are lost and in need of salvation, this fact and this need are attested on every side as the more sober-minded are coming to realize. Our progress in the scientific and cultural fields has not led to the eradication of the ancient ills which the prophets denounced, and against which Jesus spoke so clearly and so forcefully. We are still plagued by hatred of our brothers and sisters, lascivious desire, divided loyalties, aggressive self-seeking, irresponsibility in the presence of opportunity and need, and failure to tell the simple truth.

Furthermore, our lostness, which is akin to that of

people of every age, is not a purely personal affair. It permeates the social order. Racial, class, and religious self-centeredness steadfastly nourish and sustain the prejudices and rivalries which vitiate our community life; and—despite their possible temporary value—the remedies which we apply do not go deep enough to correct the ills to which they are addressed.

It is only as we find redemption in and through Christ Jesus that we are safe from betrayal by our own selfishness and pride. We cannot rightly manage God's gifts to us unless we manage them for God. We cannot know how truly to judge as between ourselves and others except to the degree that we listen to God in setting our own course. We cannot fully escape the depersonalization which is so characteristic of our age until we find the roots of our being in relation to God. Both individuals and society need redemption such as only Christ can bring.

When thinking of salvation, we generally concern ourselves with salvation from the consequences of our sin. This is not the New Testament emphasis. There, consideration of the consequences of sin is but a prelude to the offer of forgiveness to all who truly repent. This offer is divine. No matter how long we reflect on it, we never exhaust its full meaning or the wonder of the love of God which lies behind it: "God commendeth his love toward us, in that, while we were yet sinners, Christ died for us."[30]

In seeking salvation from "the sin which doth so easily beset us,"[31] one of our major hindrances is that we think of our relation with God in terms of debtor and creditor—so much due and so much to be paid. Jesus would have us think, rather, in terms of the home. The world is our heavenly Father's house and we are his family, his children. He does not require us to be worthy before we can be at home with him. But we must turn to him. He then receives us as his children in order that, in his house and among others who love him, we may become more truly his sons and daughters.

In its most elementary meaning to be "saved" means to be rescued, and the most persistent evil from which we need to be rescued is sin. But, as the late Dr. Georgia Harkness wrote some years ago,

> We need also to be delivered from frustration, inadequacies, destructive inner conflict, despair. There is no full salvation or spiritual victory unless there is a lifting of the chains, not only of sin, but also of our futility. . . . It [salvation] is positive, joyous, spiritual health. . . . We are saved to the kind of life in which we can work with God victoriously and zestfully to do his will.[32]

The key to the salvation available in Christ is that combination of surrender and reenlistment to which we are persuaded by the ministry of the Spirit of God, and which we usually call "conversion." This experience may not be cataclysmic, but it must involve deep and genuine transfer of our loyalties from self to God. If we are not God's, we are necessarily someone else's—our own or another's; but to be under the final command and leadership of anyone but God is to be lost.

> Know ye not, that to whom ye yield yourselves servants to obey, his servants ye are to whom ye obey; whether of sin unto death, or of obedience unto righteousness?[33]
>
> You cannot serve God and Mammon.[34]

In a sense, to be enlisted under God is to be saved. As John said so long ago, "He who believeth on the Son hath everlasting life."[35]

Salvation is the experience of dedication and acceptance, of repentance and forgiveness, of sacrifice and of guaranteed victory which was known among the early saints and has been the hallmark of Christian life down the ages. Those who are committed to God have found life's highest meaning and purpose. They are released from uncertainty and insecurity and lostness. The salvation available on this level needs to be sought and savored.

To be saved is to accept with gladness the sovereignty of Jesus Christ over all our lives so that we take with gratitude what he has done for us. It also means that we accept that which he wills to do *in* us and *through* us. Salvation on this level is free to all persons in the sense that no external cause can dissuade them against it. It is free because, as Peter wrote, God "hath given unto us all things that pertain unto life and godliness, through the knowledge of him that hath called us to . . . virtue."[36] This is true salvation. It is costly in that it requires us to abandon old ways and old standards—to deny ourselves and to learn daily how to follow Jesus more faithfully. But it is life of the highest order. It has its roots here but it also has its sure fruition in the hereafter.

The secret of knowing Christ is the secret of love. So many people are wrestling with besetting sins as a prelude to surrendering themselves to Christ instead of yielding themselves to his sovereignty in order to find power to meet sin. They do this because they have not yet realized the love of God and the hunger of his heart for our responsive affection. That is why the Cross and Calvary are so important. If only we can be persuaded to forget other considerations and contemplate for a moment what Calvary meant in terms of divine love for us, the barriers we ourselves put in the way will surely be torn down. When our hearts turn toward Jesus in love we begin to know him, and the more we know him the more we love him. It was in full consciousness of this that Paul wrote to the Ephesian saints:

> I bow my knees unto the Father of our Lord Jesus Christ, of whom the whole family in heaven and earth is named, that he would grant you, according to the riches of his glory, to be strengthened with might by his Spirit in the inner man; that Christ may dwell in your hearts by faith; that ye, being rooted and grounded in love, may be able to comprehend with all saints what is the breadth, and length, and depth, and height; and to know the love of Christ, which passeth knowledge, that ye might be filled with all the fullness of God. Now unto him that is able to do exceeding abundantly above all that we ask or think, according to the power that worketh in us, unto him be glory in the church by Christ Jesus throughout all ages, world without end.[37]

NOTES

1. Matthew 4:17-19.
2. Matthew 4:20-21. See also John 1:47-49.
3. John 14:6.
4. Acts 9:2; 19:9; 22:4.
5. Luke 24:26.
6. Deuteronomy 18:15-19; Acts 3:22; 7:37.
7. Psalm 16:10.
8. Psalm 19:14.
9. Psalms 2:6; 24:7-10.
10. Isaiah 7:14; Matthew 1:23, KJ; 2:6, IV.
11. Isaiah 9:6.
12. See Herbert F. Stevenson, *Titles of the Triune God,* p. 116.
13. Luke 2:11.
14. Luke 3:4.
15. Matthew 21:2; 22:40-44.
16. Stevenson, page 119.
17. Acts 1:21.
18. Ephesians 1:21.
19. Luke 1:32, 35.
20. Matthew 3:46.
21. John 20:31.
22. John 10:33-38; Matthew 11:28.
23. Daniel 7:14.
24. Matthew 1:21, KJ; 2:4, IV.
25. Luke 2:10-11.
26. Acts 5 :30-31.
27. Acts 13:23.
28. Matthew 18:11; Luke 19:10.
29. Matthew 18:12-13; Luke 15:4-6.
30. Romans 5:8.
31. Hebrews 12:1.
32. *Understanding the Christian Faith,* p. 107.
33. Romans 6:16.
34. Matthew 6:24; Luke 16:13.
35. John 3:36.

36. II Peter 1:3.

37. Ephesians 3:14-21.

Study Helps for

Chapter 52

LESSON PURPOSE

To state and emphasize the primary conditions of knowing Christ.

SCRIPTURE REFERENCES

Matthew 19:16-26; Ephesians 3:14-21.

HIGH POINTS OF THE LESSON

- Jesus Christ has had many names and titles. Their signficance depends partly upon the spiritual maturity of the person using them.
- Without Christ we are lost.
- Only those with a deep sense of their own need ever come to Christ.
- Primary conditions of understanding are moral earnestness, the sense of the present availability of Jesus, willingness to follow to the limit of our present moral insight, the enlightenment of the Spirit.

QUESTIONS AND DISCUSSION TOPICS

1. What do we mean when we state that without Christ in their lives, people are "lost"? How is this true?

2. In what ways are people brought to a sense of their need for Christ? In what mood are we most likely to become deeply conscious of this need?

3. Who are most likely to feel this need for Christ? How may we extend this sense of need to others? Who are the spiritual descendants of the Pharisees? How can these people be reached?

4. What do we mean by moral earnestness? Why is moral earnestness so important in coming to Christ? How does the story of the rich young man who came to Jesus illustrate this?

5. How may we sense the present availability of Jesus? What is the relative importance of scripture study, the personal testimony of good people, prayer, and good living?

6. What do we mean by the moral authority of Jesus? How may action without Christ reinforce thought about him?

7. What would you say to a person who wanted to become a disciple but was hesitating because of some besetting sin? How can the person work on sin? Should people recognize their obligation to follow Christ in spite of their weaknesses? What is meant by surrendering ourselves to Christ?

8. What does Christ mean in the lives of the best people you know? What does he mean in your life? When is he nearest to you? How do you share him with others?

WHAT THE LESSON MEANS FOR TODAY

Many of us know a great deal about Christ without knowing him for ourselves. Our difficulty is that we substitute loyalty to his teachings and to his purpose in the world for loyalty to him. Our religion may therefore lack the warmth of an infinitely precious personal relationship. We need to capture the glow of early Christianity, which turned the world upside down, through personal devotion manifest in our moral earnestness, creative worship, and kingdom action.